Preface

This is the true story of my life. A story about a kid from Queens with big dreams, a broken heart, and a never-ending need to feel like he belonged. I start from my earliest memories and young childhood to build the foundation of how I became a sick, suffering, and desperate drug addict who eventually found recovery, redemption, and most importantly a calm, peaceful soul. Many parts of this book weren't written from the perspective of a 57-year-old man in his 23rd year of recovery; rather, the viewpoints are from how I perceived things to be at the age I was at the time I was writing about.

Throughout the chapters in this book, I will share some of the really weird things that often go through my mind or are stored in my memory and come out at any given time. I write exactly how I think, and although I've never been diagnosed with ADHD, I am fairly positive if they had this term for kids with it back in the early 70s, my picture would coincide with the definition.

I don't believe that anyone would have ever believed that I would have turned out to be a drug addict when I was a young child, but as I think back to my early childhood, I realize there were red flags everywhere. When I think back to how often I cried when I didn't get my way or how I never felt like I belonged anywhere, or how I just wanted to be relevant to my older brother who I believe always saw me as a parasite. I remember when I felt like I wanted to die because my mother changed from being extremely affectionate towards me, from kissing me all the time, hugging me, calling me her "bella faccia" (beautiful face) to what felt like her always yelling and being mad at me. I couldn't understand what I did for her to completely change the way she felt about me. I was very young when this happened, maybe in the first or second grade, and my mother went from being a stay-at-home mom to a mom with a job. Looking back, I don't think my mom was happy about getting a job and going to work every day. What I believe today is she probably took that anger out on me.

In my neighborhood, Middle Village, in Queens NYC, most moms were considered "housewives" during that period. The fathers were the breadwinners and the head of the household and our moms took care of the house and the kids. It was the late 60's and early 70's. It was the greatest time ever to be a kid in the best neighborhood in the history of the world's existence and on the other hand, it was the hardest time to be a kid and the neighborhood was a living hell. Things went on behind closed doors in the neighborhood that were never spoken of. We would often hear the screams of friends' mothers while their husbands beat the shit out of them behind closed doors and shaded windows but we would never mention it. Kids would show up at school with bruises on their faces or arms and legs, and again, it was never talked about. Funny, but I can't remember hearing the word "divorce" when I was that young. It was something that just never happened. I do remember though, there were a few kids that moved away and sometimes they went with their mom, sometimes their dad. No one ever explained what happened or why they moved, but I guess that was just another thing that was never discussed.

Skipping forward a few years, there were a few times as an adolescent when my mom forced me to see a therapist, and I remember sessions when this period was identified by my mother and a therapist as the start of my "troubles." For me, the beginning of these troubles started in the 6th grade. This was when it was decided by some universal force whether or not a kid was considered *cool* a *nerd* or a *geek*. It was so important for me to be one of the cool kids.

That need for acceptance, the need to fit in, to feel loved, or to just be relevant was the driving force in so many decisions that created the path of my addiction and continued throughout my recovery. This book will tell the story of how this kid from Queens became a desperate, tortured soul, a hopeless drug addict, and somehow found recovery, redemption, and self-love. I'll do my best to keep this in some form of chronological order, but no promises. I've written little passages on Facebook about my past and my recovery, I would always put #mypeacefulsoul at the bottom of them. I think it's fitting for that to be the name of this book.

Where do I start a story like this? I mean, it's a hell of a story, but there are so many parts to it, so many different periods, or stages, or whatever the hell you want to call them. I guess I'll start from the beginning although there's no promise of continuity or chronological order, my mind just doesn't work like that. My first sponsor in my recovery used to tell me to find a way to deal with the things I have no control over, so that is my suggestion to you, find a way to deal with it and keep reading.

I was born in 1965, the final year of the Baby Boomer generation. I lived on 68th Avenue in Middle Village. There were around 30 kids either my age or close to my age on my block. At any given time on any block, you would see a bunch of kids playing, sometimes right in the middle of the street. I remember having a hard time fitting in with any kids from any age group. I remember fighting with a few kids almost every week. I would get into fights with Phillip from across the street, Frankie and Nicky Oppedisano from around the corner and their cousin Frankie Sindoni from a few houses up the street from my house. We would be friends for a few days, something would cause a fight to start up and we'd go at it and after a one or two-day cooling-off period, we were friends again.

I was a pretty weird kid. I was very skinny. Like, I had to run around in the shower just to get wet skinny. I was awkward and uncoordinated as well. I would often trip and fall without reason; usually just tripping over air. Being so skinny and uncoordinated was not anything that bothered me until I started interacting with other kids my age. I was never really good at sports; I didn't run fast, I would always get "tagged" first when playing tag on my block and then it would take forever for me to catch up with someone and tag them. I was always the last one picked when teammates were chosen to play baseball or some other sport or game. I hated fighting because I usually lost, but I'd get into these little fistfights with my friends at least once a week over some stupid shit that young boys have fought over throughout the centuries of mankind!

I was different though. Things kids said affected me in a way that I couldn't in any way at the time understand and I remember always feeling a need to fit in with others -an almost desperate need- because I never really felt like I did. Whenever I told my mom about the thing's kids would say, she would always say something to the effect of "All kids say mean things, you shouldn't let it bother you." As I am writing this I'm thinking maybe, just maybe, had she just said something, anything, that would help me think what those kids were saying wasn't true, I might have had a bit more confidence when I was growing up.

What I am about to write about is pretty painful for me to bring up. I've never really spoken to anyone about this except my therapist throughout the last few years. I believe the true core of my low self-esteem and lack of confidence in myself started with my mother and my older brother Jay. My brother is three years older than me and as a very young child, he was the sun, the moon, and the stars to me. He was my idol. He was good at everything. He was strong, intelligent, and most of all he was my big brother. I'm sure if you think back to your elementary through high school years, you'll remember there were those families that had between two and four boys and if you messed with one, you messed with them all. Do you remember those kids? We had more than a few of them when and where I grew up. It was just common knowledge that if you messed with one of these kids, you would at some point have to deal with his older brother. To this day, I wish I had one of those older brothers. To this day, I still harbor a resentment deep within me towards my older brother for not being one of those kids. To this day, I still seek his approval.

I loved this kid. He was so special to me. He was always so perfect to me; all I wanted was to be with him. When we were at home together we would play a lot of different games and sports together. He would always win. He was always the victor, always the best. I got on his nerves because I didn't know how to lose and when I did I would cry. I would often try and tag along with him outside and hang out with him and his friends. Sometimes he'd let me but most times they would tell me to get lost because I was too little to hang out with them. Hearing that would often make me feel small as a person. There is one time in particular that has stayed in my memory for what seems like forever. I overheard my mother trying to have my brother help me with baseball. I was terrible at baseball when I first started. I couldn't hit and fly balls would cause panic whenever I tried to catch one. Anyway, she was asking him to help by pitching to me to help improve my hitting, and he didn't want to. He was saying things like "he'll never get good", and "I don't want to do this, I want to hang out with my friends." I've learned when a very young child gets put down, rejected, or pushed away, he doesn't think "Why are these kids like this" or "What's wrong with these kids." Rather, he thinks "What's wrong with **ME**?" "Why am I not good enough for them?"

I am laying the foundation of the story of my addiction and trying to provide an understanding of everything that went into the creation of the wonderful disaster that became my life. I wasn't this sad, depressed kid walking around with my head hung low while this shit was going on. I didn't even know that it was having any kind of long-term effect on me. I was always looking for the next fun thing to do, and I did have lots of fun during these times. Most of this stuff wasn't even given a second thought until well into my recovery years.

I've forever tried to figure out just where and when I completely lost confidence in myself. I believe that between the sixth and seventh grades, I started to realize that I was a lot different than the group of kids I hung out with. The sixth grade is when the real division between the "cool" or "popular" kids and the "good" kids that never got in any trouble, that always turned their homework in on time, you know, the nerds and the geeks happened. I remember the first really "wrong" thing I did. It was mainly to establish that I was willing to be "bad" so I could stay in the popular club. My friends and I started to smoke cigarettes. I saw my friend Frank puff on a cigarette and hand it to Joey Drapala. I was astonished! I was like, *really guys? Smoking?* I remember how freaking cool it looked and I immediately said "Gimme that, I want to smoke too!". It was exactly at that point that our little crew began to distance ourselves from the rest of the kids. We began to test the waters to see how much trouble and other bullshit we could get away with. We encouraged each other to be as bad as we could be! Looking back, I realize how little self-esteem I had back then.

I was the kid in class who had to have his desk right next to the teacher. I had to be within their sight at all times. If they looked away, someone in class was getting blasted with a spitball shot from a pen-tube. At the time I'm sure none of us had any idea of the Pandora's box we were opening with our behaviors or where we were headed. All we knew was that it was so much fun to be so different from the rest of the kids. I didn't know at the time that I was trying to fit it or anything like that. It just felt super cool to be a part of that crew. This was in the winter of early 1977, just before one of the most infamous summers in the history of New York City. The summer of 77. The summer of "Sam". The summer of the NYC blackout.

The very last day of my sixth-grade school year was a monumental moment that changed the course of my life. For about six months, my friends and I were trying desperately to get the older kids to sell us weed. They kept telling us to "get lost" or "you're too young to start this shit, wait till next year." They finally caved and sold us two joints on that day. Our class went on a trip to Juniper Park that day. Joey Drapala, Maria Dassaro, Michael Viola and I snuck away from the class and went under a tree that we were able to hide under and smoked both joints.

I wish I could tell you that getting high was the greatest thing to happen in my life up to that point but the truth is I didn't feel anything. I guess I didn't know how to inhale it and I just pretty much made believe I was high. I'm pretty sure the other kids in the group did the same thing. I felt guilty, like I committed the ultimate sin. I was scared to go home because I thought my parents would see the difference in me and either kill me or punish me for life. Luckily, that didn't happen, but later that night I had a little league baseball game in the park right next to the spot where we smoked that weed. At one point a fire truck showed up and there was a bunch of firemen walking around the area and they put out a small fire. I was so scared. In my head, I was thinking that maybe one of the joints we smoked didn't go out completely and started a fire and they were going to find it and get our fingerprints from it and we'd all get caught and go to jail. I was petrified with fear believing that this was going to happen! That's how the infamous "Summer of 77" started for me.

The Summer of 77. For me, the two most memorable things about that summer were the release of the Meatloaf album Bat out of Hell and the Son of Sam killings. At any time of the day or night, if you wanted to hear a song from Meatloaf all you had to do was turn on the radio. The album was huge. Every song on the album was a hit, every song would stay on my mind all day.

At the same time, everyone in the city was scared to death of the *Son of Sam* .44 caliber killer who at the time was loose on the streets of the city. He was randomly shooting and killing women or couples sitting in their cars. Women were wearing wigs to change their hair color because he was particular to blondes. I believe he started his attacks in '76, but he went on to kill six people and injure an additional seven, until his last murder in July of '77.

It was also when I discovered what changes a teenage girl dressed in shorts and a tank top can cause in my lower extremities. You know what I mean, right? Please tell me you know what I'm talking about. Oy vey! Okay, I'll spill it for the people that don't get it. It was when I started getting woodies regularly. That soldier stood at attention about ninety times a day! My friends and I started smoking weed and cigarettes regularly. We would get super high some nights and I remember thinking that I didn't like the high as much as I liked the thrill of the moments spent with my friends throughout that summer.

It was also the summer that some of the more confident boys in the neighborhood gained the courage to ask some of the teenage girls out on dates. I was extremely attracted to every girl in the neighborhood but scared to death to ask one out on a date. I would say I was already programmed to have very little if any, confidence in myself. I was cool enough to hang out with the cool kids, but I was not at the top of the totem pole when it came to popularity with them. I would often get made fun of for being so skinny, so knock-kneed, so uncoordinated, and awkward. I can say that some of that ribbing from my friends had something to do with my lack of self-confidence. I wanted to have the courage to ask a girl out; I fantasized about it but I could never muster up the courage. In my mind though, every girl in the neighborhood was in love with me. I always dreamed about the girls being in love with me. If I ever told my friends that I liked a girl, they would laugh and say things like, "Forget it, you have no chance" and I believed them. I wish I knew what it was about me that would prompt them to say that. I wish I dared to go for it despite what my friends said. Hearing them tell me that I didn't have a chance was all I needed to keep me from trying.

A lot of my troubles at home started throughout this summer. I had a 9:00 pm curfew and my mother would get absolutely livid if I came home even 5 minutes late. Eventually, because I was usually late almost every night, she started grounding me every time I was late. I'd get grounded for 3 days, then it would turn into 5 days, and eventually, the groundings would be for anywhere between one week and then one month. Most of my friends didn't even get in trouble for being a few minutes late but in my house, it was treated like a major criminal act.

I can remember being so embarrassed about it. My friends were not empathetic or sympathetic at all. Quite the contrary, it was ammunition for them to make fun of me. I missed out on so much fun because I was grounded. When friends got in trouble, their parents may have grounded them for a few days or a week at the most. After a while, I'd find myself grounded for a month over getting home five minutes later than my curfew. I am pretty positive I had ADHD and was usually late because we were having so much fun and I'd completely lose track of time. There were no cell phones with alarms back then. There was nothing to remind me about the time and we didn't wear watches at 12 years old so getting punished and being grounded became a norm. Having it happen so often brought on severe bouts of depression.

I remember trying so hard to get them to change their minds. I would cry uncontrollably by the end of what would become almost daily pleadings and arguments. These are the first times I can remember feeling completely hopeless. I started wanting revenge at this point as well. I can remember thinking about harming myself to get back at my parents. It's sad but right up to her death, my mother never accepted that her forms of disciplinary consequences had a huge part in how I eventually turned to hate them during my adolescence. We talked about it a few times after I got clean but the results were always the same. At least my father was able to accept responsibility for some of this before he passed away. Eventually, the summer ended. Thinking back, I remember being a different kid at the start of seventh grade than I was when sixth grade ended. The summer of 77 was the first time I ever truly felt emotional pain, desperation, and despair. Somehow that changed me but not for the better.

Chapter 3. Sad Wings of Destiny- *Judas Priest*

Fall, 1977. The start of a new school year in a new school. Elementary school was made up mostly of kids from the neighborhood with a few kids of color getting bussed in from different, lower-income neighborhoods. Junior High School was different. There were kids from Middle Village (both sides of Metropolitan Avenue), Glendale, parts of Ridgewood, and Rego Park. Before this, I hung out with the popular kids and the troublemakers in my neighborhood. I wasn't the most popular of the group. I wasn't the strongest kid nor was I the best-looking kid but I was a part of the group and up to this point it felt like I belonged. At first, it was cool meeting some new people, especially the girls, but after a while, things started to change. The cool kids and troublemakers from the other neighborhoods were all trying to establish a hierarchy. There were a lot of kids testing other kids' courage, strength, and ability to fight and protect themselves.

At that time I was an extremely skinny kid. When it was my turn to get tested, whatever I had in courage wasn't enough to protect me or keep me from losing fights. Most kids, especially the kids trying to prove their dominance through strength were way bigger and stronger than me. Most fights I was involved in were over after a few punches hitting me and then me hitting the ground. My friends at the time would help me up and help me dust off, but that was pretty much all I got. No one ever really stood up for me or had my back, so I would get through the day and go home and feel sad or sorry for myself.

I wanted to yell at my friends for not coming to my aid, but I also wanted to stay within the group so I just kept my mouth shut. In my mind, I thought *what's wrong with me, what about me isn't good enough for my friends to help me?* This is when I most likely started to realize how different I was from others. I didn't know what to do and I was too embarrassed to tell my parents or my brother what was happening. I already knew at this point my brother wasn't going to be helpful. There wasn't anyone to help build me back up after the embarrassment of losing a fight. I only had my damaged ego to start the process of tearing me apart. I often wonder what it would've been like for my brother to come to my rescue just once but he never did. I wonder how different things might have been had there been someone, anyone, who showed me that I was worth so much more than I believed I was.

What kept me somewhat relevant with my peers was my ability to make people laugh. I was a good class clown. Sometimes I was too funny for my own good and would find myself headed to the dean's or principal's office after getting sent there by a teacher. A problem that was created from this was the occasional call home from the dean or principal to discuss my bad behavior and of course, I'd wind up with a week or two in the slammer (my room at home, AKA being grounded). I also found that my sense of humor made the girls laugh too, which had its ups and downsides. Every so often one of the bigger kids would get jealous of the attention I was receiving from girls so he'd have to step in and push me around a little to regain his sense of importance, you know, just to help my self-esteem out a little. With all this to figure out how to cope with, I still had to deal with being a student and pass some classes.

My grades were sucking. I wouldn't do homework and I played around in class most of the time. My friend Joey started ditching school and would try and get me to ditch too but I was too scared of the consequences so I kept chickening out. After a while though, with my grades sucking and getting fucked with by the bullies, ditching school started looking better and better. Besides, getting stoned on weed and going to class sucked. I found it was way more fun to ditch and go hang out by the train tracks or one of the many cemeteries that were all over Middle Village and Glendale. We would do all kinds of cool things when we ditched school. There was this little piece of land on the Middle Village side of the railroad tracks that separated Glendale and Middle Village. It was just outside Lutheran Cemetery, it was a little trail that led to what we called "the ooga-boogas." The ooga-boogas were like a tiny little jungle that only we knew about. We didn't have to worry about parents or police finding us. We could smoke weed openly and have a great time just being delinquent 12-year-old kids without being bothered! What started as skipping school a few days here and there wound up having us miss about 40 days in a row until some moron at the school got wind of us and called our parents.

Mom and Dad were not too pleased with me. While Joey was grounded for a week, my parents told me that I would never go out again. Ever. I was grounded for the rest of my life. I wasn't allowed to wear cool clothes anymore either. My mom went out and bought all kinds of nerdy clothes and the topping on this wonderful cake was I had to cut my hair short. The one thing I had that made everyone jealous was my hair. It really was beautiful; it was long, super shiny, and wavy and all the girls told me how nice it was!

I remember thinking *is this what life had in store for me? Am I really going to wind up being a freaking thirty-five-year-old kid living in his parent's house wearing nerdy clothes with short stupid-looking hair and still being grounded from some idiotic shit I did in seventh grade?*

The remainder of my Junior High School prison sentence between seventh and ninth grade went pretty much the same as my first year. I was always in trouble for skipping school or coming home late. Eventually, my parents found out about me smoking weed and cigarettes and of course, I was grounded for life again. I believed I would eventually die as an old man who still lived with his parents and wasn't allowed to go out. My parents had no idea how to help me through this. They reached out to therapists, priests, God almighty, and whoever else they thought could change my behaviors and save their poor souls from the embarrassment I caused. That's just it too, it didn't feel like they were trying to help, it always felt like they were ashamed of me and didn't want to be embarrassed. They never asked me why I felt the need to do all this to fit in. Whenever we did talk about my behavior it was in a way that caused me to feel like there was something wrong with me.

I don't think my mother ever considered or cared that I was embarrassed by being grounded all the time. I'm sure she never realized that I felt like I never really fit in either at home or with my friends. Something needed to change, I needed something to give me some hope that the rest of my life wasn't going to suck a big, nasty bag of dicks because that's how it felt at that point. Luckily, something happened that would eventually change the course of my life.

Chapter 4. One Way Out Babe, Lord I Just Can't Go Out That Door- *The Allman Brothers*

One of the few times my parents gave me a chance and let me out of my cage, I went with some friends to our friend John Reilly's house to watch him and some kids jam. John Reilly, his younger brother Michael, and Frankie Mortimer were musicians. They played together as a band for a little while. Watching them down John's basement and being so close to the loud guitars and drums was a defining moment for me. I found what I wanted to be when I grew up. This was it, this was my ticket out. No girls would be able to resist me if I could only play guitar like John Reilly. I would become the Rock God that I was destined to be. All I had to do was convince my Sicilian parents to buy me a guitar.

After what felt like ten years of begging and pleading (in reality, about three months) my parents caved in and bought me this exquisite, totally professional, beautiful $28 acoustic guitar, and by that I mean a cheap piece of crap. I was surprised that they signed me up for lessons too. I was never more excited in my life! I finally had a guitar and I was going to become a rock star. After about three months of lessons I asked my teacher to teach me how to play Stairway to Heaven or Purple Haze, and every week after my lesson I'd walk out knowing how to play "Mary had a little lamb" or "Joy to the world" or some other ridiculously lame piece of shit song that I never wanted to hear again in my life.

After a few more months he gave me a book with a bunch of different chords for guitar and I learned how to play a lot of different chords. I remember learning certain chords and recognizing them from songs I heard on the radio. He taught me how to play Barre Chords, which at the time were so super hard because you had to bar the whole fret with your index finger and position your other fingers to hit other notes.

After about 6 more months my teacher tried to get me to learn "Blackbird" by the Beatles. It was a really hard song to play. It incorporated a finger-picking style that I never learned and this guy expected me to have it down in like a week. Well, I couldn't get it and he got really mad and raised his voice so I quit. I think I told him to fuck off or something similar. I didn't need lessons anymore anyway; I was able to play the beginning of *Stairway to Heaven* and most of *Wish you Were Here*. Fuck him!

Chapter 5. Green Grass and High Tides Forever-
The Outlaws

I made it out of Junior High School in 1980. I didn't pass every class in the 9th grade and I had to repeat three classes. Of course, my parents used this as a reason to ground me again. I remember thinking I was super lucky because I was able to go to Forest Hills High School. I was originally supposed to go to Franklin K Lane HS, which was in a terrible neighborhood in East New York, Brooklyn. I didn't want to go there, and when the Zoning changed, I found that I could go to Forest Hills High School instead, me and the other kids were very happy about it. It didn't last too long though.

What I didn't realize when I chose to go to that school was that Forest Hills was one of the whitest, richest neighborhoods in Queens. Most of the kids that went to that school came from families with lots of money. They were usually spoiled rotten and mean-spirited.

I tried my hand at selling weed when I first went there and sold some older dudes a few joints. These guys were either juniors or seniors, all football players like 6' tall and 180 pounds each. I was just a skinny knock-kneed kid who weighed about 110 pounds soaking wet. Later in the day they came back and said the weed was shit and started World-War-Three over it. I was surrounded by five or six of them. One dude shoved one of the joints up my nose and the rest of them punched and kicked me in the face, head, and ribs. Literally, over a few joints that cost $1 each. My friends that were with me jetted, leaving me by myself to deal with these ruthless King-Kong-type assholes. They later said they took off to find some of our friends to help me but by the time they came back I was there alone and bleeding out of my nose and lip on the ground trying to remember my name.

After this, I went to school less and less, until the school called my parents wondering why I was out of school over 80 days. Then they decided to kick my ass out of the school completely. Of course, I was grounded for life again. I did the math after this one and by the time my punishment would be over, I'd have been around 70 years old. Being grounded as much as I was back then had a terrible effect on me. There were times I missed out on whole summers. I rarely was allowed to hang out with my friends after school. I was growing tired of just hearing about what went on in the neighborhood. I wanted to be a part of it and that part of my childhood was taken from me.

Luckily, God saw fit to show some mercy on my poor soul and I was allowed to transfer to a different high school. Some of my close friends went there too so I was temporarily saved. The school was a project of LaGuardia College called Middle College High School. It was perfect for misfits like me. They got it right. The school treated the students like adults. There weren't any bells between classes, we were told when the class was over and how much time we had to get to the next class. We were allowed to smoke in the cafeteria (this was when indoor smoking was still legal). The teachers called us by our first name, and we did the same with them. It felt really good to be treated so well and my grades and attendance improved for a little while as a result.

All the time I spent being grounded by my parents wasn't completely wasted. I didn't do anything but practice my guitar all day and night. I was becoming pretty good for a kid that may have had 8 months of lessons. I learned to play most of the songs I loved and was coming up with my own tunes as well. I still had that insanely cool $28 acoustic guitar. My parents refused to buy me an electric guitar. Whenever I asked for one I was told either my behavior was too bad or my grades sucked, or some other lame excuse why they wouldn't help me do what I loved more than anything else in the world. Some of my friends at the time were starting to play instruments and I'd borrow their guitars every once in a while. I had this one friend, Ricky, who always let me borrow his guitar and amp. I would teach him some songs and he would let me borrow his guitar anytime I asked. He was the nicest kid I knew. I will always be appreciative of the friendship. Sadly though, he's no longer with us. I am still friends with his brother Chris on Facebook. Sadly, the good guys always go way too soon.

One Spring Day in 1980 when I was fourteen years old my life was changed forever. I was playing Ricky's guitar through his amp which I happened to put on a chair with the speakers facing out my window so the cute girl that lived across the street knew I was one day going to be a rock star and fall madly in love with me. One day my doorbell rang and there were these 4 guys with super long jet-black hair at my door. I knew they were from the neighborhood but I didn't know them personally. I was wondering what the hell these guys that were way older than me wanted.

I was almost scared to open the door, but I mustered up the courage. One of the guys was super tall and skinny and he looked like a cross between Steven Tyler from Aerosmith and Freddy Mercury from Queen. He had super long curly black hair and it looked like he had makeup on his eyes but I couldn't be sure because his hair covered his eyes. He looked me up and down and then asked how old I was. I lied and told him I was seventeen, and he said, "Get the fuck outta here, you can't be seventeen". I asked him why they were at my door, and he said, "We were driving down this street and heard someone playing guitar, was it you"? I said it was and he told me I was really good! He asked if I wanted to come to his house and jam with them. They were in a band and needed a second guitar player! He said they were very impressed with my playing and they had to stop to see who was playing that good! I can't express how good it was to hear him say that.

What I didn't tell him was I didn't own an electric guitar or an amp, or that I was 14 and that I was grounded for the rest of my life. I had to figure out how to pull this off though, I couldn't let this pass me by. I stopped at his place the next day on the way home from school and rang his bell. I told him everything. He was really cool in a way I always wanted my brother to be towards me and said he had a guitar and amp that I could use.

All I had to do now was convince my mother and father to let me join a rock band with a bunch of guys who were way older than me. This should be easy with what you've heard about my parents, right? I have no idea why but I believed they would have let me. My parents were having none of it. There was no way they were letting me hang out with guys who were so much older and in a band. Only drug addicts are in bands was their reasoning. The one thing my parents didn't understand was that I was going to do this, no matter how they tried to stop me, I was doing it. Even if I had to fake my death, I was doing this. Nothing in the world would stop me.

Chapter 6. I got nasty habits, I take tea at three
~ *The Rolling Stones*

In what world would a fourteen-year-old kid be given an opportunity to play guitar in a real rock band and let his out-of-touch-with-reality parents stop him? It was time for me to take control of my destiny. I hatched a plan with the other guys in the band. They rehearsed in the singer "Mikey Mugz'" basement which was just a few blocks from my house. They practiced between 9 pm and midnight a few nights a week. My mom was always in bed and usually sleeping by that time. My brother never came to my room, ever. My father didn't get home from work until between 2 and 4 am. My family lived on the second floor of a two-family house; my room was next to my parents' bedroom in the front. I would quietly sneak out my window (being so quiet would become an asset a few years later too, I'll fill you in a few chapters down the road), there was a ledge under the windows. I could hang from it and my feet could touch the top of my porch, so getting in and out was easy, I just needed to be extremely quiet and careful. This was the start of something wonderful and crazy. It might have been a bit stupid, but so what? I was in a band!

I learned the value of keeping my mouth shut at this time. I didn't tell any of my friends that I had scored a gig playing in the band Naztee Habitz. I didn't want to take a chance and have my parents or brother find out so I was living this "double secret" life. I was a high-school kid by day and a rock star by night. When we jammed it was the most exciting feeling I ever had. I can't explain the feeling I had from this, nothing in my life before this point ever felt so good! For the first time, I was hanging out with really cool older kids and they didn't make fun of me, they never hit me, they treated me as an equal. These guys all treated me like I wished my older brother had. I finally knew how it felt to belong. Then on weekdays I'd go to school and get laughed at for being skinny, knock-kneed with long hair, and having terrible posture.

I was so high on life from being in the band though, there wasn't anything anyone could say that had the power to hurt me. Fuck them kids. I was in a band. I believed I would only have to endure this bullshit at school for a short time because we were headed for fame and fortune. Then all those assholes at school would be jealous of me, or so I thought!

After a few months of practicing, our singer Mikey told us at rehearsal that we had a gig. I didn't know what a gig was, so I asked and felt foolish when they all said in unison, "a show". It was at CBGB's and again, I had no clue to what a "CBGB's" was. So again, I felt foolish when they explained that it was a club in downtown NYC. At that moment, being in a band became real. In my head I knew at some point we were going to be playing shows, call it naivety, but for some reason, I thought we would be playing at parties and school dances or some other silly shit. I suddenly became overwhelmed with fear. How was I going to pull this one off? I was 14 but I looked like I was twelve years old. I was in high school and my parents were from the stone age and they didn't even allow me to join the band. Now I am going to play a show at a club on the lower east side of Manhattan, at 11 p.m.? Mugzy (what we called Mikey, our singer) had the answer. I was already sneaking out for a few months to come to rehearsal, this would be no different except they would have a van waiting for me a few houses up the street from my house. They promised to get me home before 2 am when my father came home from work. I told them all to make funeral arrangements in case I got caught because my father would kill me for sure. We had just one week to practice before what would be the very first time I ever played in front of a crowd. The rush of it all was insane. I was scared to death of getting caught. I was scared to death of fucking up and I thought for sure something terrible was going to happen. My experience in life up to that point made me sure of that.

I made it out of my house alive the night of the show. I didn't make a sound going out my window or hanging off and jumping from the ledge. The van was where it was supposed to be and we made it to the city by 10 pm. We were scheduled to go on stage at 11. The hour before was incredible. I had stolen my brother's driver's license to get in. He was eighteen and back then there weren't pictures on licenses so getting in was a breeze.

CBGB's is a tiny club. It's filthy and the bathrooms are gross with sticky floors that your feet stuck to. Other than that it was full of electricity. We were opening up for a well-known punk band and the place was packed. Until this point,

I had never in my life imagined anything quite like CBGB's on this night. There were girls everywhere, they wore super short miniskirts and wild makeup. Some girl came up from behind me, threw her arms around me, and asked if I was Naztee Habitz new guitar player and then she said I was cute. Then she stuck her tongue in my mouth and started kissing me. Her breath was a mixture of beer and stale cigarettes; she was braless and her erect nipples were rubbing up against me while she kissed me on the lips and neck. I had never tongue-kissed a girl before. I never felt a breast rub against me and never saw a girl like her in my school or neighborhood. For some reason all of a sudden, my pants felt a lot tighter in the crotch and it was harder to walk. I was pretty high; we smoked a joint on the way in the van and I drank a beer. Everything was moving so fast, the music in the club was so loud, I heard voices all around me but it sounded like people were speaking in a different language and I couldn't understand a word I was hearing. It was the most intense experience I ever had in all my fourteen years of living. For some unknown reason at the time, I felt comfortable there except in my jeans. I had the hardest erection I ever had and was doing everything possible to hide it. I thought everyone in the club would notice it and I'd die from the embarrassment. Thank God I realized my guitar would hide it and I wasn't going to die.

When we went up on the stage, right after the dude introduced the band my guitar came loose from the strap and fell to the floor-- well, actually, it fell on my feet. The volume was turned up and it made this loud and ungodly sound. I panicked and picked it back up and looked over at Mugzy and he was laughing. I thought I was going to die right there. He put his arm around me and called out the first song.

The only other memory of that night is what happened in the van on the way home. The girl that was kissing me earlier was with me in the back of the van and I remember feeling a lot like I felt at home while I was doing things to myself that my mother wouldn't approve of. What was different now was that it wasn't me touching myself…. How the hell was this happening without me touching myself? Oh my God, it felt so good but again, time was flying by so fast I barely was able to figure out what the fuck she was doing to me, and then… All of a sudden… BOOM! I exploded! It was like a bomb went off all over the place, on the guitar cases, the amps, my shirt, her shirt, her hands…. Everywhere. I don't remember anything after that. I don't remember climbing up on my ledge and going through my window. I don't remember going to sleep either. I just remember waking up the next morning trying to make sense of what had happened the night before. Mugzy called me that morning and told me that I was excellent, I played my first gig perfectly, and that I scored the hottest girl in the club afterward. At our next rehearsal, the band said they had a present for me since I did so well! They never unloaded the equipment from the van. My gift from them was a wet sponge and paper towels and they made me clean up the mess I made all over the guitar cases and the back of the van. How can life ever get any better than that?

"The reason a dog has so many friends is cause he wags his tail instead of his tongue" – Steven Tyler – Aerosmith

My God, when I look back at these times the first thing that comes to my mind is "What if one of my daughters did what I did at that age"? How would I have responded if either daughter were exposed to what I was exposed to at just fourteen years old? When I look back to these times through the eyes of a parent and with all I've experienced, I get a better understanding of why my parents were the way they were.

I got away with being in the band and sneaking out for rehearsals and gigs for close to two years. The night I finally got caught was a disaster. What I didn't know at the time was two of the guys in the band were doing heroin. They kept it from me as a way to protect me. They knew I was a bit on the wild side by this time. They tried their best to keep me from the harder drugs, but it was inevitable. Exposure to the New York City club scene at my age all but ensured I'd find my way to the harder drugs. I started taking drugs like Valium and Quaaludes shortly after our first gig. My band members had the insight to make sure I didn't get involved in anything heavier and that's why they kept the heroin use secret from me. I drank a lot too, but still didn't develop a stomach for it yet and the norm after a night of drinking was me violently puking, pissing my jeans, and passing out. Anyway, the gig was a disaster. We made mistakes all over the place. Every song was played two times faster than it should have been and it felt like everyone in the band hated each other. Looking back, I'm sure the drug use that was the cause of all that.

After getting dropped off from the gig, I was climbing up my ledge from the porch and I felt a hand around my ankle. Before I could realize what happened, my chin hit the ledge and I bit my tongue so hard my mouth was full of blood. Someone had shown my father a flyer that was posted in the neighborhood promoting the show. The flyer had a picture of the band. I was in the picture; the time and date of the show was on the flyer. My father saw this and waited in the car parked outside my house for me to come home and pulled me down from the ledge once I started pulling myself up. After my chin hit the ledge and I bit my tongue, I landed on my face on the porch. I took the worst beating my dad ever gave that night. The trauma of my face hitting the porch and his fists hitting my face has never left me. I remember exactly how it happened to this day. Needless to say, my music career was on hold for a while.

I feel the need to make this point, my parents weren't abusive. They were over-protective and sometimes went a bit overboard with consequences but they weren't bad people. They were two fairly normal people who had no idea how to deal with a kid like me. I was not some poor kid that was getting beat up at home. They were way overprotective but I provided many reasons for the way they dealt with me. There are times when what I write makes it sound like I am still mad at my parents but I am not. What I am doing is describing my thought process at the time of the story I'm telling. Now that I've clarified that, I'm not giving Mom and Dad a break either, they definitely could have handled things better. Let's just say they did their best within their parental capabilities considering what they had to deal with. After the incident of getting caught, I reached a point of no return. I was 17 years old and after spending the better part of 5 years being punished I decided I had enough. I was not going to be grounded one more day. I wasn't going to get hit by either of them one more time, not without a fight. I wasn't going to be told I couldn't do something with my friends because I couldn't be trusted ever again.

By the time I was seventeen, I was heading on a fast-moving train towards addiction. My parents knew I was headed for trouble. I don't know how many times up to this point my father had to come get me because I was too drunk to stand up and was vomiting all over wherever I was at the time. He had to pick me up from school once because I took Quaaludes and fell asleep in class and slept through a few periods until a teacher found me before the start of his class and when he tried to get me up, I was incoherent, drooling and wasted beyond the point of regaining composure. I was caught stealing money and jewelry from my parents on more than one occasion. While I felt like I had enough of being controlled by them, they also had reached a point of exhaustion trying to save me from myself.

While I was enjoying life so much as a result of being in a band with guys that were between 4 and 7 years older than me, the lifestyle I was exposed to at such a young age set the stage for utter self-destruction. Obviously, by this time my parents had enough as well. They were threatening to declare me "dependent" which would have placed the New York City family courts in charge of my life. I felt I had enough of them as well. My relationship with them sucked. I had no understanding of the responsibilities that parents had when it came to raising a kid. I was also scared of being under the supervision of the New York family court system as well. I decided to try and keep myself out of trouble until I was eighteen and was legally allowed to leave home. At the same time, my stupid ass got kicked out of school. I didn't want to find another school and have to make up about two years of classes I missed and on this rare occasion, my parents and I agreed it was in my best interest to get my GED. I took the tutorial classes and passed the test on my first try and I was a high school graduate before my friends who stayed in school and did the work to graduate properly a few months later.

Chapter 8. I Get High with a Little Help from My Friends- *The Beatles*

Shortly before my eighteenth birthday, I met the first true love of my life. One night I was hanging out with Phillip and Ritchie and Phillip asked us "Did either of youse guys (it's a NY thing) ever try cocaine?" Needless to say, I was intrigued! We chipped in and with our combined $50 Ritchie drove us to some bar in Ridgewood and Phillip went in and came out with a half gram of Cocaine. When we made it back to Ritchie's house and I did my first line, that was it, I was in love. Madly in love. It was a love unlike anything I ever experienced. We did it all and then talked (rapidly) without making any sense for about two hours after. When it was time to go home I didn't want to go. I wanted more but none of us had money so Ritchie kicked us out of his house and Phillip went home.

I, on the other hand, was not finished. I was getting more. I can't explain how strong the desire was to get more. I'd never experienced anything like that before this. There was no way in hell that I was done. That shit was just way too good. I was on a mission, let's call it a mission from God. Ridgewood was about four miles away from our neighborhood and I started walking there. It didn't matter that I didn't know where the bar was, who the dealer was, or that I was broke. I was on a mission from GOD! On the way there I managed to break into two cars and steal the stereo's out of them, even though I never did anything like that before. I somehow found the bar and I found the guy that was selling the cocaine in the bar. I traded the two car stereos for more cocaine. I did it all on the walk home. Once I was home, I stayed up the rest of the night and watched TV until around noon when I finally fell asleep. Looking back through the eyes of a person in recovery with twenty-three years clean, I should have known that shit was dangerous. I've never before been so driven to get high. There wasn't anything in this world that I loved so much as the high that Cocaine gave me. To put it lightly, I was headed for trouble. Without even the slightest bit of doubt, this was the beginning of my life as an addict.

Chapter 9. What's Love got to do with it? = *Tina Turner*

I know now that this was when my addiction made itself known to the world. I always thought that I could stop. I thought "I can drink a few beers, do a few lines, and then stop and go home". Those are just some of the lies the mind of an addict will think. I often wonder when I look back and think *what could someone have done or said that could've stopped me*? I've never found an answer to that question. I think it's highly doubtful anything could've stopped me at this point.

Throughout 1983, I had acquired and lost a few jobs. This usually happened for taking too many days off after too many nights going off the deep end on cocaine. Up to that point, I was never really involved in relationships with any of the neighborhood girls. One night in December I went to the club Lamour East with my friend Pete Manzella, a girl that I fooled around with once in a while, Fran DiBella and another girl Anne-Marie to see the band Talas. Lamour East was a huge club on Queens Blvd. It opened about 6 months before this and they were getting huge national acts like Talas who were very big at that time. They were recording a live album that night. We stayed for a little while, but then I was a little too high on Cocaine to stay, so we left. I wound up in a hotel room with Anne-Marie and we had sex and then we ended up dating. She was my first real "girlfriend".

Anne-Marie was wild. She had beautiful long blonde curly hair with slight, barely visible freckles on her face and a beautiful, timid heart. Unfortunately, she had some serious troubles at home between her stepfather and her mother which damaged her spirit and gave her a desire to break free.

There was pain within her soul, she hurt inside without a clue how to heal. We were a lot alike in that sense. Like me, when Anne wanted something to happen, there was no stopping her.

I had no idea how to be in a relationship and unfortunately, my role models were the kids I grew up with in the neighborhood. They all tended to be very possessive and sometimes physically abusive as well. Under the guidance of these geniuses, I was going to get control over her wild side and get her to submit to my ridiculous need for control. She didn't deserve the abuse I gave her; I have no excuse for that behavior. It was wrong. Anne and I were deeply in love with each other but I tried to control a soul that needed to be nurtured and free. I consider it a miracle that we lasted together for close to two years, and even more miraculously, we are still friends today.

Over the two years Ann and I were together there were some short bouts of normalcy in our lives. Because of the troubles she suffered from her stepfather, Anne was using and abusing alcohol and drugs just like me. Her mother had her placed in a daytime substance use treatment program for troubled adolescents. She was a year younger than me; she was just seventeen and using drugs just as hard and heavily as the drugs I was using. I had gotten myself in some serious trouble with a cocaine dealer shortly after we started dating and I stopped using it for a while.

The trouble happened when I stupidly tried selling cocaine so I could use it for free. The problem was once I started using cocaine I couldn't stop. This dealer I knew gave me a lot of cocaine and I was supposed to sell it off and pay him like $500 in about one week. I used it all without selling any of it. When he found out what I did it became a big mess. He was showing up at my house threatening to kill me. My parents wound up getting involved when they found out what was happening and we negotiated that I'd pay the dude off in weekly payments. This was the first time I ever got myself in trouble from using drugs and it scared me enough to stop for a while.

While Ann was in that adolescent substance use program I was very supportive of her. For a short time, we both were completely clean from any drug use. It was probably the closest thing to being "normal" that I ever experienced. We both had jobs, we shared a bank account, celebrated holidays with our families together, and were always together. Her mother loved me, and my parents loved her.

The job I had at the time was pretty cool. I got along with the boss and my coworkers pretty well. One day a few months after I started working there, we were all about to go home when we were finished working and our boss pulled out a mirror with a huge mountain of cocaine on it. I hadn't used any for close to a year at that point and once I saw that mirror I couldn't resist. He had some of the fattest lines I'd ever seen before and without giving it a second thought, I did some. I had absolutely no remorse, it was more like finding what was missing in my life and I loved it.

From the day my boss pulled out that mirror with all that cocaine, I did the first line and was off to the races. It was as if I never stopped using it at all, except the craving for more was worse than it ever was before. I brought some home with me and I did it with Anne-Marie and now we were both off to the races. It's weird, I haven't thought about this in forever, and revisiting it is making me a little sad. I wish I hadn't done some of the things I did during my early addiction. This was 1984 and it was the first and only time I ever stopped using cocaine until I got clean in 1999. It wasn't long after that day that I did something unthinkable. I was very lucky to have Anne-Marie and her family in my life.

I was getting high on cocaine after work one day and I couldn't stop. By this time, my mother was hiding her wallet between her mattress and box spring because I had stolen from her so many times in the past. I learned how to move very slowly and quietly from the days of sneaking out the window to play in the band. I went into my mother's bedroom and I stuck my arm between her mattress and box spring and stole every penny from her wallet. It was payday and I took it all.

I disappeared for three days. I wound up hiding out in a hotel room snorting cocaine and drinking whiskey and beer. I was so high and told myself I was going to kill myself after I was out of coke and booze so I wouldn't have to face anyone. I couldn't face anyone while in that state because something weird happened to me when I was high on cocaine. It was embarrassing. For some reason, my mouth didn't work right when I was high. It would move, but the words wouldn't come out. I looked really stupid when this happened and it was a dead giveaway that I was high. When I finished all the coke and whiskey, it took a few hours for me to be able to speak without looking like an idiot.

I finally called Anne-Marie and I'll never forget the disappointment in her voice. I felt like the biggest piece of shit lowlife there ever was. How could I have done this? Anne called my friend Pete, and they came to the hotel and got me. We drove to the program that Anne was in and I asked them if they could get me help. They said I would have to call their main office because they didn't take walk-ins there. It was just a day program for adolescents.

When I called my parents, my father picked up the phone and told me to fuck off and never come home. I was no longer welcome there.
I knew I hurt them and felt terrible. I can't imagine how badly what I did affected them. I never understood how they ever forgave me for it either.

Anne-Marie's mother and Stepfather were temporarily separated at the time and her mother allowed me to stay with them at their house. She was always so loving to me. The next day she had me quit that job and had her husband hire me to work in his check cashing store. All I could think at that time was "How can anyone love me, I'm such a piece of shit."

Although Anne and I shared a deep love for each other, my consistent use of cocaine and pattern of verbal, emotional, and sometimes physical abuse along with her wild spirit, we split up in the spring of 1985. It was my first and only serious relationship and I was very hurt and painfully discouraged after we split. It was my first real heartbreak.

Here's where the real fun begins. Having been exposed to the New York club scene at the age of 14 prepared me for this phase of my life. I was definitely not your ordinary nineteen-year-old. The changes in the music scene at this time were phenomenal. What I was about to get into was so wild and fun, I can't imagine not having the experience. Looking back on it as a person in long term recovery from addiction and a drug and alcohol counselor, it's so plain to see why I needed to be so different from everyone else I grew up with. I loved the attention that was paid to me because I looked so different from everyone else. I loved the attention because I felt that no one ever paid attention to me before this.

After the split with Anne-Marie I started spending a lot of time with my friend Fran DiBella from the neighborhood. We had a not-so-serious fling a few years earlier and remained friends after. Fran's relationship with her boyfriend ended around the same time as mine. This was the first of many platonic relationships I had with someone of the opposite sex. We became very close and were helpful to each other through some dark times. We both drank excessively though Fran quit doing cocaine a year prior to this, I was still using it but without a job, I never bought it. I only used it when it was offered.

Both Fran and I were in the beginning stages of becoming part of the New York City "Glam Rock Scene". The scene was pretty wild. A few Rock bands started reviving the old "Glam Rock" look of the mid-seventies, and it was a lot of fun to get in it from the beginning. We were teasing our hair to make it stand straight up from the roots. We were also dying it with wild colors as well. Fran was a natural redhead and she was quite beautiful. She very well could've been "the girl next door" but when she dyed her hair platinum blonde she transformed into this absolutely stunning woman.

My hair grew pretty long at this time. It was about halfway down my back. I dyed it jet black and was teasing it too. I started wearing makeup as well. I'd darken my eyes with black liner and dark purple eyeshadow and I'd wear dark purple lipstick. All you could see was my hair and my lips. I wore skin-tight black jeans, T-shirts that were ripped and torn, and I'd top it all off with either black, dark blue or purple leather jackets. I was WILD!

The way we looked and dressed was so different from anyone in our neighborhood. It was fun to see the shock on people's faces when we were out in public. The neighborhood kids were beyond shocked; it felt as if in some way we offended them. Some of my friends were really cool with how I looked, especially if they came out to a club with me. I fit right in the scene and there was always a lot of beautiful, wild and crazy (and easy) girls hanging with us. I almost always would end the night with some girl that I never met before. We would end up either at her apartment or once in a while I'd sneak one in my bedroom at home and deal with the aftermath of my mother's chagrin after.

My friends Pete Manzella and Frank Sindoni and a few others were shocked at how I looked and dressed but they encouraged it as well. The other neighborhood kids, the kids I hung out with between first grade up to high school saw us in a much different light. I can't say how many times I heard some dude I had known all my life scream from the window of his moving car "Gennaaaaaaaa, you fucking faggooottttt"! Every once in a while, some asshole would pull his car over and try pushing me around to try and intimidate me and sometimes even go so far as to try and hit me. Depending on who I was with when shit like that happened, the incident would either get talked down or it would turn into a fight. There were times when it would come close to a real fight, but usually it was just some idiot fulfilling his primal "alpha-male" need to feel better about himself and say his idiotic bullshit and go away. There were times it would hurt when these things happened because I was pretty good friends with some of these guys at one point but eventually, it was really easy to walk away and leave the neighborhood behind. In my mind, I was moving towards a place where I felt more at home, something until that point I rarely felt.

Chapter 11. *I'm in the middle of a NERVOUS BREAKDOWN*- Dominic "Dez" DeRosa-LACE

One night in April 1986, Fran and I went to the Limelight to see Cheap Trick. I drank a six pack of Budweiser on the way there and was feeling pretty damn good. The club was packed and the crowd was electric; it was a really fun night. I ran into a dude I knew from the local scene; his name was Dez. He was the singer of a really well-known band named Lace. After some small talk, he told me they were looking for a bass player. I lied and told him that I played bass because I would have really loved to be in that band. They were very well known throughout the city and brought in really big crowds wherever they played. We hung out together most of the night. He was a really cool dude. I lied through the whole conversation, trying to be some kind of bad dude or something. I did this often when I met new people. I didn't have a lot of confidence and needed to lie to boost my presence and look better than I saw myself. After a while we exchanged phone numbers and I promised to call him. I really wanted to audition for his band.

Later in the night I met a really drunk girl that agreed to come home with me. I had this pretty unique problem whenever I was drunk, girls would appear to be way prettier than they really were. This fact was realized the next morning. I didn't take her to my house, I took her to Fran's. She had her own little studio apartment and she let us use her bed while she slept on the floor. While this girl and I were in the bed fucking, Fran was trying to sleep on the floor right next to us. The bed started moving across the floor and by the time we were done it was completely on the other side of Fran! We somehow made the bed move completely over her sleeping body on the floor. I remember waking up the next day and laughing with Fran about how this girl looked nothing like she did the night before and we had to figure out a way to get rid of her so I could do my best to forget what happened. What happened that night was not just a one-time occurrence; it happened way more than I care to admit.

I called Dez the next day and from that point we started talking regularly. It was evident that we were a lot alike and we were becoming pretty good friends right away. The band was having problems keeping members. Dez and the only other original member, Joey the drummer, were not getting along to well. Dez said he was dabbling with Heroin and Joey found out and was pretty pissed off about it. Dez was trying to arrange a get-together between me and the rest of the band but the guitarist was currently on tour with Joco Pastorius, a fairly well-known Jazz bass player. He was having a hard time getting us together. When the guitar player was available, Joey wasn't. Joey seemed to be distancing himself from Dez and never really recognized me as someone of any importance. Whenever I would see him he would barely acknowledge me. Dez gave me a copy of the band's demo tape and a list of other songs they played and in the meantime I borrowed my friend Duane's bass and began practicing the songs. I was quite good at playing bass. Bass guitar came fairly naturally to me which was surprising because I never thought I would like to playing it.

I continued to practice at home while Dez and I grew really close. He was the big brother I always wanted. He was quite a bit older than me. He was 27 and I was 21, but we were exactly alike. We liked all the same music, we loved the local glam rock scene, we loved drugs, and even had the same taste in women. We were hanging out a lot. We got in all the clubs for free and made great use of that luxury. We would often wind up in situations that were out of this world. We talked on the phone for hours on the days we didn't hang out. At the time, I believed our meeting was destiny. I believed that somehow, we were going to get the band together and make it to fame and fortune.

After a few months Dez starting introducing me as his bass player and I felt privileged to have him say that.

During the same time, I met and became friends with a few dudes from Brooklyn. They were cocaine dealers that hung out in the same clubs as us. They were "regular" people though, they had short hair and wore normal clothes and didn't fit into the NY rock scene at all so they would buy me drinks and keep me high on coke as long as I sold their product. I would also round up people for parties after the clubs closed. Allie was one of them and he would have parties in his house. These parties would get absolutely crazy.

Dez wouldn't come back to Allie's house, he didn't like cocaine, he was more of a quaalude, valium, weed and heroin guy. I started snorting heroin with him sometimes while he would bang it (Shoot up). I fell in love with heroin. Luckily, I would only use it once in a blue moon, neither of us had jobs or money. Being friends with Dez meant the world to me. He really was the brother I always wanted. If anyone ever messed with me he would get right in their face and let them know if they fucked with me, they were fucking with him. He looked a lot like me with the big hair and makeup, but for some reason people wouldn't dare mess with him. I'd say probably because he was over 6' tall and he had this aura that let people know if they fucked around he'd fuck them up. He was fearless!

He knew a lot of what I told him about myself was a lie. I was 21 and I told him I was 25. I told him a ton of other lies, but he never called me on any of them. He never judged me though, he accepted me completely as I was. I always felt safe whenever I was hanging out with him. Dez was the most electric person I ever met. He had a style that was all his, he was definitely one of a kind. He had his own lingo, we called it the "Dez Lingo". He talked in his own way and it was totally unique. No one I ever met had such a magnetic personality. He definitely was my kindred spirit.

I became friends with a few girls who were friends of his. Angie was Dez's ex-girlfriend and they were still good friends. There was also Linda, Anna, and Debbie. I met them all by chance right after I met Dez. I was at Lamour in Brooklyn one night and this beautiful girl named Misty stopped me and told me I looked like Steven Tyler. I was instantly head over heels in love with this girl. She was just so beautiful to me. Out of the blue, her friend she was with named Debbie grabbed me and stuck her tongue down my throat and there went my shot with Misty. Gone. Debbie later introduced me to the other girls and we all became really good friends. I would run into Misty once in a great while and I would always try and get with her, but it never happened. To this day, for some unknown reason, I've never forgotten her. I tried to find her years later on Facebook, but never had any luck. I've always wondered what would have happened if it was her instead of Debbie that night. I'll never know (sigh). Actually, as I write this I feel myself wishing that she somehow reads this and we meet up. I've always considered her to be "the one that got away."

Chapter 12. All my friends they died, they died-
Jim Carol

Unfortunately, we never put the band back together. Before meeting him I never had a friend like Dez. I was never as close to anyone as I was with him. I looked up to him as my brother. We were always either hanging out together or on the phone with each other. In February of 1987, the band Queensryche played at Lamour East. This was a huge event; they were a platinum-selling national act. I got Dez a job with me at the club. We were non-union stagehands; we helped the band's road crew unload and set up the stage and then load the band's gear back in their truck. For that, we were paid $50 and were allowed in the club for free.

The following Wednesday Dez and I went to the Cat Club on 13th St. between 4th and Broadway in downtown Manhattan. Wednesday nights were the club's glam night and we went there every week. Toward the end of the night, I met two girls that were both hot; or at least I thought so. I was going to leave with them and I tried to get Dez to come with us. He didn't like one of them so he didn't come with us. This wasn't how things normally turned out and I kept bothering him to come, but he refused and I went home with them to freaking New Jersey. I fucked one of them and fell asleep after. I guess it wasn't so good for her because she woke me up the next morning and dropped me off at a subway station in the city and went to her job.

When I got home I called Dez to brag about my accomplishment and he didn't answer, which was weird. I called him a few times throughout the day and he never picked up. I figured that he may have hooked up and was with some girl. I didn't start getting worried until Friday. He still hadn't answered his phone and he never showed up at Lamour East. I was really worried at this point; we never went so long without speaking. I was worried because nobody heard from him. I called Linda, Angie, Anna, and Debbie and they hadn't heard from him either.

On Monday, after still not hearing from him, I had my friend Pete take me to his apartment in Astoria. When we got there, I was knocking on his door and there wasn't an answer. I looked through his windows and saw that the green light from his stereo was on but I didn't see anything else. I rang the bell of the superintendent of the building and asked him to let me in so I could check on him. He agreed and opened the door. I walked in and went right to his bedroom and he wasn't there. I had a momentary feeling of relief but then I heard the Superintendent say something like "Look at this son of a bitch." I went back to the kitchen and that's when I saw him. He was on the floor right by the door. I walked right past him. His nose was caked with blood and I could tell right away he was dead. He was fucking dead. He died alone on his kitchen floor. He was there for days. Alone. There was a glass of water on the table that had a syringe in it. There were three empty bags of dope and three more full bags on the table as well. Automatically it felt like the room was spinning uncontrollably. It was going so fast that I had to sit on the floor and hold my head. I didn't hear or see anything. The next thing I knew, the police arrived.

The cops made me stay in his kitchen while they searched his body. I was three feet away from his dead body watching the police go through his pockets as if he wasn't even there. Then they searched his house. His bedroom was covered in pictures of his favorite bands and pictures of the band Lace. The cops started asking stupid questions and saying some real idiotic shit. They were making fun of his pictures; they asked if we were "fags" and they were saying shit like "Look at these fucking weirdo junkies". They searched me. They made me take my shirt off to look for track marks on my veins. They asked if I wanted the do the three remaining bags of dope so I could kill myself too. They asked If I wanted to suck his dick one last time. I shut down after that.

I didn't answer them. I didn't even recognize their existence. I felt like I was somewhere else, like a dark windowless room with no light. My friend Pete called my mother and told her what happened. She called my brother, who was at the time in his second year as a New York Police officer and told him what was going on. I'm guessing he somehow got a hold of these cops and told them I was his brother because they finally stopped being assholes to me. They told me I should've told them my brother was a cop.

They finally let me leave and Pete took me home. My mother held me in her arms for a few minutes while I cried. I went to my room and curled up in a fetal position and cried for hours. My phone was ringing off the hook. My poor mother answered the phone and told everyone who that called I couldn't come to the phone and she took messages. This was so intense. I was twenty-one years old and I just found the best friend I ever had dead. I couldn't get the sight of his face and body out of my mind. I had a chill in my body, I was shivering and couldn't stop. There was no understanding of this for me. There was no way I could process this. I had no coping skills whatsoever. Without a doubt, I would never be the same after this.

The days and weeks after this were a blur. I went to the wake but couldn't bear the funeral. There was no way I could watch them lower him in the ground and fill it with dirt. I had spoken with his parents and his brother at the wake. I provided them with whatever details I knew, which wasn't much. I met with his twin brother Rob at his apartment when he went to clean it out. He offered to give me anything of Dez's that I wanted, but I couldn't take anything. I experienced a lot of trauma before this but nothing like this. I went completely numb. I felt nothing. It didn't matter how much I drank or how much cocaine and other drugs I took, I felt nothing. I had a lot of really good friends who reached out and tried to help, but I was beyond help. I didn't want help. There are no words that can ever describe what this did to me, how I felt after, or the long-lasting effects this had on my life. My heart hurt so bad. I felt so empty. Numb. Damaged to my core.

Chapter 13. Wish you were here.

We're just two lost souls swimming in a fishbowl, year after year – David Gilmour – Pink Floyd

I struggled desperately with my mental and emotional health after Dez passed away. I found no value in being alive. My heart hurt so bad and I couldn't get high enough on anything to not feel the pain. I cut myself off from people and wouldn't express how I felt to anyone. I didn't blame myself for his death, but I couldn't forgive myself for being alive. I didn't deserve life and he did. I was the piece of shit that lied, cheated, stole, and mistreated everyone close to me and he was this perfect person that was good to me despite all the horrible things I did; it just didn't seem fair.

I went overboard trying to numb the pain. My days at that time would almost always start with beer or vodka, then valium, and eventually cocaine. I was always good at getting everyone to feel sorry enough for me to pay for whatever I needed. I reached a point where I noticed some friends were avoiding me. I was either the nicest, sweetest person when I was fucked up or the most obnoxious, loudmouth idiot imaginable. There was no in-between. No "off" button either. I would just go until there was nothing left and then sleep for days. I truly stopped caring for anyone or anything. I'd steal my mother's car or her money whenever I wanted to. I would disappear for days without contacting anyone. My existence was horrible but that had no bearing on the fact that life still went on, even if I wasn't taking part in it.

My brother married his girlfriend in June and they asked me to be in the wedding party as an usher. I accepted but I had no idea what they were going to ask me to do until about a week before the wedding. At that time, I was wild. My hair was jet black and huge. You couldn't see my eyes through my bangs that covered half my face. I wore a ton of makeup too. They told me they wanted me to look "normal" for their wedding and when they told me what they wanted me to do I started flipping out. They wanted my hair completely pinned down, to make it look like I had really short hair. They said I couldn't wear makeup. Basically, in my eyes, I had to look like "everyone else" because I was an embarrassment to them. Why else would they ask this of me? I didn't want to do it. I asked to not be in the wedding party but they told me they already asked a friend of Maureen's to be my partner.

My mom convinced me to do it even though she agreed with me and believe me, that was a rarity in my house. I tried to negotiate and asked to just wear my hair pulled back into a ponytail, but they wouldn't concede. I felt betrayed by my brother. I got loaded the night before the wedding and didn't sleep at all. I did as they asked and looked like a fool for their wedding. At the reception, I drank conservatively. The last thing I remember about that day and it's been burned in my mind and my heart since, I went to hug my brother and congratulate him and he pushed me off him and said something to the effect of, "Get the fuck off me, what's wrong with you." I asked my mom for money for a cab and went home alone. I didn't even say goodbye to anyone. I didn't cry even though I was hurt and angered and felt stupid for allowing myself to change the way I looked for someone who always thought so little of me.

The next month was a blur. I was getting fucked up every night. I was sleeping with girls I would meet just to avoid going home. Then, out of the blue in early August 1987, this dude Neil who I knew from working at Lamour East called and asked me if I wanted to work as a non-union stagehand at the upcoming U2 concert at Giant Stadium. When he told me what it paid, I jumped at the opportunity. Neil owned a music equipment rental company and I worked for him a few times. He told me he was planning to move to

Los Angeles and asked if I'd be interested in relocating. I talked with my parents about it and they agreed the change of atmosphere would likely be in my best interest. They agreed to give me $1000 to do it too. I think they did this to save themselves from watching me destroy myself as much as they did it for me and I don't blame them for that. I already knew quite a few people that moved out to LA, plus I had the dude I was moving out there with so I wasn't scared or worried. I don't know why or how, but I somehow felt this would make things better for me and that I was going to be okay. I had no idea what I was getting myself into but whatever it was, it had to be better than the current situation and I was ready for whatever came my way, or so I thought.

Chapter 14. Welcome to the Jungle- *Guns and Roses*

On September 1, 1987, Neil drove up and met me in front of my house. I kissed my mom goodbye and threw my bag in the trunk of his 1969 Volkswagen Bug and we headed out to LA. We had an eight-ball (1/8th oz.) of cocaine and I had $950 in my pocket. It was a pretty non-eventful trip, the only memorable thing about it happened in a place called Bucksnort, Tennessee. Yes, you read it correctly, Bucksnort. There really is a town in Tennessee called Bucksnort.

The car broke down there and while it was getting a minor repair we went to a restaurant to eat. It was like time stopped the second we walked in. I guess they were not properly prepared for the sight of me. I was this tall super skinny dude with skintight black jeans, jet-black hair that was probably standing at least fifteen inches high with thick black makeup on my eyes. Every head in the place turned and stared at me. I was used to this sort of thing, it happened often. It happened pretty much wherever I went so I didn't give it a second thought.

While we were eating this huge dude with a cowboy hat on his head and a lobster redneck was staring at me intensely. My quick wit went into overdrive and I stupidly asked him if he was going to eat his fries and with that, he kicked out his chair and stood up and in the twangiest (great word, I know) southern drawl he said "Boy, I can't eat a damn thing looking at you!" I was used to people staring but this guy looked like he was going to hang me. Luckily, the manager saw this and came between us. He said "Your meal is paid for and we'll pack you up a doggie bag. Y'all have a nice rest of your day. Leaving that restaurant alive was probably one of the luckiest moments in my life. We went across the street to the mechanic's shop and the car was ready. Luckily it needed just a minor repair to get us back on the road. I think we dodged a bullet there!

After 5 grueling days on the road, we finally pulled up to the Beverly Sunset hotel on the Sunset Strip in West Hollywood. After checking in we went to our room and I slept till the next day. When I woke up I was pretty excited and dressed quickly and went for a walk. I walked one block and there I was, right in front of the world-famous "Whiskey a Go Go". One more block and there was the "Roxy" and right next to it was the "Rainbow bar and grill". The people walking on the street were all just like me. There was a bunch of wild-looking rock dudes with big hair. There were a lot of women too. Beautiful women dressed like it was Friday night in a club and it was in the daytime! I knew right then and there that this was what heaven must be like. I called my friend Laura from NY. She moved out there a few years before me and invited me to her house. She gave me her address and I took a cab and met her and her future husband Casey at their apartment. Laura dated Dez before I knew him and she was full of questions about what happened. She asked if I was shooting dope and asked to see my arms after I told her I wasn't. Her Boyfriend Casey and I started talking a bit and he told me he could get me a job where he worked as a telemarketing salesman. Laura and I got pretty drunk, and she kept asking questions about what happened to Dez. I felt like I was being interrogated by the police and after a while, it became too much for me to handle. It was still such a sore spot for me and talking about it just hurt. I told them I needed to get back to the hotel.

My first week there was spent establishing some connections and finding an apartment. During the night I'd walk around the strip and hit all the clubs. Things came together fairly quickly, I secured a job in telemarketing and another job through one of my New York connections, Steve Habl. He was the production manager for the band Kiss. In his off time from Kiss, he was the production manager of the club Lamour East. I called him when I got to LA and he set up a meeting with Gene Simmons and I was offered a job to house sit for Gene while he was gearing up for a tour. I was originally supposed to get hired to go on the tour as a roadie but I was a week late and all the spots were filled by the time I made it. Neil and I found an apartment in Hollywood and we paid the deposit and first month's rent. I was ready to start this new life. I was 3000 miles away from home, 21 years old, and on my own for the first time. I was far away from my parents. I was far away from all my friends and bad influences as well. It didn't take long to get the ball rolling and it didn't take long for my demons to come out from their hiding place.

LA was a den of iniquity wrapped up in a beautiful package. It was really beautiful with the scenery and all, but it didn't take long for the sleazy, dirty underbelly to show itself. My job at the telemarketing office had weird hours, we started between 430 and 5 am so we could reach customers on the East Coast before they left their offices. We sold fasteners (anchors, nuts, bolts, and screws) to electrical contractors so we had to catch them early. I lived within walking distance of the office.

One day walking to work I saw what looked like really a few beautiful prostitutes, but as I approached I noticed something a bit scary. These women all had unusually deep voices for females and they were all pretty damn tall. When I was right next to them I could tell they weren't biological women. Back then, I don't believe that the label "transgender" was even a thing. One of them caught me looking and said in the thickest Mexican accent *"Oooooooh honey! Can joo tell I'm a fag? Are joo a fag? Lemme tell ju something, joo got the cutest walk, now come on over here and gimme a keess"*! As I was running away, I kind of thought it would be best to take a different route next time. I ran across the street and a cop car pulled up next to me and the officer asked me why I was running. I told him I was scared of

the transgender prostitutes. I thought they were chasing me.
He got out of the car and told me to stand with my arms up
against the wall. He asked for ID. I didn't have one, but I gave
him my name and address. I told him I was only in LA for like
two weeks and that I just moved from NY. He handed me a
ticket and told me I had two weeks to pay for it or I'd have a
warrant. I asked, "why the hell are you giving me a ticket?"
He told me it's illegal to cross the street when the light is red.
I thought he was kidding. I was in disbelief, but he told me I'd
get a ticket any time a cop saw me do that. I looked at the
ticket, it was a freaking $15 fine! As I walked the rest of the
way to my job, the Guns and Roses song *Welcome to the
Jungle* played over and over in my mind. There was much
more in store for me.

Chapter 15. I'm a Liar — *Henry Rollins*

My first few months in LA were cool. I didn't have
any drug connections and I wasn't making a lot of money
with either job (house-sitting for Gene Simmons was pretty
cool though). I was limited to a few beers here and there. I
spent most of my time with my NY friend Laura and her
boyfriend Casey. I didn't mix well with my roommate Neil so I
tried to avoid him as much as I could. He wasn't a bad guy.
He was just too normal for my rowdy, loudmouth, obnoxious
lifestyle. I worked a show with him one night and the
Whiskey. He rented a bunch of equipment to a pretty well-
known band called London. London was managed by AMI
Productions and I met their rep Tony Recasino and the owner
and CEO of the company, Steven Machat.

        This company managed some of the biggest names in the business and Steven's father co-managed the Rolling Stones back in the 60s. Tony and I hit it off well that night. He loved my image and he said over and over "You have a really strong Rockstar look, you're going to be famous someday". I went to their office/home on Mulholland Drive and it was stunning. It overlooked both LA and the valley. The walls of the office were covered in Gold and Platinum albums from various bands that they managed over the years. To say I was "star-struck" would definitely be an understatement.

        I called a friend in NY, Tommy, he was the guitarist in Lace before I met Dez. I told him about who I met and he was very impressed. Tommy just left a band named "Smashed Gladys" who were signed to Elektra Records (a fairly stupid move) to form a new band called Knockout. They just finished recording a demo and he asked if I could get a copy of it to Gene and AMI. Tommy was telling me he didn't care much for the bass player in the band and if I would get them connected to either AMI or Gene Simmons, he'd fire the bass player and the band would move to LA with me as their bass player. I totally wanted that gig. Tommy was a super cool guy and from what he told me, the songs were really strong and their image was awesome. I wanted to be in a band and play gigs in LA. After a lot of hell after losing my best friend, things were looking better in LA.

        I received the copies of the tape and after giving them a listen. I was pretty impressed with the songs. I got copies for both Gene and Tony. I played the tape for Gene in his house. Right away he didn't like the singer's voice but said the songs were promising. He offered to pay for a new recording with the advice they should fire the singer and find someone better.

The response from Tony from AMI was quite different. He was wild over it; he said his boss Steven loved it as well and they wanted to manage the band. He swore they could get us a record deal within a year. When I called Tommy with the news, he was super happy and promised I'd be the bass player. We planned for Tommy and the drummer Jimmy to fly out and meet with Steven and Tony to discuss how they could help the band if we were managed by them. This was so cool and I needed something good to happen after all that happened with Dez. I played with one or two bands after Naztee Habitz broke up but they sucked. I was so looking forward to playing in a good band and with AMI productions as managers, with all the gold and platinum records on their walls, I was sure I was going to be famous.

About 1 week later, I went with Tony to pick Tommy and Jimmy up at LAX airport. When we got to the hotel, Tommy and Jimmy said they needed to talk with me about something important. They told me Tommy got way ahead of himself by promising to make me the bass player and they weren't getting rid of their bass player. Tommy apologized with some bullshit story. I was hurt by this. I had already told quite a few people that I was going to be in this band. I was fuming mad and left. I didn't go to the Rainbow that night and I didn't go to the meeting the next day.

Tony called me a few days later and asked what happened and why I didn't come out with them. I asked him if Tommy or Jimmy told him anything, and those little wimp bitches didn't tell them anything. I told him what happened and he told me that AMI was poised to sign them to a management deal but if I said the word, he wouldn't sign them because of what they did to me. I asked him not to do that. I didn't want to be responsible for something like that. The fact that I was the bigger man meant something to Tony and he promised me he'd set me up with a paying gig or something similar. Unlike my "friend" Tommy, he kept his word. He called me a week later with an offer to audition for a paying gig on an international tour. My world was about to get rocked.

Chapter 16. Don't you know that you are a Shooting Star- *Bad Company*

I auditioned and was hired on the spot. After 4 weeks of rehearsal, I was going on tour to England, Ireland, and Spain. The singer was in a pretty well-known band from England and then had a huge hit as a solo artist in the early eighties but hadn't done anything since. To avoid causing any embarrassment he'll remain anonymous. The tour was very small. We were playing small theaters, not arenas, and there were a few club appearances thrown in too. There wasn't a lot of money put into this tour, we stayed at three-star hotels and all the equipment went under the tour bus which was not much more than a glorified Winnebago.

The first two shows were sold out and had great crowds but the rest of the shows were played to half-filled theaters or clubs, and the crowds were not very enthusiastic. There were a few times I went on stage with a severe hangover but they were cured by the after-show parties. The best part of the tour was the parties. There were really beautiful women and people with lots of drugs. As usual I was the loudest, most obnoxious person at each party! I spent most of my time with the 3 guys in the road crew. The other musicians in the band were all way older than me and they were "sober." I wanted no part of sobriety and the road crew knew how to party.

When I came home, I had four weeks of paychecks waiting for me and it was more money than I ever had in my life. My boss at my telemarketing job held my position for me so I was able to start working right away too. I checked in with Tony and Steven from AMI to thank them for providing me with the opportunity. They told me that wonderful things were said about my playing on the tour and I would probably get more work as a result. Things were looking good!

Chapter 17. It's so Easy, When Everybody's Tryin' to Please me- *Guns and Roses*

Right after returning from the tour, I found a strip club that would become my home away from home for the next few years. The Alladin was one of the clubs that Motley Crue used for the "Girls, Girls, Girls" video. I started going completely overboard with my drinking and cocaine use. I'd meet strippers and go on days-long binges with them. I was missing work and quickly spent all my money from the tour. I wound up homeless for a day or two as well. I slept in the car that my boss had let me use. My boss took the car back and fired me for the first of many more times to come. He just wanted me to straighten my act out. I was a good salesman and I was making decent money for me and the company so he would always hire me back after drying out for a while.

I needed a break so I convinced my mother to let me come home for a while. I told her some bullshit story about why I needed to come home and she allowed me to. This was another pattern that started, I would burn all my bridges in LA, come home to NY and get my shit back together and go back to LA. It happened way more times than I'd like to remember.

I was hired for a few more tours over the next few years but they were nothing spectacular. Touring in rock bands is not as glamorous as it may seem. Most of the time spent on the road can be quite tedious. We would either be on the tour bus traveling to the next destination or stuck in our hotel rooms waiting for the next performance. The duration of our time on stage would vary depending on whether we were the headliner or the opening act, but it usually lasted between an hour to ninety minutes. Some bands would celebrate after each show for a few hours, while others would head straight back to their hotels. As for me, I would party after every performance, either backstage or in the hotel. There were always a lot of women around, and it was rare for me to spend a night alone. My problem was I never had an "off" button and when most people had enough, they'd call it a night. Not me though. I'd keep going until my body would just say " I had enough" and just physically shut down. I was fired from the last tour because of my drug and alcohol abuse. My attitude sucked and my playing suffered so I was fired mid-tour. Of course, I lied and blamed the band for my shortcomings.

Between 1987 and 1990, I frequently traveled between Los Angeles and New York due to my struggles with drinking, drug use, and toxic relationships with dancers. The root cause of my problems was my inability to quit using cocaine once I started. Whenever I used cocaine, all my responsibilities went out the window. If I had to choose between paying rent or buying cocaine, I always chose cocaine. Even if I had to choose between spending time with my family or indulging in cocaine, I'd choose cocaine. If I happened to be in a relationship with a girl, and her best friend or sister had cocaine, I'd choose cocaine over the relationship. People around me started getting tired of my erratic behavior, but I was too sick and foolish at the time to realize it.

I moved back to LA in October 1989. My mother helped me get my apartment by paying the security deposit. A few months after I moved in, my boss fired me again. I was missing work and showing up fucked up sometimes as well. I started selling bootleg t-shirts at concerts with a friend who was a silk screen printer whom I met during one of my many cocaine and alcohol binges.

We were selling t-shirts at a Janes Addiction concert in Santa Barbara and I got caught by the police and was arrested. I had a warrant in LA for one of those goddamn J-Walking tickets that I didn't pay. The police held me on the warrant, and I was in Santa Barbara County jail for a day. They wouldn't release me until I paid $750 in bail. I called everyone I knew and of course, no one had that kind of money so I called my parents. My mother was pissed off but I was relentless. I told her would have been beaten, killed, or raped if I wasn't bailed out. I was scared to death and true to my nature, I convinced my mom to send the bail via Western Union. After going to court on the charge, I was fined $200, and the court returned $550 to me for the remainder of the bail. Let me lay the background before I talk about what I did with the money.

In the building where I lived in Hollywood, there was this black dude with dreadlocks that I'd run into once in a while. I would hear him fighting with some girl over there a lot and there were always people coming in and out of his apartment at all hours. His apartment was right across the hall from mine. Sometimes he would walk through the hallway in the building making these really weird coughing noises. Every time he saw me, whether I was coming or going, he'd ask me for something. He'd ask for a cigarette or change of $5 for the washing machine, a beer if I had some while walking in my apartment, and even a quarter for the payphone outside. I mean every single freaking time I saw him he was asking for something! I had no idea who he was, but I soon found out. He was a very well-known musician. His name was Ivan Neville. He was most recently the keyboard player for Keith Richards (Yes, THE Keith Richards) solo band, "The Expensive Winos." His father Aaron Neville was a famous singer from the band "The Neville Brothers" and he also had a huge hit song from the 60s called "Tell it like it is." Ivan had an album of his own that had a hit in the Billboard top 30 called "Falling out of Love" and there was another hit called "Not Just Another Girl" from the same album. I went from hating this guy to becoming all too willing to give him anything he asked for.

One day I was playing my guitar, Ivan heard me playing and knocked on my door. He said he liked what I was playing and that it reminded him of Keith Richards. We started talking about music and what we've done in our careers. I told him about going on tour a few years before and about some of the bands and some songs I played on as a hired musician. He asked if I wanted to come to a recording studio he owned to check out his music. I said of course I did! When we got there, he played me a song he was working on for his second album and asked what I thought would work on guitar for it. I listened to it once and showed him my idea which he loved and immediately recorded me playing it on the 16-track tape with the song!

Later that night, he came over with a few people who were partying at his apartment. He pulled out more cocaine than I had ever seen in my life so I was like, OF COURSE you can hang out! They were freebasing, which is a way of smoking it after putting it through a process that made the cocaine pure and the high was 100 times more intense than snorting it. I was hooked from the first hit.

When that $550 check came from the bail refund I should have done what I promised and sent it to my mother. That was the right thing to do, right? Yeah well, we're talking about me, so the right thing went out the window along with all the money in about 7 minutes. I went to Ivan's apartment, and we smoked it up in a few hours. I became addicted to smoking cocaine very quickly. Within a few months, I was evicted and fired (again). Ivan let me stay at his apartment across the hall from mine. That's one of the things I absolutely love about Ivan. He had the biggest heart, even at the height of his addiction.

I was very sick from using this time, I lost a lot of weight even though I was under weight to begin with. Things got out of control really fast. By the end of the summer, Ivan went to rehab at the Betty Ford clinic and I went out on the road to sell bootleg Rolling Stones t-shirts during their "Steel Wheels" tour. The tour was on a route that would have carried me back to NY where I was going to clean up and get my act together again.

The very last show before I was going to go to NY was in Pontiac Michigan. I wound up getting caught by the police. What happened next was terrible. These cops took me to the police station and strip-searched me. Then they held me in a holding cell and wound up taking all my money and told me I could leave. They let me keep like $3. The police station was very far away from the Pontiac Silver Dome where the concert was. It took me hours to reach the guys I was with, and thank God, they paid for my taxi back to our hotel. I was dead broke; I didn't even have a way to get to NY. They were going to drop me off in Buffalo and I would take a train to NYC. Luckily, the guy I was working for took mercy on me and gave me money for a train ticket and gave me $100. I was grateful for that but scared to death at the same time.

I got into NYC late the next night and took the subway to Queens and spent the night in a hotel. The next day, I went to see my friend Pete. He owned a little corner deli around the corner from my mother's house and then I went to see my parents. I rang the doorbell and my father came downstairs and told me to go to hell. They found out I received that bail money and never sent it to them. I was told, "I don't care where you go, but you can't stay here". I was out on the street. Homeless during the coldest winter NY had seen in 100 years.

That night, with nothing but a bag of dope and a subway token, I slept on the subway for the first time in my life. The F train was my home for the night. I thought about how and why I got there, but I was too sick and stupid to hold myself accountable. No, this wasn't my fault. My parents were fucked up for not letting me stay with them. It was my brother's fault; he wouldn't let me stay with him either. Instead of learning my lesson and changing for the better, I was hurt and angry and looked to get even.

What I did next was terrible. After about one month of sleeping on subways, I called my mother and lied about getting beat up on a subway train the night before and begged her to let me stay with them. She wouldn't let me stay but she paid for a hotel for a week. I was supposed to find a job, make enough money, and pull myself out of the situation in a week. I was in no way capable of that. My seriously sick thought process had me thinking my parents should know I couldn't do that and they should've let me stay with them. That wasn't going to happen. They weren't buying what I was selling so I just became an evil asshole and stayed in this room ordering room service all week. I think the bill came to $1500.

For that act of stupidity, my parents were finished with me. They went to court and filed an order of protection against me in the NYC courts. I could go to jail for calling them, or for being within ¼ mile of their residence. My brother was done as well. He wouldn't accept a call from me. As usual, I blamed them. It was their fault. How dare they try and buy me off with one week in a hotel. How was I supposed to get my act together in just one week? Well…. Back to the F train I went for another few weeks. When I was a kid we used to call homeless people "bums" and now here I am, living on the train like a damn bum.

I vividly remember my eyes filling with tears when I approached the Woodhaven Blvd subway entrance. I remember the empty feeling in my heart as I walked down the steps and waited for the next train. I would cry while getting on the train to look for an empty car to sit in so I could hopefully fall asleep without being bothered. I think the worst thing I remember about sleeping on trains was when one morning, I woke up in a subway car filled with people going to work around 7 am. I noticed a pair of eyes looking at me with disgust. It was almost like I could feel them staring. The eyes belonged to a friend of my brother; his family lived downstairs from my family in our two-family home. I practically grew up with him and here he was looking at me like I was an animal and not saying a word. He was just staring at me with a look of disgust. I felt so small, so embarrassed, I just wanted to crawl in a hole and die. I exited the train without saying a word with my head hung low in shame. Feeling shame is so damaging to the psyche. As I write about it, I can feel that feeling all over again.

My friend Pete had the kindest heart and for some reason, he bought my bullshit story about why I fucked my parents over in the hotel. He saved my ass. My friend Laura and her husband Casey moved to NY and Casey was still working for the telemarketing company that he got me my job with. He was leaving his job and he offered to sell me his customer base for $1000. Pete stepped up and paid for it so I could start working. I called my old boss in LA and told him I now had Casey's customer base. I told him that I bought it from Casey and I could either come back to work for him or sell to these accounts through his competitor. He welcomed me back with open arms! I made really good money from this and saved enough to move back to LA.

I made it back to LA in October of 1990. My friend Anna, a beautiful girl from France (accent and all) let me live with her in her condo in the Hollywood Hills. I really wanted to get back into music and to live as peaceful a life as possible. I was tired of the chaos, so I tried my best to stay away from the strip clubs and cocaine dealers. Ivan lived close by and was sober and working on a program of recovery. He recently married his girlfriend Gretchen and they had a baby together. It was nice to hang out with him without us freebasing cocaine and living with all the drama that comes with that lifestyle.

Life was fairly normal the first few months back in LA. I was checking out some local bands, looking to get involved in one. Anna and I, along with a coworker of hers went to New Orleans for Mardi Gras in February 1991. Mardi Gras was an awesome experience. I was constantly getting surrounded by people who thought I was Steven Tyler from Aerosmith or Tommy Lee from Motley Crue and true to form, I lied my way into free drinks and dinners and even a few girl's beds (come on, give me a break here, you wouldn't have done the same at 25 years old?). It felt like I was a Rockstar. When living in the lie was better than living in the truth, I chose the lie. Always.

My last night in New Orleans I met some strippers and wound up too drunk to walk, let alone anything else. They put me in a cab and told the driver where to take me. My only memory after leaving them was waking up on the floor outside of our room and Anna and her friend were laughing at me.

Upon returning home, I placed a call to my grandmother in Florida. I called her almost daily since I moved to LA in 1987. I knew she wanted to go back to NY but none of my family was able to take care of her. Besides her and my Aunt Lee (my father's sister) and my cousin Sandra, I had no contact with anyone else in my family. My parents and I hadn't spoken since the hotel incident. My brother and I rarely, if ever, spoke to each other. My Aunt Lee, her daughter Sandra, and my grandmother all knew about my problems with my mother and father and my drug and alcohol abuse but they never judged me. They always made me feel like family. I found out my grandmother passed away while I was in New Orleans. I remember feeling sad and then really angry that no one tried to contact me to tell me. I remember feeling like the biggest piece of human feces on Earth. My parents hated me so much that they didn't even try to tell me about the death of my grandmother. I was incapable of holding myself accountable for what I'd done to my parents because I was still caught up in my addiction at that time. To me, it was just another wrong on the part of my terrible parents. I thought *no wonder I'm so fucked up.*

Shortly after we came back I met a dude that would become my toxic twin. My ride-or-die and best friend for years to come. He was looking for a bass player for a new project he was starting and I met him and the singer at his house one night. From that moment forward we were inseparable. His name was Tommy Azevedo. He was originally from Hawaii as was the singer Rocci. They had played together on and off for a few years and had a great song writing chemistry. They had another dude from Hawaii, Paul Schofield, a great drummer lined up to play in the band as well. After our first rehearsal, we all knew that something really special was in the works. We settled on a name that Tommy had envisioned, Vertigo Children and we were ready for business!

If there were ever two people that should never have met it would be me and Tom. We were so much alike and instead of us trying to keep each other out of trouble, we encouraged the wildest behavior imaginable. There was no "off" button and once we got started there was no stopping the train until it wrecked. We were extreme, obnoxious, rude, loud, foul and any other word you can think up that described our debauchery. We continually tried to outdo each other with rude, vile behavior. We weren't the type of people who would consider any consequences before we acted on a behavior. Instead, we would dare each other to be as extreme as possible.

The only time we were serious was at rehearsal. We played our instruments with our hearts; our rehearsals were taken as seriously as live shows and we wrote lots of songs together. Outside the rehearsal studio was quite different a story. We took our drinking and our cocaine use to levels far beyond imaginable. There were times that we didn't sleep days while continually drinking and snorting cocaine. I remember one time after a two-day binge we were cleaning up the mess and counted over 100 empty beer cans. I couldn't tell you how much cocaine we did but I do remember going back and forth to our dealer's house multiple times.

The first time I realized that Tommy and I were truly toxic terrors was during the band's first photo shoot. The photographer wanted to do it early on a Saturday morning which would have been fine but Tom and I were up drinking and doing cocaine all night before. We didn't get any sleep and we were going on purely alcohol-induced adrenaline. It didn't take very long for the photographer to throw in the towel. We were being obnoxious and making fun of him the whole time he was trying to get our pictures done. After he left we went with Rocci in his car to his girlfriend's house. She was a stripper and supposedly some of her friends (also strippers) were there. We were out of cocaine for a while and were drinking Jack Daniels and beer excessively.

I don't think either of us could put together an intelligible sentence by this time. For some reason Tom didn't like one of the girls and was being really mean to her. I don't remember what she said but Tommy's response was pretty vicious. He called her a skank or something to that effect and said the last thing she would taste in her life was the bottom of his boot before she flew off her balcony. I thought that was hysterical and in my idiotic drunken state started laughing uncontrollably and that was it, I wound up projectile vomiting off Rocci's girlfriend's balcony on a woman and her dog as they were entering the building.

Needless to say, she kicked us out and Rocci lost it on us. He was yelling and screaming at us and told us to fuck off as he drove off without us. We walked the few miles back to Tommy's house and continued as if nothing happened. There has never been a friend in my life that I've partied with as hard as I did with Tommy. Episodes like this happened with us regularly. People liked hanging out with us if we were sober, but no one would last more than an hour or two if we were partying.

The band was excellent. We were all top-of-the-line musicians and Rocci was an incredible singer too. The first round of songs we wrote were a little on the commercial side but still very good. A friend of Rocci's came to a rehearsal and loved us. He turned out to be a movie producer of small, low-budget "B" movies. He had one movie that was ready to come out on video tape (remember them?) and asked us to write a song for the ending credits. Rocci wrote it in one day, and we recorded it the next day in about two hours. I played the tape for Ivan; he liked it too. I asked him if he would help us and produce a demo for us in his 16-track studio. He agreed to do it for us, and we went in his studio to record shortly after.

We recorded two songs in one night while drinking and snorting cocaine (Ivan recently relapsed and was getting high again). The recordings turned out excellent. Ivan's long-time friend and bass player, Nick Daniels III sat with me and helped me come up with incredible bass lines for each song. Ivan brought out the best of our creativity and together we turned two ordinary songs into really well written songs, both with potential to be hits. The songs, "Midnite Summers Dream" a dark, moody ballad and "Baby-Baby", a pop/punk song, came out excellent in the recordings. Both songs had excellent lyrics and they sounded amazing after Ivan mixed them. Ivan was a lot of fun to work with. I was intimidated at first because of his stature but between him and Nick they helped me become a much better bass player and band member. They taught me the valuable lesson of always having the common welfare of the band and the song come before my personal needs. That is a hard pill to swallow with an ego like mine but they helped it make sense to me and the rest of the band which is in part the reason the demo came out so well.

Chapter 19. It's a long way to the top if you want to Rock and Roll- *ACDC*

That demo tape helped us get the ball rolling by getting our name out to the industry. Tom's girlfriend Leann worked for a famous producer, Bob Ezrin. He produced early Kiss albums, early Aerosmith, and also Pink Floyd's The Wall. Shelly Yakus was the head engineer at A & M Studios where Leann worked for Bob. Shelly approved a "spec deal" for us, which meant we could record in A & M Studios for free, and the record label would have what was known as "first right of refusal" to either sign or refuse to sign us to a record deal. If we were refused a deal, we could then take possession of the tapes and shop them to other labels. The least expensive studio there costs around $3000 per day, and depending on the room, the cost could reach over $5000 per day, and we were recording there for free! We recorded in the actual room where the song "We Are the World" was recorded. We were all excited about this opportunity.

For the next few weeks, we practiced the three songs we chose to record over and over, perfecting the arrangements and our individual parts as we went. There were times each of us fought over certain parts. We were all pretty egotistical and we each thought our contributions were the best. I fought extremely hard over a part in the song I wrote, "Mystery Achiever". I went as far as showing Ivan what I wanted versus what Rocci and our new Drummer Tony thought I should play. Ivan once again stressed I should play what's best for the song, and the common welfare of the band over my personal thoughts. So, I caved and played it the way they wanted. We all had to sacrifice our personal thoughts on a part or arrangement to the majority of the band's beliefs.

When we went to the studio, we were ready. We had the songs basic tracks all done on their first take. After that, we worked on all the overdubs, vocals and background vocals, guitar solos and percussion additions and it all went really quick. We went from start to finish and mixed perfectly in three days. We were all really proud of what came out. The finished product had completely captured our vibe and sounded amazing. All we had to do now was wait for the record label to hear it. It was all down to two people's opinion of the recording, Shelly Yakus and the A & R guy from the label.

The day the label people listened to it we were at Tom and Lean's house waiting like puppies waiting on a snack for her to come home and let us know the outcome. When Lean finally came home, we almost attacked her because we were so anxious. When she told us the news, it wasn't great but wasn't bad either. They couldn't decide solely on the songs even though they really liked them. They wanted to see us live on stage in front of a crowd and then they'd make their decision on whether or not to sign us. We were happy with the news, even though we all wished we would get signed solely off the power of the songs and recordings. I was a little worried though, like I said earlier, we never played a show. This was the closest any of us ever came to getting a record deal from a major label. It was really exciting and I was completely caught up in it.

When we heard the news about what the label thought, I was heartbroken. They declined to sign us. They loved the music but thought Rocci was boring to watch. Leann told us in the most caring way and tried to have us remain hopeful. When I watched the video of the show, I agreed with the label. Rocci was an unbelievably good singer, but to me, he was lame as a frontman. He was no match for the energy that Tom and I put out.

I allowed this to get to me a lot worse than I should have. I started drinking a lot more, I found some people that were doing heroin and I would go on heroin binges with them once in a while. I kept that secret from everyone I knew though because no one would accept it. I would disappear on binges for days and lie about where I was after. I started playing in two other bands at the same time as well. I loved Vertigo Children but couldn't get past dealing with the rejection from the record label. My heart wasn't into it with the band anymore. Tom and I were still best friends and still as crazy as ever, but my love for the band was lacking. I tried my best to stick it out but after a few months my drinking, drug use, and obnoxious attitude became too much for them to handle and I was fired. I spent two years with these guys, they were my whole world for the better part of them. I was mad as hell at them for firing me but deep down I also knew I deserved it. I think this was the first time I ever took some responsibility for my actions. Not completely, but I did own some of it. I was starting to get tired of the lifestyle but not in any way ready to let it go.

Chapter 20. Can you take me to the fire, it gets so dark and cold in this old city= *Little Dickens*

I played in a few other bands while in Vertigo Children, one of the bands was "Little Dickens." I was living in a house with the singer/rhythm guitarist Matt. Four guys were sharing the house, with three of us in different bands, and I played in Matt's band. Matt and Steve (the other roommate) also sold cocaine. All we did was drink beer, play music, and snort cocaine all day and night. We always had a lot of people over. There were lots of women who brought groceries, cigarettes, and beer for us. Besides the cocaine, there were other drugs in the house that guests would bring like Percocet, Valium, Ativan, and other sedatives. It sounds crazy, but at that time with all the cocaine that was in the house, the pills were life savers because they'd knock me out so I wouldn't stay up doing cocaine for days at a time. Shortly after I left Vertigo Children, Matt moved out of the house and Steve brought in another roommate and I had to find another place to live. The new guy didn't want all the people in the house like it was before. I stayed on people's couches (mostly strippers) all over Hollywood and the valley for a while. I wasn't working and was always broke. I was still in Little Dickens with Matt and he always made sure that I ate and he'd always buy beer and share his coke with us. We hung out together almost every day.

My drinking and drug use were way out of control. I'm sure it had a lot to do with my mental and emotional state. I kept getting kicked out of whoever's house I was staying at because I stole or didn't pay my share of bills. If I stayed with a woman I was dating (not really dating, more like fucking), I would usually cheat or not come home for days while binging. I hadn't spoken to my parents or my brother in years. I was still very good friends with Tommy from Vertigo Children and we would always get completely fucked up whenever we hung out.

Eventually, Matt let me move in with him but that didn't last too long. I would steal so much coke from him and I would disappear for days with girls that were doing dope and coke and it just became too much for him (anyone in my world often felt the same, I had that effect on a lot of people). It was ugly when he kicked me out. He pretty much did it literally, and by that I mean he woke me up and told me to pack my shit and get the fuck out. Then with a swift kick from his boot to my ass (literally), out the door I went.

I was falling apart from all the drug and alcohol use. I was a complete mess. As usual, I found my way back to New York. I was homeless. -Again. One would think that after all the chaos, homelessness, and insanity I'd at some point realize I needed to stop getting high and maybe change some behaviors? Nope. Not me. There was still more defiling of myself yet to come.

Chapter 21. And it's sure been a cold, cold winter- *The Rolling Stones.*

When I look back now I can see how the end was near by this point. I had pretty much done everything that I always told myself I'd never do. Everything was so much different than when it all started in 1986. The "glam" thing was over. The eighties music at the end of the decade sucked, it all sounded the same, everyone looked the same, and there was no originality whatsoever. The Seattle "grunge" scene had taken over and that was what everything was about. I remember being tired and finally thinking that I was never going to make it to be the big-time Rockstar of my dreams. I thought about dying a lot. I welcomed it. I never told anyone that I had those thoughts, they were my little secret, my way out of this mess without having to say goodbye to anyone. I wouldn't have to face anyone either. I thought of myself as a failure all the time. There was very little of my original drive left in me. Music was all I had at the time and the only reason I didn't give up.

Here I was in 1993, 27 years old and back in NYC again. Ugh. I was getting tired of moving back and forth across the country. I still had not spoken one word to my parents. In my sick mind, I was still mad at them. I did see my brother. I showed his wife and him some videos of the band Vertigo Children. Neither of them seemed to be interested in them. I remembered leaving their apartment thinking that I didn't even know them. I stayed at my good friend Chris Traina's house for a few weeks and then I went and stayed with my old friend Ivan Neville.

Ivan was living in Manhattan, recording his 2nd album "Thanks". He was dropped from the record label that released his first album. They dropped him even though the album was fairly successful with a top 30 hit and a song in a very successful movie. He was dropped because of the drug use during the recording of his second album for the label. He had multiple stints in rehab and was missing a lot of sessions during the recording. Getting dropped from a major label did not help him to stop using at all. He was using more and more, but instead of freebasing, he was using crack.

Crack is a much cheaper form of smokable cocaine but every bit as powerful and addictive as freebasing was. I stayed with Ivan, his wife Gretchen, and their daughter Ivy Jo for about 6 months and fell deeper and deeper into addiction. We all did. Ivan didn't have anywhere near the money he had back in 1989 and we struggled to stay high. We all did some dirt for money and we were living in a very toxic environment. There were days that Ivan was supposed to be in the Power Station recording studio at 4 pm and it would take us hours to get him there. The way we lived at that time was terrible. We were getting high with his 4-year-old daughter in the house. Ivan and Gretchen fought constantly.

I would reach levels of paranoia so bad that I'd sometimes hide in a closet for hours. It was a miracle that we didn't get arrested. My brother was a narcotics detective in the New York Police and his precinct patrolled the area where I would go out to buy crack. I was always terrified of getting caught either by him or by a police officer who knew him.

Whenever I would meet old friends, they would tell me that I looked terrible. It was very distressing for me, so I started avoiding going to my neighborhood just to avoid hearing such comments. One day, I took Ivan's daughter with me to Long Island to spend some time with my friend Linda and her husband. Upon seeing me, Linda expressed concern and told me that I looked like I was dying, which was true. She then called our mutual friend Laura to inform her about my condition, and Laura urged me to come to New Jersey to stay with her and her family. Although I was hesitant at first, I knew that things were out of control at Ivan's place, and it was only a matter of time before something terrible happened. I was scared to death of going to jail, but at that moment, I felt that I would have welcomed death with open arms. So, I left Ivan's house and moved to New Jersey. Little did I know that I wouldn't see Ivan for the next eight years.

Moving in with Laura and Casey saved my life. They let me stay there for a month or two, I had to leave the house when they left and I had to get a job right away because whether ready or not, I had a time limit and they weren't stretching it. At the time I was mad about that, my sick mind thought I should be able to live as I wanted but today I understand and I know they did the right thing. Thank God for them. I found a job at a restaurant as a waiter and stayed clean the whole time I was at their house. I gained some weight back and was fairly happy to be out of the craziness and chaos of Ivan's house even though I missed him and was worried about him.

My friend Chris in Queens was moving in with his girlfriend but wanted to keep his little studio apartment in Maspeth and offered to let me stay there for $75 a week. I was making enough to afford that, and even though I had to take a bus to New Jersey to get to work I still jumped on it so I could be near my friends in Queens. Eventually, I got a job at Red Lobster on Queens Blvd. My biggest problem was that I took myself with me everywhere I went. Change of scenery meant nothing. My addiction lived within me and followed with me where ever I was.

Chapter 22. Back in the New York Groove- *Ace Frehley*

I hated being back in New York. It was winter and it was freezing cold. I didn't want to see anyone except for Pete and Chris and another friend Frank DiMarco. Pete was my best friend for a long time, he bailed me out of a ton of shit over the years and was always there when I needed him. I met Chris at Lamour East back before I moved to LA. We both worked there part time as non-union stage hands. We hit it off quickly and I met Frank through him. We were true knuckleheads. Chris occasionally sold cocaine, and Frank and I would usually snort more of it than he sold. Chris and Frank were really good friends to me and were always a lot of fun to hang out with. We'd get pretty fucked up but for some reason, whenever I hung with them we never really went overboard.

A few weeks after moving into Chris' apartment, I went to the city after work one night. Without giving a second thought, I bought some crack, a stem (to smoke crack in) and choirboy (Copper mesh to use as a screen). I was walking around Times Square dipping in phone booths and hallways smoking crack and drinking a 40 (40 oz Beer). Addiction is baffling, I hadn't done anything like this in months and I can't even say what prompted it but I started doing it a few nights a week. That night and pretty much only that night, I went home when I ran out. After that I'd spend all my money every time I went out and smoked crack. Going home after running out was a challenge because it was so hard to stop once I started. I remember walking around Manhattan trying to figure out how to get more money. The drug was starting to make decisions for me which always ended terribly. I got myself fired from Red Lobster and luckily found a job at Lenny's Clam Bar in Howard Beach which was pretty far from Chris' house in Maspeth. To get to Howard Beach from where I was living was a two-bus ride and I figured with the hour-long ride that maybe I wouldn't go to the city after work and smoke crack. It didn't stop me. Addiction doesn't allow common sense to get in the way of getting high. Ever.

I was able to maintain the apartment because as a waiter I'd get paid every day. I would always pay Chris the rent every Friday night after work. I was still going to the city a few nights a week and would spend all my money on crack. One night I was in the city and I was under a building marquee taking a hit, and some dude came up and asked me a question that I didn't hear. He saw I was hitting a crack stem and pulled out a knife and held it against my throat till it broke the skin. He took my stem and whatever crack was in my hand and walked away, he even said "you should know better" while walking away. He didn't get everything from me though, I still had money and crack hidden inside my pants where he didn't look. Looking back at this today I realize how sick I was. Addiction truly turned me into a sick motherfucker.

I eventually had Pete smoking crack with me and we went on a rampage for about a month. Luckily, an old friend from LA called me; it was right around the time of the OJ Simpson car chase in the summer of 1994. He was living in Pennsylvania and was trying to get me to go down there to start a band with him. Scott was someone I worked with at the telemarketing company, his ex-girlfriend was my former roommate. Scott and I had our moments when we were pretty good friends, and there were times when I wanted nothing to do with him.

New York wasn't working well for me so I decided to go to Pennsylvania and give the band thing with Scott a try. I was in NY for longer than I wanted to be anyway. I started missing my parents and figured that I'd try and contact them before I left for PA. Surprisingly, my mother didn't hang up when I called and of course, I lied and told her I hadn't been using cocaine for a few years or something to that effect. I told her I was moving to Pennsylvania to start a band with an old friend from LA and we would be moving back to Los Angeles after a while. She was receptive and it was nice to hear her voice after a few years of no contact. Before I left, I met with them and my brother and his wife at their house. My brother brought his baby, Victoria. She was around 8 months old at the time. We had a nice family dinner together for the first time in years.

I went home and packed and for the first time in a very long time, I cried. Don't get me wrong, I was not in any way taking responsibility for the terrible things I'd done, I was just sad at how things turned out. I guess by not seeing them or speaking with them I shielded myself from having any feelings about them. Seeing them brought down the shield. I hadn't cried like that for a long time. I may have wanted to at times, but I wouldn't allow myself to feel anything; that's where the drugs and booze helped.

Addiction is ugly. The worst part of the disease to me is how it kills the human spirit. I don't believe that anyone, unless they are an addict or someone in recovery will ever understand how a person can want a drug so bad that they will do things they know are terribly wrong to get it. The painful part is having to live with the guilt and shame of knowing I couldn't stop myself before doing it. I was totally powerless and life was not in any way manageable. It was becoming more and more obvious to me that it was my addiction that was the core of my troubles. I was losing the ability to hide from the truth and the truth always hurt.

Scott picked me up the next day and off I went to Mount Holly Springs, PA. Being raised in Queens and living in LA for a few years did not prepare me for what I was about to experience. Mount Holly Springs is a tiny little town about 20 miles south of Harrisburg, which is the capital of PA. The town had two stoplights, four bars, and not much else.

When we got to his house, we unpacked his van and Scott showed me where I'd be staying, in a one-bedroom apartment in a house that his father owned. He was going to turn the apartment I was staying at into a tattoo shop and I would stay in the bedroom rent-free. He started showing me his tattoo equipment and telling me how he was making really good money from it. He showed me how to set up the tattoo machines and how to use them. I tried telling him that I had no talent whatsoever when it came to drawing but he continued on as I continued to pound down Budweiser's like they were water. Anyway, throughout the night he continually told me how easy tattooing was and that he was going to show me how to do it. He went upstairs to go to bed, and I don't remember falling asleep, but I do remember waking up.

At some point during the night, I put four tattoos on my legs. I woke up with a slight hangover and felt a burning pain in my legs. When I looked to see what the hell was hurting me so badly, I saw them. Four of the ugliest, stupidest, terribly done tattoos imaginable. They were just stupid. I felt like an idiot. I had a ridiculous-looking yin-yang symbol, a tribal that looked like a 3-year-old did it, and a comedy/drama theater mask that you couldn't tell which one either of the masks was. Scott came down and when I showed him he laughed his damn balls off. I wasn't ready to see the humor in it yet but eventually did. Scott was laughing hysterically for what seemed like an hour and then I started laughing too. As I write this, I am smiling and chuckling. I've done some ridiculous shit in my days, this was definitely one of the most stupid of them all.

Scott and I got down to writing some songs. Scott was a really good drummer, his playing often reminded me of John Bonham from Led Zeppelin, and Bonham was the best drummer of all time. Scott's style of playing made it easy for me to come up with really cool grooves. We started the search for a guitar player, and believe me, the pickins were slim! This area had a very small rock scene, and whatever talent was available wasn't very good. Nowhere near the caliber of players we were used to while in LA.

We met this one dude in a club in Harrisburg. We gave him a tape with three songs to learn and set a date for him to audition. I remember he showed up with this little practice amp and I immediately thought this guy has no idea of what the fuck he's getting into. Let's just say I wasn't wrong. He couldn't play through one song. These songs were so simple, and he couldn't get through one. I was dumbfounded.

In LA, I've auditioned for bands without ever hearing them before and without having a tape to learn the songs either and I'd learn the songs on the spot. Both Scott and I had played with a level of musicians with that capability. This guy didn't come close. All his bragging and he couldn't learn the simplest songs. Oy Vey! I remember laughing all night with Scott about that disaster!

Scott and I went out to a strip club one night and I met these two really cool girls. We hung out with them most of the night. I was attracted to them both, but one of them was more my type so I made my interest obvious. Her name was Laura, and her stage name was Pheonix. She was absolutely stunning. She had long natural strawberry blonde hair, perfect white skin, and piercing blue eyes that cut right through all my bullshit right to my heart. Usually, I'd lie to every girl I met to make myself look better than I was. I never had enough belief in myself to just be me. With Laura though, I found myself completely incapable of lying. There was something about her that made me feel very comfortable in her presence. The other girl Heather, was quite beautiful as well. We all hung out until the place closed. They told us that they both had kids and had to get home to them and they were going to leave without me and Scott! Something like that was a rarity in LA and I was quite intrigued by meeting a girl that wouldn't fuck the night I met her. I got Laura's phone number and we said our goodbyes.

I started speaking to Laura on the phone quite a bit after that first night. I was telling her how hard it was for us to find a guitar player. She told me about this guy, his name was Scott, and how he was an excellent guitar player. She found his number and I called him and we hit it off. He was a lot younger than Scott and I, but that didn't matter to us. We set up a day to meet. He was in a band that was playing at a club in Harrisburg the following weekend so we decided to meet that night. What an awesome way to check out a potential bandmate!

We went to the club and my look attracted a lot of attention, as usual. I got pretty drunk and I met this girl and soon after we started kissing. I became my usual obnoxious self and not realizing where I was, I followed her into the ladies' room. A bouncer came in and pulled me out and told me that was unacceptable. After he walked away what did I do? I walked right back in there again. The bouncer saw this and came and kicked me out of the club. He was walking next to me and had his hand on my shoulder and I pulled his hand off and told him "I'll walk out of here, but not with your fucking ape hand on me."

He didn't take too kindly to that and we were about to get into it when another bouncer saw what was about to happen and came between us. He was cool and said as long as I was leaving, no one would touch me. As I walked through the door the first bouncer, the dude that kicked me out, pushed me through the door. My stupid drunk ass became infuriated at this and started calling the guy all kinds of names and challenging him to come out. I remember calling him a "steroid pussy freak" and he didn't like that so he came out and shoved me and I fell into the marquee and the glass on it broke into a million pieces. Scott came out and saw what was going on and got pissed at me and left me there to fend for myself. What a fucking dick, I should've known from that point that Scott was a douchebag and never had anything to do with him ever again. My friend Tommy from Vertigo Children would have never left me there alone.

After that, these fucking bouncers came out and held me down. They called the police and when they showed up, I was given a citation for disorderly conduct. I tried to have them charge the asshole that shoved me but they wouldn't. So here I am in Harrisburg, 20 miles away from Mount Holly and Scott left me stranded. Luckily, a friend of the guitar player we were meeting at the club said he'd drive me home. Halfway back after realizing I lived pretty far away, this guy starts saying some bullshit. He said I owed him more than the $10 I promised him and then he actually said I owe him a blowjob. At that point, I shut up and when we got to my house, I went in and got the $10 and threw it in his face and told him to fuck off.

He came after me and busted through the front door and tried to grab me, but I got the jump on him. He had his arms around my waist and his head was buried in my chest. He had pretty long hair, and I wrapped his hair in both fists and punched him in the head with his hair wrapped in my fists. Scott heard the commotion and came out, I was yelling to get this guy off me while I continually punched him in his head, pulling his hair with each punch. Scott was able to break us up, the dude went home beat the fuck up and I finally went to bed. I woke up the next morning with a hangover from hell.

Scott came down and tried to apologize for leaving me, saying he couldn't chance getting into any trouble while fighting for custody of his daughter. All I could think at that point was that none of my friends would have ever left me like that. I never really felt the same about Scott. I was never really able to fully trust him again.

We finally did get to meet the guitar player; his name was Scott too. He was only 21 years old. We called him Scott Jr. We were creating some pretty cool music together during our rehearsals. Scott Jr. and I got along great and started hanging out more. I talked to Laura every day and we decided to meet up one night. Junior knew both Laura and Heather so it was comfortable for all of us and we had a great night. I slept over at Laura's house with her that night and for reasons unbeknownst to me, I fell head over heels for her. Before this I wouldn't allow myself to have feelings for any women. I was either just too scared to get hurt or I was just with so many women that I didn't want to get tied down. I wish I hadn't fallen so hard for her; I had no idea how to be in a relationship. I had no idea how to behave around a kid and her son was about 1 year old at the time. It was very strange to find myself in this situation and while I did love her, it was also very uncomfortable.

The next few months kind of flew by. Laura and I got pretty close as Scott and I grew further apart. Eventually due to being an obnoxious drunk Laura had enough of me and ended the relationship. I was severely heartbroken and depressed. I struggled to let go of her. I tried to get back with her a few times over the years but she wasn't interested and I don't blame her. Scott, now back with his pregnant wife and daughter had lost interest in the band and I just wanted to go back to LA. To say Pennsylvania was a letdown is an all-time understatement.

By this time, I had lost count of how many times I moved in and out of LA. Over the next two years, I moved back to Pennsylvania and back to LA two more times. I took myself wherever I went and the monkey on my back came everywhere. This fact still hadn't been realized by me yet. While I was still incapable of taking personal responsibility for my problems, the past 8 years of problems were taking their toll on me, both physically and emotionally. I was tired. I promised myself (again) that this was it. If I was not successful within a year or two, I would move home to NY and change my life forever. I recently turned 30. I never ever thought or believed I would live that long. In a way, it was disappointing that I did. Looking back now, it was sad that I felt that way. One of my favorite sayings was "Drunk by noon, dead by thirty."

This time around things went a little better. I was still telemarketing but for one of my former bosses' competitors and this guy did it right. He was a serious businessman who recently moved to America from South Africa. He was importing his products directly from overseas manufacturers. I was able to outsell our competition and still make good money. I was making more money than I ever did before in LA.

I found a roommate in the valley and we got along well and finally, I was responsible for all of my bills. I immediately started hanging out with the old Hawaii crew, Tommy, Toby, Rob, and his brother Johnny. We all lived very close to each other and hung out together every day. We would all meet after work and decide on dinner and it was like a family thing and everyone had their job in putting it together. This was the closest thing to having a family for me in years. I will forever cherish the times we all spent together over those two years. This is one of my favorite memories of LA and it for sure was the happiest I ever was out there.

Within a few months of moving there, I ran an ad in a local musician magazine looking for a band to audition for or musicians to put something together with. I received a call from a very well-known singer named Terry Illous. He was the singer of the band XYZ, an 80's hair band that had found some success. They released a few albums on a major label and had some airplay on MTV with their videos. I met him and Jeff Northrup, another well-known guitar player/producer and they started a band named Ground. Their original bass player, Phil Soussann, who played with Ozzy Osbourne had left right before the band had some upcoming showcases for a few major record labels. When they played me some of their songs I was blown away. The music was awesome and Terry's singing was simply amazing. I really wanted to be in this band. They gave me two tapes with 3 songs on each and they gave me a week to learn them and audition. I stayed home all week and practiced them and when the audition came up I was ready. I nailed the songs in the audition and later that night Jeff called and told me they wanted to try me out for a few gigs. I was so excited over this. Finally, something really worthwhile had come up for me musically.

We rehearsed for a few weeks before the first gig which was at the Coconut Teaser on the strip. We had a great crowd show up for us, and we performed perfectly. I really felt like this was the best band I was ever in and we all got along genuinely well. What I believed helped was that I was friendly with the guys in the band, but we weren't close friends. We never hung out outside of rehearsal. It was strictly business with them. My friends were always supportive of me and everyone came to see us and were blown away just like I was when I first heard them. We played a second show to the same response, and it truly felt great. We had a third show lined up, and our drummer dropped a bomb on us two weeks before it. He quit because his other band was going on tour. I was sick over this because he was a seriously good drummer, he made it so easy for my style of bass playing to shine.

Terry and Jeff were a lot less worried than I was. They set up auditions for drummers and we auditioned three and chose one that seemed to fit the bill. I thought the original drummer was way better and his style fit my bass playing better, but I went along. I felt I was too new in the band to offer my opinion.

The day of the show, Toby and I did our regular Friday after-work routine of going to the Star-Garden strip club for a few beers. My stupid ass had more than a few beers and got drunk as fuck. I needed to sober up so I went home and fell asleep for a little while. I woke up feeling like shit and went to Tommy's house and drank a few more beers and did some cocaine. I was somewhat wrecked by this point and wired from the coke, so I made another brilliant decision and called some stripper chick I knew and she came over with some Percocet. By the time we went to the club, I was fairly fucked up. The guys in the band never saw me like this and were worried, as they should have been. Needless to say, for the first time ever I was too fucked up to play and I made a million mistakes during the show. I was so embarrassed after. My friends tried telling me it wasn't that bad but I knew I was terrible. I'd never screwed up on stage as bad as I did and I felt like the world's biggest loser. Later that night, after getting more fucking drunk and coked up, I called Jeff to apologize. He told me they decided to find another bass player. I couldn't blame him. I fucked up a show. This knocked me right off of the cloud I had been on since joining this band. This was the first time that I considered getting sober.

I actually made a few calls about going to rehab which was something I never thought I'd do. I never went though, after a few days I just figured this is who the fuck I am and I'll never change so fuck it. My two famous last words. "**Fuck it**". They've done me lots of good throughout my life and they were my "go to" words whenever I fucked up. I understand today that was just my way of avoiding the obvious truth that I didn't want to face.

Chapter 25. This is the End, Beautiful Friend, The End- *Jim Morrison, The Doors.*

After this, I started thinking about moving home to NY. I was making decent money from my job, and I was already working from home so it wouldn't have been that big of a change for me. I was too tired for someone only 31 years old. I had spent ten years trying to make it in music and I came close a few times but never to the point where I could make a living from it. I was feeling the pain from the past ten years more than ever. My friends were the best at this time. I'll never forget how they were really understanding of what was going on with me and they never tried to steer me away from my thoughts. They were just there to listen and be supportive. They kept me sane and from going off the deep end. I started having suicidal ideations at this time and these guys will never know how they kept me safe from acting on them.

While sitting at home deep in my thoughts one day, I got a phone call from Scott. He recently came back to LA and was in a band with this weirdo Jerry and a singer from one of his previous bands, Doug Starr. The band was way different than any other band I've ever played with. The music was really good but different than anything I've ever done. It matched the time, it was a cross between Pearl Jam, Led Zeppelin, and maybe the Stone Temple Pilots. I liked it. When I auditioned, they told me they had a gig lined up a week away. I didn't have much time to learn this stuff and there were like 12 songs. I managed to pull it off. Somehow, my style of playing was perfect for this music. Everyone in the band was impressed and they all thanked me for joining and helping them out of a jam. We played that first gig and received a great response from the crowd. Someone from one of the local music magazines was there and they gave us a really good write-up and we started having different bands and venues call to offer us gigs.

Scott and Jerry were pretty much arguing all the time. Jerry was a seriously mentally ill person with delusions of being someone way more important than he could ever dream of being. He was a really good sound engineer and a decent guitar player but he tried to make himself seem as someone of importance in LA when the truth was no one could stand him. Scott believed a bunch of Jerry's bullshit and then when Jerry couldn't produce any of what he promised, Scott tried to take control of the band. Scott suffered from the same delusions as Jerry and the two of them fought constantly. After a few more shows together, Scott went back to Pennsylvania supposedly for something having to do with his kids. He called shortly after and stated he wasn't coming back. Jerry was staying with me at the condo that Scott co-owned with his ex-girlfriend Anna my former roommate and all of a sudden, he got weird with me. We were supposed to discuss the possibility of replacing Scott but his attention turned towards me and my cocaine use. He accused me of some really weird shit and he wasn't making any sense at all. It was obvious to me that he was seriously mentally ill. He tried starting something with me so I threatened him with a baseball bat which put a stop to his weird behavior and he finally moved the fuck out which made me quite happy.

This was it. This was the final straw and I decided to go home. Ten years of hangovers, drama, and getting kicked out of where ever I was staying all had taken its toll on me. I planned to first move to Pennsylvania because the cost of living was inexpensive and I made pretty good money so I could save to move to NY. I spent another two weeks in LA, saving money and preparing to leave. I hung out with my Hawaii crew every day, the only hard thing about leaving LA was leaving these guys. They were the only family I had known in ten years. I knew I was going to miss them terribly.

On my last night in LA, the guys took me to the Star Garden, our favorite strip club. As a going-away gift, the girls all brought me up on the stage with them, put me in a chair on the stage, and gave me the best multi-girl lap dance ever! Then, they tied me to the stripper pole and soundly spanked my ass with a paddle. It was truly the best sendoff I could ask for. The next day, exactly ten years to the day I left NYC for LA, September 1st, 1997, with a sore ass and a bad hangover, I drove away from LA forever. I somehow knew I was never coming back.

Chapter 26. Can't Find My Way Home- *Blind Faith*

After a four-day drive, I pulled into Mount Holly Springs in the early afternoon and went right to the apartment I rented from Scott's father. I fell asleep on the floor. The apartment was unfurnished and empty. My bed and some other belongings were being brought out by a long-distance moving company and were supposed to arrive the following week. I had some money and bought a used convertible couch and Scott helped me drag it to the apartment. It was a small one-bedroom apartment, perfect for me and the rent was cheap. I was just happy to have an apartment and was ready to start my plan to get home to New York. I truly believed I wouldn't be in Mt Holly for more than 3 months. Boy was I ever mistaken.

It didn't take long for the depression to hit me. To this point, I hadn't given too much thought to leaving music behind. The reality of it all was starting to sink in. I started feeling like a failure for all the opportunities that I fucked up from drinking and drugging. I started remembering all the potentially wonderful relationships I didn't care enough about staying in and was suddenly feeling lonely. This was a different type of loneliness though, the only way I can explain it is that it felt permanent. I had horrible thoughts of living alone forever without a woman in my life and it was sort of scary. I remember asking myself why the fuck am I like this? Why am I never truly happy? Why do I fuck up every good opportunity that comes my way? Then finally, the most important question at that moment was, "Why the fuck am I sober right now?" I was going through way too many feelings for me to deal with and felt the need to get fucked up. One good thing about Mount Holly at that time was there were four bars all within walking distance. I got myself good and fucked up to the point of vomiting all over myself right outside my apartment when I got home. The hangover the next morning was terrible. I could barely move and anything I would try to eat or drink couldn't stay down. This was becoming a regular thing. As were my walks to the bar every night.

Mt. Holly was a strange little town. It was a very white, very conservative little town. I don't remember ever seeing many kids around. There never were any kids playing out in the street like when I was a kid. The people there had no idea what to think of me. I no longer had really big hair or wore makeup, but I still, in no way came close to looking like I was from there. I still had a New York Accent at that time, it was kind of a protection for me. It may sound hard to understand but I felt vulnerable in PA. I didn't know anyone and I didn't want to get fucked with, so in my sick mind, if people knew I was a New Yorker they wouldn't fuck with me.

Just another example of the sick thinking that I dealt with most of my life.

After a few weeks of going to the bar most nights of the week, I met the dude I was looking for. I met Dave. You know Dave, right? Dave was the dude that knew where to get the drugs! There wasn't an abundance of sniffing cocaine in good ole Mount Holly or the next town over, Carlisle, but there sure was a lot of the coke you smoke. You know, that good old crack cocaine! So here I am, in Mt. Holly Springs PA, where the men are men and the sheep are scared (I know, I know). I'm living in a town with two stoplights, 4 bars, and the dude who knew where to buy the crack. How could a guy like me, a severely depressed alcoholic with a thirteen-year cocaine addiction go wrong in a little one-horse town like this?

Chapter 27. I used to do a little but a little wouldn't do it so a little got more and more=
Guns and Roses.

Two things that I never knew about Mt Holly until this point was that everyone in the little town is an alcoholic. Everyone. At one time or another on any given night, you'll find almost everyone in the town at one of its four bars. Everyone from the grandmothers and grandfathers, the chief of police and the other two cops in that station to the underage teens and their parents. So, when I say everyone, I mean everyone! The second thing is, almost everyone in that damn town smokes fucking crack! Mt Holly had no idea what hit them when I came into town.

My dope fiend skills were top-notch. You can take a kid out of the city, but you'll never take the city out of the kid. Within a few weeks, good old Dave wasn't the only guy in town who knew where to get the drugs. I was making pretty good money at that time, working from home telemarketing anchors, nuts, bolts, and screws and I only had to work a few hours a day so I could spend the rest of the day being a full-fledged dope fiend. What was wonderful at the time, I was able to smoke way more crack than I paid for by being the guy who scored drugs for everyone else in that little town. Anyone who used me to get their drugs got way less than they paid for. *I know you don't have to tell me, I am a full-on genius. I do, however, appreciate that you recognized this fact. Thank you!* I don't know how I accomplished this without raising suspicion from Scott, but I did.

Around the Christmas/New Year holiday of 1997 going into 1998, Scott and I were talking and he had this idea. When he owned his tattoo shop and started doing body piercing, he knew that the jewelry cost a lot less than he paid for it. At this time body piercing was getting popular, but nothing like it was a few years later than this. His idea was for us to start making the body jewelry. It seemed to be fairly simple, just a round steel hoop with a bead in it or a straight bar with a ball screwed on each end. I must say, it was a pretty genius idea even though at the time we had no clue exactly how genius of an idea it was.

We started researching where we could buy the steel, the beads, and the balls. After finding this information, we learned we can make a ton of money off the needles.

Scott got a loan from his father and bought a few cases of the needles we thought body piercers used for piercing. The needles he bought were what he used when he learned how to do body piercings, but they weren't what most piercers were using. The needles Scott bought had a hub on the back end so they could be screwed into a syringe. We tried our hand at selling them to tattoo shops in states other than PA and wouldn't you know it, we sold about five thousand needles in less than two weeks and we made a ton of money. Scott split the profit down the middle with me and I was impressed by how easy it was to do this. We were selling the needles for more than one dollar less than most piercers were paying for them and we were still selling them at over five times their cost!

We ran into a snag after the first round though. Some of the shops that bought the needles from us called us and wanted to return them because they never used needles with a hub. Scott and I were pretty shady when we first started this. We didn't put our phone numbers on the invoices and the company name we used was fictitious. Our sales pitch was that we worked for some huge needle manufacturers and we were just getting started selling to piercers because our main business came from hospitals. When the shops that were able to get our phone number did call us to complain, we acted like customer service guys for this company and say we would get it fixed for them. To throw them a curve, we sold them MORE needles at half price to make up for our mistake. Within a month we were making between one thousand and fifteen hundred dollars a week. We were definitely on to something, but we needed to fix the snags.

My drug use was getting a lot worse because I was making more money than I ever imagined. I would use all night and get on the phone and sell fasteners for my regular job in the morning and then sell piercing needles in the afternoon. The hangovers were becoming unbearable. It wasn't easy being a crack-head with a job. I went through a private hell trying to keep this secret from Scott and his father. I talked about what happened to me when I was high on cocaine, that my mouth wouldn't work right and getting words out of my mouth was ridiculously hard because my lips and mouth would move but the words wouldn't come out. I looked like I was some kind of mental case. I had to hide this from everyone. It would usually take me about thirty minutes for that thing with my mouth to stop so I wouldn't look so stupid when I talked to people while I was high. I was always telling Scott I would be down in a half hour when he called me. I lived upstairs from him. I would lie about being in the shower or not feeling well and needing to get myself together or some other weird made-up story. I was truly falling apart and didn't know how to stop. This shit was getting seriously bad and it was about to get worse. What's even crazier was the hair-brained scheme I came up with to try and make things better. I thought if I could get my hands-on pills like Percocet or Xanax to help me come down from the crack, I wouldn't have so much trouble hiding this from Scott. As my sick mind thought I was getting smarter, the reality I was getting sicker and dragged deeper into addiction.

Meanwhile, were both earning a lot of money, so much that I eventually quit my other job selling screws. My drug use continued to get worse. I would get so high and paranoid that I'd stand by the front door, peeking out the peep hole while standing on one foot balancing myself for like thirty or forty minutes at a time. I would also hide in my closet, sweating to death, holding a gun while being scared to death because I thought they (the police or Scott) were coming to get me. I reached depths of depravity that were at one point unthinkable. Throughout the year 1998 this continually got worse and worse, until I reached a point where I could no longer take it. Something needed to change quickly; I was unable to hide what a mess my life had become.

Chapter 28. We are here because there is no refuge, finally from ourselves- *Taken from the Gaudenzia Philosophy.*

December 31, 1998, a friend and I were driving to his place with enough drugs in the car to put us in jail for a long, long time. A cop made a U-turn and pulled up behind me and hit his lights. I told my friend to dump the stuff out the window and I'd run. He said "I ain't throwing out shit, just fucking run." It was then that I said the first prayer that I said in years. I said to God, "Dude, (Yep, I called God dude!) if you get me out of this I'll get straight, I'll stay clean." I opened my eyes and just then the cop pulled up right next to me and took off down the road. It felt like forever but for real the whole thing probably took 10 seconds. I had to pull over and just sit silently for about 5 minutes. I was literally shaking and I almost shit my pants. My friend was telling me to get back to his place but it was like I couldn't even hear him. Somewhere inside, I knew God had stepped in.

When we were finally out of drugs, I called the Cumberland County Drug and Alcohol commission. I told them I needed help and if I didn't get it, I would be dead within a week. I told them I was smoking crack and taking opiate pills every day. I told them I was drinking alcohol by the gallon. I repeated over and over that I was dying. The person on the phone took my information and seemed to be very understanding. She told me a bed was opening in a rehab in Harrisburg in less than three days. I told her I wanted to go. I needed to go. I pleaded, *please, get me in there*. I received the call the next day and they told me they could come and get me tomorrow at 9 am. I breathed a sigh of relief and went to a friend's house to get high and drunk. walked home around 4 am. The rehab called around 8 am and said they were on the way. I started to panic. I started to fear that I couldn't go through with it, but I knew in my heart that I needed to go.

I went downstairs to Scott's house and told him what was about to happen. He swore he had no idea but I didn't believe him. He asked, "Why are you so weak and why couldn't you just stop?" I didn't bother to even try and explain. I told him if he needed me to leave the apartment and if he wanted to fire me it was fine. I'll get my stuff when I am out of rehab in 28 days. He promised it wouldn't come to that. The dude from the rehab showed up, and in my last act of stupid defiance, I threw my shoes into my bag with my clothes and went out to the van barefoot and lied and told him my shoes were at my friend's house one block away and asked if we could stop there so I could get them. He knew I was full of shit but took mercy and allowed it.

I went in, took my last hit off the crack pipe, took a swig of Jack Daniels, put my shoes on, went back to the van, and went to rehab. I remember walking in the doors and hearing a voice in my head say, "It's over". I immediately felt a weight come off me and for the first time in years, I felt safe. They took me to a room and searched through my things and took me to see the nurse. The first thing she did was put me on a scale. I weighed 108 pounds. She said, "Dude, I'm not kidding, you're dying. Please stay here for the duration. You don't have to die this way". After this, the house manager dude took me upstairs and showed me to my room. I was sleeping before my head hit the pillow.

Chapter 29. Someone saved my life tonight…. *Elton John*

I had been sleeping for a few hours and someone came into the room and told me I had to get up and come downstairs for the group. I was groggy and tired, I hadn't slept in days and pleaded with the guy for mercy but he wasn't having it. I had to go to the group session. I had never in any form of treatment before this, I had no idea what to do or say, I just sat and listened. Everyone who spoke said something that reminded me of myself. They were talking about being powerless over addiction and if anyone could understand that; it was me. I never heard anything like the discussion that was taking place but I totally identified with everything that was being said. It felt comfortable, almost like I knew these people that I just met for a long time. Someone asked me a question and when I answered, I broke down. I never; ever discussed my drug use with people. Any time someone brought it up I'd start an argument or tell lies to avoid the confrontation. I'd say anything to avoid having the conversation. But here in treatment after hearing people talk about things they've been through, it felt natural. This was strange to me. After less than an hour in this group session in a place I'd never been and with people I didn't know, I felt at home. I knew I needed to be there.

After a few days, I started to understand how the place operated. We would get up early and have breakfast, then a cigarette break, and then do the morning meeting. This rehab was what was called a Therapeutic Community, or TC. It was run by the clients. We worked our way through the process of the Therapeutic Community by having different jobs and responsibilities. Everyone took part in the organization of the day's activities and the structure of the curriculum. It took a little while, but I was catching on. The counselors would run the groups and sometimes offer insight or direction, but mostly just monitored us.

One of the counselors was starting to see right through my bullshit. When I shared in group sessions it was more of me trying to fit in than talking about my real issues so he started pushing buttons to get a reaction out of me. I wouldn't allow him to get to me. I was too smart and strong-willed for him, or so I thought. Finally, I don't remember how, but he found the button that broke me and man did I get pissed!! All 108 pounds of me got up in this 225+ pound man that was sober for 13 years face as if I was going to kick his ass. I was pretty sick and definitely stupid back then. He should have swatted me away like the insect that I was but instead, he kicked me out, told me to get packed and leave. How dare he say that to me?

I was upstairs packing my clothes and it dawned on me, here I go again. The self-righteous know-it-all that I am is getting kicked out of another place. At that point, I was kicked out of almost everywhere I had ever lived. I was kicked out of almost every band I played in. I was kicked out of every meaningful relationship I ever had, and here I was again, getting kicked out. Again.

I was crying pretty hard, I was finally upset with MYSELF because, at that time after ten days clean, it was plain as day that all this shit was my fault. It took so long to finally realize this. It wasn't my parents' fault for kicking me out for stealing everything. It wasn't the fault of the assholes that kicked me out of their houses for getting high when I should have paid rent. Not the fault of the stupid bands I played in for showing up to gigs completely wasted and barely able to perform. Not the beautiful women that I loved so much that kicked me out (usually because I screwed around with their friends). It was because of ME. It was my fault. My attitude. My behaviors. Just like everything they talked about in rehab. It was then that Jim the counselor came upstairs and talked to me and let me stay. He showed mercy when he should have kicked my ass out. I think this was the first time anyone ever showed me mercy. When I asked him why, he said he believed in me. I've never in my life heard those words directed at me before. Ever. That doesn't in any way mean I was getting a pass for almost getting physical with Jim. My learning experience for that was having to sit in the "thinking chair" for twenty-four hours. The thinking chair was a four-foot-high chair painted bright yellow. In other words, a dunce chair.

I was in rehab for a few more weeks after this and I started taking treatment seriously. Jim was a great counselor and through our talks, I came to realize how close I was to dying. He explained things to me in a way I could completely understand. I felt like he knew more about me than I knew myself. I left there after about 26 days. They made me leave early because I wouldn't go to another rehab like they suggested. They wanted me to go to a ninety-day facility but I was unwilling. They made sense, I mean, I used drugs regularly since I was 14 years old. I created a lot of damage for myself and my family and there was no way in hell that 26 days in rehab cured me. But according to my brilliant thinking, I had 26 days clean and completed all my treatment work. I worked all of the Narcotics Anonymous 12 steps while I was there and I was ready to go out to the world and share my wonderful recovery knowledge with all that needed to be saved. In plain English, I was an idiot. I was still too sick and stupid to understand that. I would learn this for myself soon enough.

Chapter 30. Then, as it was, then again it shall be- *Led Zeppelin*

Scott came to Harrisburg and picked me up at Common Ground. We didn't really talk much on the drive home, but he did talk about business and how things were rapidly growing. He didn't seem interested to know or hear anything about my treatment experience. I had asked him to help me clean out my house and he said he had too much shit to do so I prepared myself to deal with it alone. I remember feeling nauseous when I walked up the steps. When I walked in I nearly vomited, it smelled worse than a bar after a busy night. It wreaked of stale alcohol, cigarettes, and dirty clothes. Almost every night when I was getting high after I ran out of crack, I'd spend about an hour searching for more on the damn floor. Every night I got high I'd swear I lost a $50 crack rock. I never once found it but wouldn't you fucking know it, while cleaning the place I found a pretty big rock of crack. I held it in my hand for a few minutes weighing my options. I felt nauseous. I flushed it down the toilet.

Immediately after doing so, I started crying in a way that I've never done. It was more like wailing. The past 20 years flashed before my eyes. All the trouble, heartache, and pain I caused was running through my veins. I started to feel what my parents must have felt from the years of my destroying everyone's life. I don't know how to explain what happened but to me it felt like God gave me a real glimpse into all I had done over the past 20 years. Nobody prepared me for this. My counselor had said, "At some point if you stay clean, you'll be overwhelmed with feelings when you start to realize how your life really was." I was feeling this right now, maybe an hour after getting out of rehab. I started wishing I hadn't flushed that crack. I was pacing and the overwhelming desire to get high was more powerful than anything I ever felt. I was about ready to say "fuck it I'll go to that 90-day rehab, just get me the fuck out of this house." I actually called the rehab and asked to speak with Jim but he couldn't come to the phone. I thought, *fuck it, this isn't going to work. I'm going to go score and get high.*

Scott knocked on the door and unbelievably, he started giving me shit. He was mad because I didn't go right to work as soon as I got home. It was always all about him. The fact that I was just in 26 days of intense treatment meant nothing. I needed to get on the phone and make money for him. I completely flipped out on him. We wound up walking down the street so his kids couldn't hear us. We were so loud and came so close to getting physical that the Chief of Police heard us and drove up to us and got out of his car to try and talk us down. I swear, I could've killed him. I was so hurt and angry. It was all too much for me to handle so I went to sleep. I woke up at 6 pm and drove to my first 12 step NA meeting.

The first week after treatment was rough. Almost daily I'd get overwhelmed with feelings of sadness, anger, and anxiety. These all are things I wouldn't allow myself to go through before rehab. Anytime one of these feelings would appear, a six-pack of beer and some cocaine would drown them all away. After rehab, after my first thirty days without using anything, I was feeling all this and had no idea what to do with it.

The rehab set me up in outpatient counseling as part of my aftercare program and I let the counselor know what I was going through. He told me that this is what going to meetings is for. He explained that if I was to share these things in a meeting, I'd get support from the people in the meetings. I remember thinking, *this dumbass has no idea where I come from or who I am*. All my life I was raised to believe that men don't have these feelings. If they do happen to feel that way it's a moment of weakness and I should

NEVER discuss it with anyone. I was raised to never allow someone I didn't know to learn anything about me. You only trust your friends and even then, only your closest friends.

I went to a meeting on my 30-day clean anniversary. I sat way back in a corner hiding, not wanting anyone to notice me. I did like listening to people and when some of them spoke it felt like they were speaking directly to me. I totally understood them because my experiences were similar. I didn't speak at all but when they did the "clean time" count at the end, I stood up and received my very first key tag for having thirty days clean. Narcotics Anonymous gives key tags to people after different clean anniversaries. When I left the meeting, the only thing I could think about was the really beautiful woman with the green eyes who sat across from me and received her thirty-day clean key tag too. I hoped to see her again.

In rehab, we talked about getting involved in relationships often. People who had experience in recovery would say that getting involved with someone when you first get clean is a bad idea. The counselors and the house managers, most of whom were in recovery, said the same thing. I had no idea how this thing was supposed to work. I believed that meetings were kind of like an extension of rehab. I thought it was still treatment but it wasn't. I wanted to stay clean, but those fucking people were weird. This one weirdo old biker dude tried to hug me after the meeting when I got my key tag. I was like what the fuck, is this dude gay or something? Why the hell is an old biker dude that I don't know trying to fucking hug me? It was getting easier for me to find the differences between me and the people in the meetings. I started feeling like I didn't belong.

I didn't know at the time, but that's how an addict's thinking works. Our thinking works against us. Instead of realizing how similar I was to those people and how they could help me, I was building my case against them. My brain at that time was wired to find reasons for me to get high, even though I didn't want to. It's hard to explain to someone not in recovery how this works. I tried telling my mother how it felt like I didn't fit in and that I sometimes thought I wanted to get high as a result. She got mad and yelled, "why would you WANT to get high after all the trouble that drugs caused you all your life"? Explaining addiction to someone who's never experienced it on their own is impossible. It's looked at as a moral failure, not a disease. Addicts were thought to be weak people, too weak to "just say no".

No one who has ever experienced addiction will ever understand how the mind of an addict works. I didn't go to a meeting for two nights after getting that key tag. I was sitting at home, looking out my window, and saw my old drug dealer drive away from the house of my friend who lived across the street. The one and only Dave. The guy that helped me start getting high in Mt. Holly in the first place. It didn't take seven seconds for me to knock at his door and it took less than a minute to take my first hit of crack after thirty-two days of abstinence. I smoked crack with him all night, and I drank beer and vodka all night too. I was so ashamed of myself after that I wanted to crawl into a hole and die. I got a bunch of phone numbers from people at the meetings, but I couldn't call anyone. I called the rehab and spoke with Jim and then I drove there because we had an after-care meeting and I spilled the beans to the people in the aftercare group. Most of them were in rehab when I was there. I wasn't alone though, two others said they got high too. The guy running the group told us that staying clean is hard at first and the people that want to stay clean will go to a meeting and share about the relapse.

I mean, really? Go in some freaking church basement with a bunch of strangers and tell them I was too weak to hold my ground and not smoke crack? I told myself I couldn't do this. *That's just not me.* I asked if I could talk with Jim and I went to his office with him. I was able to tell him what I was thinking. He was the only person I knew who understood me. He was patient and didn't get mad at me for wanting to get high. He helped me understand that I used drugs for so long that it's the only coping mechanism I had and it's going to take time and effort to build and develop new coping skills. A lot of the treatment work I did in rehab was about this but I didn't think that shit applied to me. I was learning that it did. Jim explained that telling on myself in a meeting would help me by letting the people there know I need support. He promised that I wouldn't get judged and people would reach out to me after to share their experience, strength, and hope. I left his office a little more motivated and willing to give his suggestions a try.

I went to a meeting that night. The first thing I noticed was she was there. That girl with the green eyes. I don't know what it was about her, she was very pretty but not my type at all. To this point, I only ever hung out with the girls that went to rock clubs or girls that were "exotic dancers". This green-eyed girl was different. She was dressed nicely. She was sober. I was sober. I couldn't think about anything else, and then I remembered I was supposed to tell on myself and get all this sympathy and understanding from the people in the meeting. I had to take my mind off her and concentrate.

For the first time in a meeting the words "My name is Mike and I'm an addict" came out of my mouth. It was near the end of the meeting and I disclosed to a bunch of strangers and fully clothed women that I had used two days before. It was embarrassing. After the meeting, I'm expecting all this fellowship shit to happen. Not one of them fuckers came to talk to me! Fucking Jim, the house manager Mike and my outpatient counselor Bill, they all fucking lied to me.

It was all a conspiracy to get me to make an idiot of myself. I was done with this bullshit. Fuck this, I knew I shouldn't have trusted anyone. I fucking knew. As I was getting in my car, some weirdo guy that looked like the "shit happens" smiley face, Jack, called my name and walked over and handed me a piece of paper with his phone number and it also said, "Next time, call me BEFORE you use". I got in my car and then that green-eyed girl waved me down and told me I needed to get a sponsor, and she handed me her phone number! I felt a little better and drove home.

Chapter 32. I went looking for trouble, and boy, I found her- *Type O Negative*

I went to a meeting the next day and of course, I didn't say a damn word. I did my good deed for the day! I love writing about this because I'm remembering what a damn knucklehead I was back then. Anyway, that "smiley face 'shit-happens' dude" Jack was there and I said hello to him, and that green-eyed girl was there. I was playing it cool with her, I was going to get her interested in me by ignoring her. Where I came up with these ridiculous ideas is beyond me but I'm famous for them.

I waited a few days before I called her. Her name was Barbara. Barbara Jo. She called herself BJ. *Wait what? BJ? For real?* This love affair is over. Throughout my whole life, I only knew BJ to mean one thing. How the fuck can I hang out with some chick that calls herself the initials of the word blowjob? Again, I love remembering the stupid idiotic thought process that I possessed back then. It took a lot for me to talk to her without thinking about blowjobs. I have to be honest though, she turned out to be a pretty cool person.

After speaking to her for some time, I learned a little about her. She actually knew Scott; I guess they grew up living close to each other. It turned out I almost met her once in LA. She moved out there with her boyfriend around the same time I did. One day, he was supposed to meet Scott at the building we worked in to talk about forming a band. I waited there with him but left after a short time. It turned out, she married that guy and they had a kid together and recently broke up. She moved out of LA the same day I did and she drove the same route as me to get back to PA and to a town very close to Mt Holly Springs.

This was it! This was my destiny! I met the woman I was going to marry! We were in the same place at the same time, we left the same place at the same time, and were both trying to get clean and recover from addiction at the same time. I truly believed this was destiny. We started speaking a lot. She kept pressuring me to get a sponsor. My outpatient counselor did too but I couldn't get a grip on that concept yet and anyway, I wasn't interested in that shit. I was interested in one thing and one thing only. Sex! I had a few days clean at that time and I knew of no other way of thinking. We went to meetings together every day. I went out with her after a meeting one night and I met her daughter, Lindsey. This kid was awesome. She melted my heart right away and turned me into some kind of freaking ball of mush. I was falling in love. Not so much with BJ, but I was falling in love with the *idea* of falling in love. I was falling in love with the *idea* of having a family. That's not to say I didn't like or have feelings for BJ, I did, and they were more than just wanting sex.

This getting clean thing, going to meetings, and building relationships was growing on me. I was making more money than I ever dreamed of with Scott and I had money in the bank for the first time. I met a girl I really liked; she had a kid that made me all mushy inside. I was gaining weight. I weighed about 140 pounds which was heavier than I ever was before. I believed with all my heart that all this was meant to happen as if it were planned by God himself. Then, God smacked me upside my head with a severe dose of reality. It happened the day after I got my very first "60-day clean" key tag.

Chapter 33. My angels, my devils, a thorn in my pride= *The Black Crowes.*

When I used a few days after getting out of treatment, (I learned it wasn't exactly a "relapse" because I wasn't clean long enough, it was more of a learning experience) I managed to achieve a milestone. I stayed clean for sixty days in a row. Life was improving; I'd never experienced what was happening over these sixty days. Things like waking up without a hangover, still having money in the bank on payday, eating every day, wearing clean clothes, buying things other than drugs, things that are most likely normal to you were completely out of this world to me at that time. I was enjoying it.

BJ (still at that point incapable of not thinking about blowjobs when I said her name) was hanging out with me all the time. It was nice to be able to take her and Lindsey (her daughter) to dinner and do some normal things with them. The day after I got my sixty-day key tag, BJ called and asked if she could borrow $100 because Lindsey was sick and was prescribed medicine and she couldn't afford it. It felt super good that I had it and was able to help out. I was always so used to being the one asking for help from others that I actually felt lucky that she knew she could come to me for it. She came over and I gave it to her, and we agreed to see each other at the meeting later that night.

I went to the meeting and I was anxious to see her, I guess you could say I was in "puppy love" at that point, but she didn't show up. I recently got my first cell phone and I tried calling her after but she didn't answer. I drove past her house and she wasn't there.

I left a lot of messages for her and she never called. I eventually went to sleep that second night still without hearing from her. Finally, the next morning she called. She did relapse. She asked if I wanted to come over and get high and I turned her down and then she asked for more money and I turned her down again. I told her when she's ready to stop, I'd gladly see her at a meeting. I couldn't believe I actually said that because I never turned down getting high before. She told me to fuck off and hung up. I've never been sober and had my feelings hurt and it sucked. Some people in the meetings noticed we were getting close and warned us that getting together in a relationship wasn't healthy but I thought those knuckleheads were stupid. That actually made sense to me, and what I mean by that is, I heard them but I wasn't taking their advice. I think after about 5 days she showed up at a meeting. She apologized for what she said and I melted like a marshmallow in a fire.

BJ and I started hanging out regularly again. We went to meetings together and hung out after them all the time. I had made some friends in recovery by this time and there was this older dude, Paul, who was really cool. He was clean for eighteen years and he was originally from NY. When he shared at meetings it felt like he was speaking directly to me. He was a Vietnam veteran, he didn't speak much about it, but he often spoke of the aftereffects of it. I asked him to be my sponsor and he agreed. It only took me four months to do this even though it was what everyone suggested I do first.

After her relapse, BJ and I were getting closer in a more intimate way. I wanted this but at the same time, I was scared to death. I had been with many women in my life, like really, a lot, but never intimate. That doesn't mean that I didn't do a lot of fucking in my time, it meant that I rarely, if ever, had feelings for anyone I was with. The world of sex, drugs, and rock and roll was way different. It was almost a rule not to fall in love, or for that fact, not to even fall in "like". Most often, these relations were a two- or three-day affair at the most.

So here I am with a little more than sixty days clean and catching real feelings for someone. That shit was fucking scary. I didn't like feeling vulnerable. Not at all. I didn't know or understand how to experience it. I didn't feel like I could talk to Paul about it. I thought he'd either laugh or tell me I was stupid. Feelings of inadequacy started ganging up on me and I couldn't speak to anyone about it. It was ingrained in me to never let anyone know anything like that about me. I asked myself over and over, again and again, how the hell am I going to deal with this. BJ had the perfect answer. She came over one day and said, "let's get drunk and fuck". I thought, *wow, what a fucking genius idea,* and *why did I not think of that first?* Have you ever read the story of Pandora's box? I have my own version, just keep reading. It's coming up in the next few chapters.

Chapter 34. Strange Brew, Kill what's inside of you- *Cream*

We did it. What everyone in the twelve-step meetings told us not to do. We did what both of our sponsors told us not to do. We did what my counselor told me not to do. We did it. We got drunk and fucked. When she suggested it, we planned on meeting up in a few hours. I went downstairs and tried to explain to Scott why we both needed to drink even though we were trying to be in recovery. I wanted to borrow his corkscrew. He wouldn't let me use it and told me I was stupid and not to do what I was about to do.

We not only got drunk and fucked, but we also smoked crack as well. I can't speak for her, only myself, but I believed at the time that maybe the crack would make it all go away. In reality, I had absolutely no coping skills and was overwhelmed with feelings and I did what came naturally. I got fucked up so I didn't have to deal with what I had just done. Looking back, I totally understand why it happened. I was 33 years old with the coping skills of a teenager. Before this, I was only in one really serious relationship and that was back when I was 18. I didn't know in any way how to cope with having feelings for someone. I didn't know how to be intimate. I had no idea how to behave after having sex. Getting high was the natural thing to do. It was definitely better than trying to go through all that while sober.

Within days we were an "item". Within days her daughter Lindsey was calling me daddy. Within days we drank and smoked crack again. I didn't know what to think, how to feel, or what to say to anyone. I wasn't used to any of this. Before this, accountability was for other people, not me. I learned in treatment that people who stay clean need to be held accountable by their peers and need to hold themselves accountable as well. The only thing I was sure of was I didn't want to use anymore.

Somewhere inside I wanted to go back and have a "do-over." I wanted to go back to the day before we did the deed. Magical thinking never helped before and it didn't this time either. I called my sponsor Paul and told him what we did. He knew immediately the day it happened because neither one of us was at any meetings for a while. He had no judgment, no long story to tell, no advice other than to show up at the next meeting and start over. I told him I was afraid of what people were going to say to me and what they were going to say about me as well. His knowledge and experience eased my worried mind. He said what we did happened with a lot of people in early recovery over a thousand times before and it will happen a thousand times again and that most likely half the people in the program did the same thing in their early recovery.

We opened a Pandora's box that neither of us was prepared for. BJ and I started a pattern of behavior and a huge wave of problems that would drive not only us but our peers crazy as well. We would have these arguments that usually started over something stupid, she would accuse me of staring at a female in a meeting, or I was being too nice to a female and she'd accuse me of things that weren't happening. I would try and ease her worrying but nothing worked. I would always wind up losing my shit, get loud and storm out. That would trigger one of us to go out and use. Then we would use together and then go to meetings and blame each other for our use. I was getting a lot of "white key tags. A white key tag is given to someone who either comes to a meeting for the first time or is coming to a meeting after a relapse. White represents surrender. In Narcotics Anonymous people receive key tags to acknowledge reaching recovery milestones, like 30, 60, and 90 days clean. After 90 days, there's a key tag for 6 months, 9 months, 1 year, and 18 months and then they get one each year to recognize multiple years in recovery.

This pattern between BJ and I went on for some time. While it was happening, I was building the business by hiring a few people from meetings to sell Body Jewelry over the phone to tattoo shops. I was making insane amounts of money for both Scott and me by doing this. Even though we were making so much money, that asshole was getting angry and giving me shit because he didn't believe I was involved enough. Just a year ago we were both barely squeaking by from selling fasteners for my boss in California and now we were making between $3000 and $5000 a week and here he was getting on my nerves because of how I was living. Now he's telling me that I wasn't investing enough time in the company which we started together.

When I look back it all seems so insane. I was barely capable of getting more than 10 days in a row clean and I had this crazy lady telling me I didn't love her because I was looking at every woman within a twenty-five-mile radius with lust in my eyes. I was managing three dudes that were working out of my spare bedroom and I was dealing with this guy that I started this thing with and he was always telling me I wasn't doing enough.

So what did I do? What genius idea did I come up with? What was my answer to all this? I took BJ and Lindsey to the beach in Ocean City Md. I drove the four hours to Ocean City and we consumed a 12-pack of beer along the way. I went into the hotel to get a room. When I came back I told BJ that I flirted a little with the girl at the counter and got us an ocean-view room for the weekend at a super low rate. I believed I was a genius for doing that but I didn't get the response I was expecting.

After we got in the room and put Lindsey to bed, BJ started crying hysterically and saying I was going to sneak out and fuck the counter girl. She was saying that I didn't love her and that she should have known better than to trust a lying cheating asshole like me. This went on for hours. It was getting light out and we were still going through it. In the midst of all this, I came up with the world's greatest idea of how to put a stop to all of it. I can prove my love, squash her fears, end the fight, and go peacefully to sleep with this one insanely genius move. I'm sure you're asking "What the hell did he do that was so smart" right? I fucking asked her to marry me. What a brilliant idea! With that one ridiculously stupid move, I changed the course of my whole life.

After the weekend we returned to PA. I told Scott the wonderful news that we were getting married and he fucking fired me. I was dumbfounded. I had made him so much money the past four months, we were friends since 1987 and he fucking fired me. We argued for some time until he changed his mind and allowed me to keep my job but it was going to cost me. The three guys that worked for me now worked for him. Just like that, he was taking what I started away from me and I had to accept it. I begrudgingly went along with it but I was also going to make sure this would never happen again. I made plans to move out of the apartment I rented from his father. I found a beautiful four-bedroom house about twenty-five miles away from Mt. Holly and was moving in on June 1, 1999. I truly believed I was solving all my problems with this move

Chapter 35. But as the eagle leaves the nest, it's got so far to go= *Led Zeppelin*

The house was stunning. It had 4 bedrooms, a living room, and a family room with a stone fireplace and a sunroom that overlooked four acres of land. There was a double deck in the back, and the topper was an indoor pool. I've never lived anywhere so nice in all my life. BJ and I were planning on getting married and this was a beautiful house to start a family. The only problem was BJ and I living together. It didn't work. The first week was like a honeymoon and after that, it was a nightmare. I wanted to stay clean and she wanted to drink. She would tell me that we could drink and smoke weed and not do heroin or crack. I knew better than that. We would get into fights after work over this.

Sometimes I would give in and sometimes I wouldn't. We would break up on and off and she would go back to her apartment, she wasn't due to move out for a few more months so she didn't break the lease because was in her mother's name.

I hired a guy named Billy and he was a really good salesman. I let him move in downstairs while he saved his money to get his apartment. He was making me a ton of money. BJ and I broke up one more time and this time, she went to work for Scott so we wouldn't see each other. This caused trouble between Scott and I. Scott would also let her call customers that were mine and lie to me telling me she sold them off of a cold call. I truly believe that Scott lived for two things, drama, and control. He loved what was happening because it wound up making him more money. I was getting very angry over it and I knew he was full of shit. He was working BJ and me against each other to his advantage. I don't know why I wasn't willing to just cut my losses with her and move on.

Eventually, we started talking again and she came back, but it didn't last long. It was right before July 4, we were using and I allowed her to use my bank card for cash to go buy some dope and some crack. She took out like $200 more than I told her to. I found out right away and that was it. I made her leave and tossed her clothes that were there out with her, I was done.

I started using on my own then and stopped going to meetings. I was spending practically everything I made on dope and crack. I started shooting dope rather than snorting it. It didn't take long for me to become physically dependent on heroin; I was doing more and more of it every day. I met a dude one day while I was copping in Harrisburg and he convinced me to go to Philadelphia with him. It's so weird how easy it is to trust someone you've never met when buying drugs. He said the dope was better and cheaper so I gave it a try. I found a connection through him there and I was able to call this dude in advance and drive there to pick up however much heroin I wanted. Billy was on work release from a DUI sentence and I had to pick him up and drop him off at Cumberland County Prison every day. Everything was happening so damn fast and before I knew it, I was spending around $500 a day on drugs and booze. The crack made it possible for me to stay awake and work. The dope helped me sleep at night and the alcohol-fueled the whole thing. In less than one month I lost all the weight I gained and spent all my money and was living day to day. I convinced Scott to pay me three or four times every week, so as the money came in, I spent it. I was literally in hell.

I knew that there was a better life if I would just stop using. I would wake up in withdrawal every day. There was no way I could live through that sickness. I often found myself asking God to let me overdose and die. When I first stopped going to meetings a few people called me every day trying to get me to come back, but I never answered calls or returned messages. I was too ashamed. I lost too much weight. I stunk because I stopped showering. I truly invited death, but God had other plans for me.

August 10, 1999, after a binge of heroin, crack, Budweiser, and Jack Daniels, I was out. Nothing left. The dope and crack were gone. I tested every open beer can in the house (of course, I drank a few sips with cigarette butts in the can) and the bottle of Jack was empty as well. I was scared- no- I was literally frightened to death of the upcoming pleasantries of my inevitable withdrawal. I was already feeling it in my bones. Sometimes, the fear of withdrawal is worse than the actual sickness but once withdrawal hits, it's terrible. I gave up crawling on my floor looking for crack. I had this awesome way of getting my face and eye completely level with the floor so I wouldn't miss even the tiniest pebble of fallen crack. I spent my normal 2 hours or so doing that and smoked every piece of lint and anything else resembling crack and surrendered to the fact that I wouldn't find anymore. I had a $100 bill left with no chance of getting any more money until the next day. This was going to be a rough day and my anxiety was going through the roof. I was getting sicker by the minute. I was pacing, looking through the empty dope bags, scraping my stem, the common ritual of craziness after running out of drugs. I planned to run into Harrisburg to grab a bundle of dope and sweat my way through the day. I was curled up in my bed, sweating like crazy while convulsing from withdrawal and my phone rang. It was my sponsor Paul. He just returned home from vacation. I guess he heard I wasn't at any 12-step meetings. I stopped attending when I started using about a month ago. I did not want to answer. I didn't want to hear the bullshit and have to explain myself to him. I declined the call and laid there in my bed curled up in a fetal position crying and occasionally got up to vomit in the bathroom toilet.

I started thinking about the past 8 months. I went to treatment in January. I was tired of how I had spent the past 15 to 20 years always in search of "just one more". After treatment there were many spurts of recovery, I'd get 30 days clean, and 60 days once or twice, but I would usually find a reason to use. The reason usually involved BJ, who was attempting to recover as well. We broke up over the 4th of July holiday and I started using and couldn't stop. I quickly went from 2 bags of Heroin a day to between 20 and 30 a day. Every day. I remember telling myself that during those little episodes of abstinence that I was really happy, and asking myself *why the fuck are you living this way? There's a better way of living. Go back to meetings, fool!* The only time I felt like shit was when I was using (or fighting with BJ, which always facilitated using). Paul called again, and again and I declined the call.

The withdrawal was getting worse and I needed to run out and cop that last bundle (A bundle is 10 bags of heroin). I was telling myself that I'll call Paul tomorrow and get back into going to meetings after. The pain was getting really bad at this point, there was no way I could talk to him now. I needed to go buy heroin. I was scared to leave though; I was spending less time on my bed and more time in the toilet vomiting and releasing liquid fire from the bowels of hell out of my ass at the same time (withdrawal is so lovely). It was at this point I realized that I wouldn't be able to leave my house because I'd probably shit myself in the car. I was so fucking pissed at myself for not leaving earlier. I was in full blown dope sickness at this point and reserved to the fact that I was going to be sick until I got my paycheck tomorrow and make my way back to Philly. If you've never experienced withdrawal from heroin before, try to imagine having a seriously bad flu with a high fever while puking and having diarrhea at the same time. I was shivering and sweating at the same time. My bones hurt so bad and all I could do at that point was rock back and forth while holding my arms around my stomach.

I was in my bed crying, praying for God to just end it all and asking *please God, just take me now* over and over. Then that damn fucking phone rang again. It was Paul again. I picked up the phone but didn't answer. I just held it there and screamed at it to shut up. I was literally yelling at the phone telling Paul to leave me alone. I was dope sick and needed to get through the damn day and then I heard his voice come out from the phone speaker and say "dude, what the hell are you doing?" I had accidentally answered it in my momentary fit of rage, and now I had to talk to him. *Fuck me, this sucks* I thought, *what the hell am I going to say to this guy*? I answered him and told him I'd been using for the past month. I told him that I had $100 left and was going to cop (buy drugs) with it as soon as I could stop shitting liquid fire and vomiting whatever else was left in my stomach. I asked him to call me tomorrow and promised that I'd get clean and start going to meetings again. All I needed was "just one more".

He said what I believed at the time to be the stupidest thing that I had ever heard in my life. He said something to the effect of, "if you don't use, and don't spend that $100 and go to the meeting tonight, you will stay clean every day for the rest of your life, but if you go spend that $100 you may never get clean and probably die from this disease." *Really? Fucking Really Paul?* I'm here sick as a dog, literally dying, and this crazy old coot is telling me not to use. Like, *don't spend that last $100? REALLY?* I told him I didn't think I can do that and once I stopped bleeding liquid satanic fire out of my ass I was going to go cop. He was insistent that I didn't use though. He kept saying "Mike, you can die. Mike, you'll just keep going and never stop." Eventually, I lied and gave in just to get him off the phone and I promised not to use.

I asked if he could come over and he said he couldn't. He was on vacation with his family for a month and needed to unpack. He said I can call him whenever I needed to and he would send some of the guys from our crew over to get me to the meeting later. I got off the phone and I was trying to figure out how to get out of this stupid freaking commitment I had just made. I didn't want any of those guys from my sponsorship family coming over. There were empty dope and crack baggies everywhere. There was crack stems and needles, empty beer cans, and the empty bottles of Jack too. I was a mess. I lost about 30 pounds; I hadn't showered in at least a month and I smelled like unwiped ass. *This is ridiculous* I thought, *I'm getting the fuck out of here before he calls or any of those dudes show up.*

Well it took about two hours for me to gather the courage to walk out. Why did it take that long, you ask? Anyone that has had the pleasurable experience of being up for 4 or more days smoking crack while shooting dope and drinking booze will understand why it took that long. If you never had that experience, then you'll never understand. As I was getting in my car I saw this car coming up my driveway and I knew who it was. It was fucking Blaine. This 19-year-old kid with 6 months clean that Paul sponsored. He was in my support group. I thought it was like 3 in the afternoon but it was almost 7:30, the time my home group meeting started, and this fool was coming to get me. *Fuck me, kill me now!* I was finally courageous enough to go cop that last bundle and here comes freaking Blaine. I tried my best to lie my way out of going but this son of a bitch called Paul and together they talked me into going to the damn meeting. I was wondering if it would hurt any more than I was already hurting if I jumped out of Blaine's pickup truck while he was driving but couldn't bring myself to do it.

So I'm in this NA meeting and people are sharing a bunch of gibberish. I heard words but couldn't make out what anyone was saying. I did happen to see some people making faces like they were wondering where that horrible smell that permeated the air in the room was coming from and I remember feeling really embarrassed and crying. This one dude that looked exactly like the "Shit Happens" smiley face, Jack, kept poking me in the ribs telling me it gets better if I share about it. I felt like telling him to die of hemorrhoids or something, there was no way I was going to open my mouth in this meeting. If I did that everyone that wasn't sick from my body stench would most certainly get sick and possibly die once I allowed my breath to enter the meetings air space. In fact, I told myself *as soon as this meeting is over I'm going home and getting in my car and driving to Harrisburg to buy that heroin* but this fucking son of a bitch smiley-face mother fucker kept poking me in the damn ribs. If I wasn't so weak, I'd have cracked him, but I could barely hold my head up because I was so sick. I was hurting really bad. I was dying from embarrassment. My ribs were hurting from this fucking smiley fuck face poking me so when the chance arose, I blurted out "My name is Mike and I'm an addict." I have no memory whatsoever about what I said although I do remember crying and it being very hard to speak through the tears. I remember the faces of empathy from everyone listening to me. I remember the people hugging me after (despite my foul odor) and telling me they loved me.

Now it's time to go home and then get that bundle from Harrisburg, right? I was actually feeling a bit better and just waiting for these fuckers to stop talking and take my ass home. They had different plans. We wound up at Paul's house sitting by his pool and talking. Paul was sharing about his recovery and how he loves his life today. Blaine was sharing some hope as well. I have to admit, it was nice. I actually felt really peaceful. Even though my insides were turning into a rollercoaster and I stunk like a fish market on a 90-degree day, it was nice and I felt like I belonged there.

So Blaine finally took me home and somehow God saw fit to let me sleep that night. That was my last night of sleep for a few weeks as I went through the most torturous, painful withdrawal imaginable. But I stayed clean. Somehow.

I went to two or three meetings some days. I hung out with Blaine, Jack, Bill, Andy, Brian, and Paul every single day. I eventually made it through the withdrawal and the following weeks of no sleep and started sleeping through the night. I was eating every day. I was showering every day and working every day without the use of any mind- or mood-altering substances. I saved the $100 bill from that day for exactly ten years, and on my ten-year anniversary I saw some homeless dude with a sign on 2nd street in Harrisburg. I pulled up to my tattoo shop after attending an NA meeting to get my 10-year coin and gave it to him. I told him that he could do whatever he wanted to do with it. I also told him what Paul told me, which was that if he didn't buy drugs or alcohol with that money, if he'd spend it on a room and food and then go to an AA or NA meeting, he could possibly stay clean every day for the rest of his life. I have no idea what happened to him and I think of him often.

Chapter 37. It's a new dawn, it's a new day, and I'm feeling good- *Nina Simone*

It probably took 6 weeks to be fully detoxed and to feel somewhat human again. The people in my support group were just wonderful to me. They called me and spent time with me every day. We went to meetings together. Sometimes we went to multiple meetings a day. I called Paul every day. I was building a genuinely cool friendship with Blaine.

We were from completely different worlds, he was from Chambersburg or Shippensburg, not sure which, they're all the same if you ask me. He came from a place with lots of land, grass, mountains, and hills. He was a hunter, a fisherman, and a painter, and he enjoyed the outdoors. I, on the other hand, was about 12 years older than him, from New York City, a musician who at one time wore makeup and had big hair. What we had in common was we shared the same desperation to stay clean. Both of us let our addiction take us to places so far from where we came from and to places that we never imagined going to. The common bond of addiction and the desire to recover was the glue that kept this group of men together.

I still had to deal with BJ working for Scott though and he was fueling the fire between us. He seemed to take some sick joy from the game he was playing. The longer I stayed clean and hung out with the different men in my recovery support group, the easier it was to start seeing through Scott's façade. I was starting to hate him. He was rapidly changing into a sick version of himself. He seemed to be all about having control over people. He would call me from time to time and tell me about BJ and her troubles. I kept telling him I was done with her and he shouldn't have her working for him because he was supporting her addiction. Keeping her employed just provided money for her to get high. She wasn't paying her bills or feeding her daughter with the money she earned.

He didn't like hearing that and I think that it made him stand his ground with her more. I didn't speak to him nearly as much and most of our communication was after the close of business every day. I would send him my orders via fax every day. He would call to thank me and tell me how good I was doing. Other than that, my life was centered on recovery and I spent my time with my support group.

My support group, my crew- Bill (the old biker dude who tried to hug me at my first meeting), Jack (Smiley Face), Blaine, Andy, and Paul were truly awesome people. I'm sure none of us would have hung out together on the street, yet we all shared the same common bond of reaching a point of desperation from addiction that made us willing to do anything and everything for our recovery. We all spoke at great lengths about how we all went far beyond our expectations and barriers as our addiction progressed and how we found justification for doing things that we would never have done if sober.

To finally tell someone how shitty it felt to reach my hand between my mother's box spring and mattress to get at her wallet and steal her money and have them understand this was amazing. To have someone understand and not judge me for that was so liberating from the damaged spirit and tortured soul those behaviors created.

I often refer to these first few days and weeks clean as my favorite times in my recovery. There were no real responsibilities except to do my job, which I was and was making more money than I ever made in my life. Then I just needed to show up to meetings every day, call my sponsor Paul every day, and talk to my support every day. It was a wonderful time that I am forever grateful for. Most of what I learned from this time has stayed with me to today. They're the basic spiritual principles of recovery. There was and always will be quite a bit more to learn. I know this for sure. The basic principles of "living one day at a time," "get involved," "be of service to others" and "how the therapeutic value of one addict helping another is without parallel" will always be the foundation of my recovery.

Chapter 38. Just cause you can, don't mean you should- *Joe Bonamassa*

The next few months went by fast. I hired a few more guys to work for me and I turned the sunroom in my house into a very nice office that comfortably fit 4 of us. The two new guys, Bo and Paul learned their job fairly quickly and both were earning themselves more than they've made ever before. They were both people in recovery and both considerably younger than Billy and me. Billy was starting to become a problem. I had to ask him to move out of my house to protect my recovery. I had asked him a few times not to bring alcohol into the house because I wanted to avoid anything that could trigger me. I had asked him to move because he brought beer into the house more than a few times. I felt bad for having him move out and I gave him some money to cover the expense. He found a place nearby and I agreed to continue to pick him up and drive him back after work.

As Paul and Bo continued to advance and improve, Billy seemed to fall off. His attitude was changing, he was always bright and happy, but that started to change. I learned he was talking about me behind my back. I wasn't mad angry about that, I talked about all my bosses behind their backs so I understood. I eventually decided to let him go.

Billy immediately went right to Scott complaining about me and of course, because of Scott's love of drama and control he hired him, creating more of a rift between him and me. I was infuriated at this. Scott pulling this shit meant that anyone I hired could behave any way they choose, not follow the rules and not worry about losing their job because they can go right to Scott and get hired. Another fight ensued between us after Billy called on customers who were mine. In Scott's eyes, he was always right and I was always wrong. I thank God for my support at that time. I still hadn't developed coping skills, and honestly, these men helped me stay clean through a rough patch in my recovery. My growing distaste for Scott was causing me to pull further away from him. By this time, I didn't even consider him a friend. Looking back at our relationship now, I've come to realize he never really was a friend.

Around the same time, my sponsor Paul called to tell me that BJ finally reached out for help and that He and Bill (old biker dude) were picking her up and taking her to treatment. Within three months, BJ was in three other treatment facilities and left each of them. I didn't care at the time. I loved her but I was so angry at her at the same time.

Eventually, Scott did fire her, she was turning in sales that never happened to get more money. It didn't take long for the bullshit orders she turned in to come back as returns. He told me he was going to hire her back if she completed treatment. I have to give it to Scott; he truly loved the drama he created. I believe he thrived on it. At least that's how it felt to me at the time. He would often say that I should respect that even if I disagree. He had me by the balls because I was making so much money that I wouldn't dare leave. After all, I'd never make this kind of money anywhere else. Or so he thought.

Chapter 39. Can you see the real me, can you, can you- The Who

Putting the situation between Scott and me aside, with BJ in treatment and out of my hair (I still had hair back then), life was really good. I was in the process of building a relationship with my parents. I was clean longer than I'd ever been and I was feeling like a part of something in our little recovery community. During the previous months when I was using, I wrote a bunch of bad checks and I was working towards paying them back (a few local magistrates were threatening jail time if I didn't). Even though I felt like I belonged in the recovery community, I still often felt the need to fit in as well, which was a life-long issue.

A lot of people in meetings were quite vocal about the positive changes in their lives. I thought to fit in I'd need to do that too. The problem was, even though life had improved I still had a ton of troubles. There were thousands of dollars in bad checks I was paying off. I was dealing with the issue with Scott, BJ, and my parents. I had a huge ego at the time but it was a front. My ego, my self-esteem, and my belief in myself were all damaged. There I was in meetings pounding my fist on tables, talking all loud about how great my life was because I was clean. I was full of shit, just like I was in rehab when my counselor Jim called me out. Everyone knew I was full of shit and while I believed I was pulling the wool over their eyes; they all saw right through it.

I went on a camping trip (the first time in my adult life) with Paul and the rest of our crew to Front Royal, Virginia. We had a great time together too. We all got tattooed, and we had some excellent cookouts and some awesome nighttime fireside chats while we were there. And again, here I am, talking a line of bullshit about how perfect my life was. Afterward, Paul pulled me aside to talk to me. He was trying to tell me that I should share about the problems I was going through; how I sometimes struggled to stay clean as a result of them and that I needed help. I gave my typical answer which was "I know," and for the first time in our relationship, Paul called me on my bullshit. He was pissed off and said, "You know, you know, that's all I ever hear from you"! He also said, "As long as you know everything, then you don't need a sponsor. I can't help you with the things 'you know'. I can only help you with what you don't know." He went on saying "Your life is NOT perfect. It's a mess." "Your parents have no trust in you. You're this close to going to jail for all the money you robbed writing bad checks, and you're in love with a woman who's incapable of returning the love!" Paul never spoke to me like that and I was pretty mad, but he was absolutely right. It hit me pretty hard and I started feeling everything he said and I told him I couldn't talk about that stuff. I'm embarrassed about it; I'm hurt over it and I don't know how to fix any of it. He poked me in the chest with his finger and said, "Now I can help you" and "These are the things you need to become able to talk about in meetings because this is the real you. The real Mike Genna, a 33-year-old teenager that wants to be a man with no clue how". He gave me a lot to think about, and it was on my mind for days. I loved him for that. He was speaking from his heart and told me what I needed to hear because he wanted to help. For a minute, I wished he was my father.

Chapter 40. Heaven beside you, Hell within- *Alice in Chains*

I had a lot to think about after that camping trip. I wanted to grow up. The thirty-three-year-old teenager thing hit home. I started getting more honest in meetings and in my talks with Paul. I also started going to counseling. When BJ and I broke up I said some terrible things to her and continued to do so on the occasions we spoke after breaking up. I wanted to be a better person; I didn't want to be that person who needed to hurt those who hurt me. My therapist was awesome, she had a way of telling me how good I was doing and that made me want to continue to grow. I had a long way to go but I was doing things to initiate personal growth that I never imagined doing before I got clean. The inevitable happened around this time. BJ started calling me from treatment. She apologized, she was sorry, she wanted better for herself and she knew she fucked up. She loved me and still wanted to be with me. "We" rented that house; it was for "US." After a while of her doing this, I started buying what she was selling so to speak. I would talk to Paul about it and I'd talk with my therapist as well. Neither of them told me NOT to get with her, but both said it was in our best interest not to do it right away. There was a lot to contend with and I wasn't prepared for all the feelings that were happening. Up to this point in time, I was never prepared for any kind of feelings and I avoided feelings all my life. So as these feelings were happening, I found I was getting triggered quite a bit.

One evening it hit me hard. I was home after a meeting and out of the blue, the thought of using hit me. That thought triggered a craving and I was immediately obsessed. My mind went into overdrive, the voices in my head were telling me that *I was a failure my whole life. I might as well use, it's inevitable. I can't keep this recovery thing going forever, I've never been able to before, so why did I think I can now?* These thoughts were overwhelming. I was trying my best to deal with it, but I was losing the battle. I was pacing, telling myself "Don't use." "You'll get over this", but I couldn't stop the thoughts. I went out to my car and started it and I was in tears. I didn't want to do this. My mind wouldn't stop, the voices went on and on. *"You can't stay clean". "You're not like those people in the meetings." "They're winners, you're a loser."* I went back in the house and paced more. The argument in my head was deafening. I went out and started the car a few times, and went back in the house a few times. What was happening was so surreal. Finally, I did something that until this point I've never done. I called Blaine. I was in tears and I told him how crazy I was and how walking back and forth, starting and stopping my car, and about all the thoughts that were going on in my head. I told him everything. He laughed and responded with two very simple words. He said, "Come over." That was it. Just "come over." Nothing else needed to be said. Just "come over."

I drove to his house, sat and talked with him in his living room, and fell asleep in the damn chair. I woke up the next morning and it was over. I didn't feel like using. The voices were silenced. There were so many lapses in my first eight months after treatment, and people would say "You need to call someone *before* you use, not after." I guess they were right. That was the day that I finally started believing I could do this. I can stay clean and get through anything without using. Although I heard many people say that in meetings before, I never truly believed it until this happened.

Chapter 41. With or without you- *U2*

BJ was calling a lot while she was in treatment and I had pretty much forgiven her by this time. I was scared of her getting out and coming home. I loved her but I knew deep down that we shouldn't be together at that time. I was just starting to get some real recovery and gaining some clean time which is was different than just abstinence because being in recovery, with all the support at meetings and sober friends also helped my mood and self-esteem. I'm not a religious person in any way but I do believe there is a God. I have to believe someone intervened that New Year's Eve night when I didn't get arrested with all those drugs in my car. I also have to believe that there was a divine intervention after I survived my last relapse with how freaking much dope and crack I was doing every day. I truly believe God stepped in again when I received a phone call from BJ.

She was getting ready to complete treatment and her counselors at the rehab set her up with a halfway/recovery house in Lantana Florida. I wanted her back but I wanted to stay clean more. When she told me about it, I was all for it. In fact, I paid for her first month! My sponsor Paul was very happy with this outcome. I'm sure he didn't want to deal with all the drama that would've happened if she came back and stayed with me. This gave me the opportunity to stay clean longer and gain some coping skills and stay around my support. My therapist thought it was a great idea as well.

Things between Scott and I were getting better, I had completely lost trust in him, but as long as I was twenty miles away, I felt safe. He had asked a number of times to come to my house to meet the two guys that were working for me but I always found a way to avoid it. Deep down I knew he wanted to meet them to get inside their heads. He was becoming more and more devious and I was more than happy to keep my distance.

I often question why Scott was such a significant part of my life back then. By this time, I knew without a doubt that Scotts only interest in anyone was what they could do for him. I no longer believed him when he'd say that we were partners in the business. Looking back at our relationship I believe that my always wanting a "big brother" and seeing him as such for a time is why he became so significant. He had the potential to be that to me. I think that once he started showing his true colors and how I felt let down by him so many times brought up a lot of the resentments that I had built over my brother Jay over the years. I never felt significant to my brother and I never let go of the pain of not being significant to him. I believe that Scott had become equivalent to my brother. I often sought approval from Scott since starting the business and since I rarely felt like he provided it, I would try harder to get it, just as I did with my brother in my teens. I found I couldn't be happy either with or without his approval just like I felt with BJ.

The few months that BJ was away were my most stable months since I went to treatment. I was making a ridiculous amount of money; all my bills were paid in advance and all my bad checks were paid off. I had money in the bank, like, a lot of money. Thousands. I never imagined I would be able to do that. I spent 10 years in LA and only once did I have my own place, and I was evicted in less than six months! I still remember the thrill I had every time I bought clothes, or groceries or pretty much anything! I never bought myself anything in LA, I always had people taking care of me.

BJ called me a lot once she made it to Florida. She came home from treatment for one day, spent the night with me and left to go to Florida the next morning. I paid her rent directly to the house she was going to stay at in advance. I was too smart to actually give her cash. After she arrived and started getting plugged into the recovery community there, she started calling me and telling me everything I wanted to hear (or what I thought I wanted to hear). Her birthday was coming up, and I wanted to buy her something nice so I went to the same store that I bought my watch at and bought her a nice gold bracelet. When she received it, she called and thanked me but told me she couldn't wear it because her ex-husband bought her the same one and it reminded her of him. That shit hurt. I told her to just sell it and get herself something else. At the same time, I was getting close to her daughter Lindsey. She was still calling me daddy and I'd have her come over and stay with me a few days a week. I really love her; she was always such a sweet kid and had been through so much drama since her mother left her father.

From what I learned, after BJ left her husband in Arizona, she took Lindsey to LA and they stayed with some guy she was seeing out there. This guy was very abusive to Lindsey. He wanted BJ but not her daughter. My understanding was that Lindsey was traumatized by her experience with him. BJ wound up leaving him and drove back home to Pennsylvania. They left LA on the same exact day I did.

Anyway, after the bracelet thing, I was pretty hurt and was contemplating just ending it. I didn't want to hurt Lindsey though. I didn't want to be just another man her mother knew that hurt her, so I kept seeing her a few times a week. After a few weeks, BJ called me telling me she needed money, that she got kicked out of the recovery house because she tested positive for alcohol. She swore she didn't drink. I wasn't buying her story, so I called the house myself. I was told she was removed for bringing a man in the house and for having alcohol in her system. I was done. I told her to do whatever the fuck she wanted to do, but I wasn't going to be a part of her plans. I told Lindsey I wasn't going to see her mom anymore but while her mom was away, she could come over to my house anytime she wanted to. I didn't know what else to do.

So of course, BJ went into overdrive trying to repair things with me. I didn't take her calls for a few weeks but after listening to message after message, I finally spoke with her. She had this magical way of knowing what I wanted or needed to hear and saying it. I was never in a real relationship other than Anne in NY when I was a kid. I had no idea how to deal with what was happening. Paul told me over and over to stop talking with her. He would tell me things like, "Mike, you're doing so good, and your life is attractive to others. Just chill on BJ and believe me, someone will come around and treat you better." I wish I had listened but of course, I didn't.

I felt myself starting to feel lonely. I had lots of friends that I hung out with all the time, I just didn't want to go to bed alone. BJ was calling constantly and her persistence was working. She was supposed to stay in Florida for between four and six months, but she wanted to come home now after two months. She missed Lindsey, she missed me, she missed her mother was what she said over and over. She wanted to move in with me and I wanted her back as well, but I definitely was apprehensive about it.

Our history together was not good. We both used a lot and blamed our use on each other. I foolishly told her to come back and move in with me. We definitely weren't ready. Before this, every time I lived with someone had terrible outcomes. But that was when I was using, I'm more grown up now is what I told myself. She drove home from Florida one week before Christmas.

BJ's first week back was amazing. BJ, Lindsey, and I picked out a Christmas tree together, I've never done anything like that before, so it felt nice to do it. We had a wonderful first Christmas together, I loved that I was able to buy presents for everyone, even my parents, my brother and his wife and daughter Vicky, and Scott and his family as well. Before this, I was always the one who received presents but never bought them for anyone. I was always the one in LA who didn't go home for the holidays and was usually alone and drunk or high on dope over the holiday, so this was an incredibly nice experience for me. I even gave the guys working for me $100 bonuses.

On New Year's Eve, I started to feel anxious and couldn't understand what was happening to me. I was very tense and felt like I was on edge. We were supposed to go to my friend Jack's (smiley face guy) house for a party later that evening with other people in recovery. It was around dinnertime when I realized what was happening. This was the very first time in my life that I ever celebrated New Year's sober. Exactly one year before was when I thought we were getting pulled over with heroin and crack in the car and today, I was going to a sober party with my girlfriend and her daughter. Out of the blue, I found myself planning to sneak out of the house and get a hotel room, buy some booze, and go to Harrisburg and buy drugs. I truly wanted to do this. The thoughts were running around in my mind so fast I couldn't even slow the thinking down to have a reasonable thought interrupt the process. I was clean for almost five months at this point. I had never been clean that long in my life and for a little while, it didn't mean anything to me.

As I stated earlier, I believe that a higher power has intervened on my behalf many times. That night, I believe one of those interventions happened. I've never been diagnosed as schizophrenic, bipolar, or with a multiple personality disorder, but I have heard voices in my head before and they usually are calming and caring. When I walked through the door of Common Ground, the rehab I went to, there was a very distinct voice that told me "It's over". That night, the same voice appeared and said, "Call someone". That voice interrupted the thought process that was triggering me to use.

That interruption gave me the break I needed and I called Paul. I told him I had been thinking about sneaking out, getting a hotel, and getting high. I told him I wanted to do it. His answer was stunning. I had to step back and ask him to repeat himself, ensuring that he heard me. He said "So?" I was like, "Paul, did you hear me, I said I want to get high. I'm doing what everyone told me to do and calling someone before I use"! Again, he said "So"? And I'm like, "That's all you have to say, Paul, 'so'"? "Where's the support, where's the common sense telling me I'd be throwing everything away if I used? How come you're not telling me not to use? Why is the only thing you're saying is 'so?'" He replied that I already just said the words I needed to hear, why did he need to say it too? I asked him, "So what you're saying is that I already know using will fuck up everything that I accomplished these four months and it will go down the toilet?" "Yes Mike, that's what YOU'RE saying. You know this.

So go enjoy your night, tomorrow's another day. I'm sure the craving will be gone" and he hung up. He didn't even say goodbye, he just hung up. Paul had a way of being completely senseless while making perfect sense at the same time. I didn't think about using, I didn't glorify using, honestly, from the second he hung up, I stopped thinking about it at all. I've grown to appreciate the voices in my head.

Within the next two weeks, the honeymoon was over. I remember sitting in my living room one night and the phone rang. BJ answered and the next thing I heard was "Who may I ask is calling" and that was the last normal sentence spoken for the rest of the night. The next thing I heard was BJ yelling "Who the fuck is this? I am Michael's fiancé! What do you want from him"? My heart immediately sank. The next thing I heard was "Your fucking girlfriend Sherrie is on the phone for you!" Sherrie was a friend from NY, I was friends with her for years. I spent maybe three seconds trying to say hello but the sound of objects flying into walls and breaking took over the whole house. I apologized and tried to find out what the fuck just happened. The next four to six hours were spent defending myself against an onslaught of insults, accusations, and other nonsense. This was the first of countless of what I called "you don't love me" fights. This shit went on until 3 am. Lindsey kept coming out of her room asking us to stop fighting. I felt terrible for her. I've never before in my life had to deal with something like this. I wasn't even sure if I was talking to the same person. The way she flung insults and accusations at me was indefensible. After unsuccessfully trying for God knows how long to de-escalate the situation, I started to escalate instead and matched her verbal aggression. I don't remember how it ended, which was usually the case after one of these situations. If I think back to my teens, I remember this is exactly how my father behaved when he and my mom had arguments. I remember waking up the next morning feeling bad.

I spent the next few months desperately trying to avoid these confrontations. At any given time, BJ could start and blow up a situation to something unbearable. There were times it happened in front of the guys that worked for me. There were times when what was happening spilled over into the meetings we were attending. We wouldn't fight in the meetings, but she would often share inappropriately about me in front of me at them.

What happened next in this scenario was disastrous and it gave BJ all the ammunition she needed to continue this behavior. She learned that I subscribed to a pornography channel on the satellite television network I had in the house. Up to this point, I never attempted to hide anything. I had a lot of porn VHS tapes in plain view. She knew it existed. One time before I moved from Mt Holly, BJ and I came into my apartment and turned on the television, and a porn tape was playing. One of the guys working for me at the time was watching it while I was out. Nothing was ever said about porn up to this point. Now, all of a sudden, it was an issue. So at this time in my life with around 6 months clean, pornography became an issue.

I think much differently today about porn than I did back then considering the circumstances of where I was mentally and emotionally back then. Anyway, I felt BJ had no right to tell me what I can and can't look at and I refused to get rid of any of it. Our fighting was so bad that I felt the need to leave the house instead of fighting sometimes. I rarely ever watched porn. It wasn't like I would have it on the television when she was home. It was just that I wouldn't tell her I'd get rid of it or promise to stop. This was infuriating to her and she would go and put our business out in meetings and by calling my sponsor and other friends.

While I don't condone pornography today, I still won't condone her behavior or the demands that she was putting me through. She recently moved in with me, she immediately changed my whole house to make herself feel more comfortable. I felt she was lucky that I even forgave her for everything she put me through before and while she was in Florida. There were a lot of things she did that bothered me but I didn't put her through anything like what she put me through to try and change her. But if BJ didn't get what she wanted, then all hell would break loose until she was satisfied.

Blaine and I had plans to go to South Carolina to buy fireworks for the Fourth of July celebration that was coming up in about two weeks. A few days before we were to go, she started in and didn't want me to go. That was another thing that went on often. If I ever hung out with my support group without her then her suspicions would rise and another four-day "you don't love me" fight ensued. This was no different, for two days she was on me about it. The bickering was non-stop and I was near the end of my rope.

The day I left with Blaine to go to South Carolina, within minutes of us leaving my phone started ringing and she was crying. She was threatening to harm herself, threatening to leave (which I invited) and other crazy things trying to get me to come back. Eventually, both Blaine and I had to turn our phones off because she called us both. If I didn't answer, she'd call him. Anyway, after about four hours, I turned my phone on to check my messages and there were literally 50 messages from her. In her last message, she sounded like she was high.

If you've ever done heroin, then you know what the "heroin voice" sounds like. I called her and again she sounded high. She wouldn't confirm that she used, she just cried and continued to blame me for the whole thing. In the 4 or 5 hours since we left, she called around 100 times. I was done though. I told her to move out and not be there when I got home. I turned my phone off until I got home. She wasn't there when I got home and I was perfectly okay with that. A lot of future problems might have been avoided had I just moved forward at this point. I just couldn't.

Chapter 43. Cause you had me in deep with the devil in your eyes= *Aerosmith*

I sometimes felt like I had died and gone to heaven, but then BJ would do something and I'd feel the heat of hell all around me. My sponsor and I spoke every day, it was a routine by this time. I remember him pointing out how much happier I am when I'm focused on myself and my recovery. I didn't know how to completely leave her, or maybe she figured out how saying the "right thing" would get me to momentarily forgive and forget. She came back home after about a week. My therapist was working with me to build some coping skills and she was also showing me how to de-escalate our arguments. Sometimes they worked and sometimes they didn't. As I look back on this point in my recovery, I can't help but think about how my self-esteem kept me from making better choices back then.

It was getting close to my one-year-clean anniversary which can't be described any other way than a true miracle. When I used drugs, I used to live and lived to use. I can't explain it any other way. The many times I'd use after treatment were often so painful because before then I never dreamed that I could go without using. After learning how it felt to not use for weeks or months at a time and then giving up and using would hurt my spirit. I'd get so depressed during those times. Reaching the one-year point without taking anything mind or mood-altering was beyond my wildest dreams. Our little recovery community had a custom of sharing your story once you reached one year clean and it was done in a fairly large auditorium at a local hospital. I signed up to speak for my anniversary and was super nervous as the date drew near.

When the day came for me to speak at this meeting, all my friends in my support group and a whole shitload of people from the area showed up for it. I was so scared to do this. Getting up in front of thousands of people to play music was simple but getting up in front of about three or four hundred people in this auditorium to talk about my life was frightening as hell. I told my story from the point of entering treatment to the first anniversary. I don't remember much about it. I do remember when I finished the chairperson sitting next to me had a few tears in his eyes and turned his head to me and held his forehead to mine and thanked me and told me I did great.

I felt like I was on top of the world. Local treatment facilities would bring their clients to this meeting every week and I remember a lot of the people in treatment approached me and asked for my phone number and were all telling me how they got a lot from my story. I didn't know about all that but I do know how wonderful it felt to let that all out. My sponsor gave me this huge hug after and told me something to the effect of all that I had been through that has led me to this point and this is God's purpose for me. He told me that I had such a relatable way of sharing which made everyone in the room connect with me. No one has ever in my life said anything so nice to me before and I cried when he said it. I want to say I cried because I was thankful but the truth is, I cried because I didn't believe it. This was the early stage of realizing how little self-esteem I had.

Maybe one week later BJ called me while I was running errands and told me to come back to the office. She needed me and it was important. I remember driving back and was scared of what I thought was the next four or five day "you don't love me" fight. When I got there, it was something completely different and unexpected. BJ told me she was pregnant and handed me the instant pregnancy test. I was going to be a father. Holy. Fucking. Shit.

From the onset of our relationship, BJ had said many times she didn't believe she could get pregnant and now she's pregnant. More than anything else, I was scared. I had a little more than a year clean at this time which is still a "baby" in recovery terms. Throughout all the madness I truly loved her and believed that we would be able to work through anything. I bought a ring and asked her to marry me. I called my parents and told them. We agreed to get married at the house and we figured out everything we needed to do it and by the first week of September, we had pretty much everything set up. We were going to get married on September 23, 2000.

Chapter 44. The lunatic is on the grass…
= Pink Floyd, Brain Damage

We planned on having the ceremony at the gazebo in front of our house and we had a plan B for bad weather. The day started very cloudy so we decided on having the ceremony in the pool house. The pool was housed in a huge structure built as an extension on the side of the house. The sides were all glass and there was a beautiful view of the tree line and hill surrounding the back of the house. The pool was covered with wood planks that were strong enough to support all our guests. We covered the planks and decorated the pool house beautifully for the day. Next to the pool house was a tent we rented for the day; it was big enough for over 100 people. If it rained, there were windowed sides that could be pulled down for protection.

My office was right next door to a limousine company and I rented a 1939 Rolls Royce to pick BJ, Lindsey, Marty, and BJ's mother up and take them to our house. We had somewhere in the area of 75 guests. My parents, my brother and his wife and daughter Victoria came and they brought my father's sister, my aunt Ann with them. Scott was my best man and BJ's sponsor Marty, was her maid of honor. Paul walked BJ down the aisle. It was truly a delightful, lovely day. We didn't go on a honeymoon but we spent the weekend in a beautiful bed and breakfast in Hershey.

What makes that day hard to believe is what went on over the two or three weeks before it. While we were planning, we were constantly at war with each other. My therapist suggested a couples/marriage counselor and we went to him a few times. In our last session with him, BJ got mad and flipped over a table in front of the couch we were sitting on and left. She took the car and left me there in Harrisburg without a way home. What he said after she did that was astounding, so much so that I remember it word for word almost 24 years after. He said "What I'm about to say to you I've never said to anyone. If you tell anyone I told you this, I'll deny it." He said, "Do not marry this woman. You cannot and will not ever relieve her of the pain she is in and you will forever be blamed for it". He went on to say "If you do marry her, your life will be a living hell, you will never have a period of more than two or three weeks that you're not at each other's throats." He then said, "even if you don't marry her, she will be a permanent thorn in your side over the next eighteen years when dealing with your child, but you will have a much better life". I was speechless after he said that. He didn't even charge me for the session. I didn't take his advice.

Over the next nine months, I went through periods where I wanted to either kill myself, kill BJ, or move away to LA or somewhere else far, far away, or find a hole to hide in.

I'd have welcomed anything that would get me away from this woman. Something happened to BJ as a result of her pregnancy which is inexplicable. I thought she was crazy before this, but her mental illness up to that point was like a bad mood compared to how it became after her pregnancy. What I went through those nine months is to this day one of the most painful experiences in my memory. I had sought help everywhere. I would call her sponsor Marty at all hours of the day or night, pleading with her to help us. I would also call my sponsor and the men in my support group multiple times every day, begging them to take me away, to come get me, or to let me come to their house. I'm searching for something to say that can properly explain what went on over those nine months and I can't find the words. Chaos falls miles short. Disaster doesn't come close. I can't think of any other time in my life where I felt so powerless, so angry, so enraged, and so sad all at the same time.

I had a box of pictures I saved over the years. There were pictures of Dez with me and Joey the drummer from Lace. There were pictures of me with a few famous rock stars, one was a cool picture that I cherished of Steven Tyler from Aerosmith and me with our arms around each other. Tons of pictures of me on stage with different bands. Pictures of me with all kinds of women and lots with strippers and porn stars. They were memories of the days of the NY and LA club scene and different tours I was on. They were cherished. I loved them, they were proof that my crazy days were so cool. Who wouldn't keep pictures of that stuff?

I was looking for the box, but it was nowhere to be found. I started freaking out because none of the pictures could ever be replaced. I asked BJ if she had seen it and she told me she threw them out a few weeks before. She said I shouldn't have or want memories of those days because I was a drug addict and a sex fiend. "Why would any married man want pictures of his past conquests with women?" she asked. I can't explain what this did to me. It didn't just hurt or make me angry; it went deeper. I felt like I was invaded and deprived of my precious memories. As soon as I raised the subject it became another fight. She seemed incapable of understanding that she shouldn't have done that, especially without warning. It was another fight that I just surrendered to and did my best to move forward but honestly, I was enraged and held a silent resentment for years after this.

I chose to rid the house and my computer of all pornographic material, which amounted to maybe three video tapes and I canceled the porn channel on the satellite tv. Even that turned into a fight because I gave the videos away rather than throw them out. Everything turned into a fight. I started looking at my shoes whenever we left the house to go anywhere because if at any time, any woman whether beautiful, ugly, tall, short, fat, or skinny ever came into my line of vision, BJ would know and there would be one of those four day "you don't love me" fights. At any time, anything I said could be taken wrongly and would be a reason to argue. I never in my life felt the stress I was under at this time. My therapist tried desperately to help me cope. My friends in my support group were worried that I wasn't going to maintain my abstinence during this time and yet they were so supportive. To this day I believe with all my heart that the combination of my sponsor, my support group, and my therapist saved my life.

While there was a mountain of chaos at home, there was also a rift building between Scott and me. The business was growing so fast, we were making so much money while at the same time we were growing apart. Scott loved the drama between BJ and me, he would often speak out of both sides of his mouth, he would agree with BJ when he spoke with her, and then turn around and agree with me whenever we spoke. He was also doing a ton of unnecessary shit with the business. He would purposely ship out orders wrong, so the customer would call and complain and in his sick mind he would use the opportunity to sucker the customers into spending more money under the guise he was giving them a special deal to make up for the mistake. He was taking it too far and we didn't need to do that. We were legitimately making a ton of money, and I believed this was going to hurt us in the long run.

Scott was sticking his nose where it didn't belong by calling my employees and speaking with them. In reality, I was an independent contractor and he hired my company to do a large amount of his sales. These guys were my employees, not his, but he thought differently. He was getting weird, and he was trying to convince me we should all be under one roof. With my experience with him taking my employees from me to work directly for him, there was no way I would do that. He was constantly burning us by passing out our customers to his sales staff in his office. I don't know why he would start shit like that, but he truly loved to be at the center of controversy. I never intended to leave and start my own thing.

Scott invited BJ and me to lunch at a place by his office to discuss the benefits of me moving my office to his office and combining it. At lunch, he was acting weird, like he was some kind of super entrepreneur and that none of us would be where we were if not for him. He brought this douchebag Martin that he hired to help him run things. I fucking hated the dude and never hid that. He would call my office to try and give me shit about something and I consistently told him to fuck off. About fifteen to twenty minutes into the lunch, Scott dropped the bomb that if I didn't move my office to his immediately, he'd fire me. I told him I'd consider it and let him know in a day or two, but he insisted and withheld my pay from me, which amounted to around $8000. He thought if I couldn't pay my team they would leave and go to work with him, leaving me nothing.

This was by far one of the stupidest decisions of his life. I had plenty of money saved and my crew was bothering me to leave for months before this. When I got back to my office, I called him and said, "No need to fire me, I quit." He lost it, he was threatening me with a lawsuit because he knew I was starting my own thing and going to compete against him. He ran such a shady business and ripped off so many customers that he knew I had the upper hand and would hurt his business.

With everything going on in my life at that time, it felt so good to be free of him. Within five days, my mother cosigned a ten-thousand-dollar loan, and combined with my savings, my new business "Premier Body Accents" was up and running. In our first three days, we sold enough jewelry for me to pay the crew for the last week of working for Scott even though he stole $8,000 from me. I also rented a new office a few doors away from us that was bigger and better with more room for a larger sales crew. We were ready to rock and roll right from the get-go.

Chapter 46. Cheap Holiday- *The Sex Pistols*

In recovery, I learned that the disease of addiction grows in the dark and dies in the light. That means if you're holding on to secrets, especially dark secrets, they will only get worse until you expose them. Another way of explaining this is if a person is entertaining thoughts of using and not talking about it either to a sponsor, a support group, or in meetings, those thoughts get worse and can lead to actually using. If that person were to expose that thinking, the thoughts would eventually die down because they're inviting their support to stay close and support them through it until the thoughts no longer exist.

Recovering from addiction is similar to walking up an eternally downward escalator. What I mean is, if you're walking up this eternal escalator while the steps are going in the opposite direction, walking at a steady pace will keep you continually moving slowly forward. If you try and get to the top by walking faster, you will eventually get burnt out and start moving backward. It's the same if you just stop walking, you'll start moving backward. When I am steadily working towards my recovery by attending meetings and having regular contact with my sponsor and support group and exposing negative thoughts, my chances of staying in the recovery process are very good. If at any time I stop working on my recovery, eventually the negative thought processes start and continue to grow and my chances of staying in the recovery process become smaller and smaller.

I was experiencing negative thoughts and was too ashamed of them to tell anyone. I had thoughts of suicide. There were thoughts of giving up and using drugs. There were also thoughts of just up and leaving and going back to LA. None of this would have had a desirable outcome. I was extremely caught up in my image, which was one of a successful man with a solid recovery and lots of money, cars, and other shiny things that made the outside look like everything was perfect. I didn't want to be seen any other way. It's not hard to understand if you think of the person I was before finding recovery. I was scared to death to be seen again as the dirty, shady, underhanded disappointment to my parents and friends. I never wanted to be seen like that again. Since I never experienced being what I envisioned myself as at that time, I was too afraid to lose the image. My silence about what was going on in my head provided the negative thinking space to grow into monsters and demons.

Approximately one month before the birth of my daughter Lauren and after another of the many "you don't love me" fights, I found myself driving around aimlessly. I went to Walmart and looked at the different guns and tried to figure out the process of buying one. I was thinking a bullet in my head would be a better end to the hell I was living through. I was looking in a pharmacy at different drugs I could overdose and die from. I was thinking that maybe driving into oncoming traffic and going head-on into a tractor-trailer might do the trick. My sanity was slipping through my fingers like I was trying to hold ten pounds of sand in both of my hands.

While driving around Harrisburg I drove past something that sparked a huge lightbulb in my head. It was a massage parlor. I drove around the block and passed it again. I did this maybe three or four more times until in my head I was telling myself this is exactly what I need. All I had been doing was trying to take care of everyone, all my employees' needs, BJ's never-ending needs, Lindsey's, everyone. I was taking care of everyone and no one was taking care of me. A massage is exactly what I need. Someone to take care of me. Someone to care about my needs. After driving past it a few more times I went in. It wasn't what I was expecting, nothing sexual happened but it sparked a hunger that needed to be fed. It didn't take more than three days to find what I was looking for. I found a massage parlor that offered "happy endings."

Until Lauren was born, every time BJ and I fought, I'd storm off and do the unthinkable and visit a massage parlor. It stopped after Lauren was born. It never did what I wanted it to do, which was make me feel better. Even after having one whole year clean, I was still capable of evil, and even worse, doing so without feeling any remorse. That is until I felt it, and when I did, it hit hard.

Chapter 47. "My, my, my, don't tell lies, Keep fidelity in your head"– *The Rolling Stones, 'the spider to the fly.'*

Thursday, March 8, 2001, I received a call at the office from BJ, her water broke, and it was time. I drove home like a maniac, picked her up, and drove to Harrisburg Hospital. Lauren Kasey Genna was born a few hours later. She was perfect. It was immediately noticeable that she looked just like me except for her beautiful blue eyes. Her birth went easily, within 30 minutes of BJ starting to push, this little angel came right out. The very first thing she did, as soon as the nurse laid her on the table to clean her, was poop. A tiny little poop right there on the table. I've told her this so when the book comes out and she reads it, she'll allow me to live. I hope!

She was such a beautiful little baby; she looked just like me except she had beautiful blue eyes. I felt an attachment to her immediately. I would just stare at her while she slept or when she was in my arms. I would repeatedly say over and over to her that I would never not be there for her. She would never feel like I felt as a kid, she was going to know without a doubt that she was loved. Up to this point, I've never felt a connection to anyone like I did when holding her.

We took her home the next day and for the next week, we all sat around her day and night. I was in love. I was also feeling terribly guilty about what I had done, and I had no idea what to do with the guilt. There was no way I could tell anyone and I knew I could never do it again. I was trying to deal with it without showing that anything was going on in my mind. Other than that, it was a peaceful week. I didn't go to work for a week. I just sat with my little family in amazement at how beautiful Lauren was. Lindsey was so excited about her and watching her was a joy.

About a week after I went back to work, I came home after work, got the mail, and went into the house. I handed BJ her mail and I went into the kitchen to open mine. Suddenly, BJ came into the kitchen and I could see just by the look on her face that something terrible happened. She "handed me a card and yelled, "What the fuck is this?" I looked at the card and nearly dropped dead on the spot. Someone that knew us saw me go to the first massage parlor in Harrisburg and wrote in the card that I was spotted going in there and that she was better than those "jack-off whores." I lied and lied over the next few hours, trying to calm the situation. The next morning, BJ woke me up and had my check register in her hand and was asking me to explain a bunch of cash withdrawals and was asking where I spent it and where was the rest of it. I couldn't think and couldn't explain myself either. I felt there was no way out and told the truth. I thought she was going to kill me. She told me to leave the house and demanded all the money in my bank account.

I felt terrible. I was guilty, but I wasn't insane. I wrote her a check for five grand (even giving her that much was stupid) and left. Before I was a mile away, my phone started ringing. First my mother, then my sponsor, then her sponsor. It was one after the other, back-to-back without a break. I didn't answer any calls. I didn't go to the office either. I just drove for a few hours. I finally called Paul, and he told me to come to his house. When I got there I was in tears and shaking. I apologized for lying to him. He was understanding and told me that whatever happened between BJ and me, I would get through it without using or harming myself. I called my mother from Paul's house; she was the first person BJ called and told. I felt like a lost little boy speaking to her. She took it better than I expected and while very concerned, she was very understanding.

A guy that worked for me, his name was Paul, called me and told me BJ was trying to get him to give her the company's bank information. She was trying to empty the account, there was over $50,000 in there and a lot of it was already spent in checks that were going to clear over the coming few days. I called the bank and made sure she couldn't access the account and they put my mind at ease. Her name was not on the accounts so if she tried, she'd be denied access. Of course, she tried, the bank called and told me afterward.

I felt terrible. I felt like I was a horrible person. I was beating myself up. I spent a lot of time with Paul. He was really helpful. I finally went to the office and answered the phone all day. Everyone and their mother were calling me. My friends were so supportive and understanding that it confused me. I thought they would hate me for what I did but quite the contrary, they held me up and helped me keep my chin up.

BJ wanted to work things out but I was unsure. It was so crazy but at the time I didn't believe I could stay with her the way things were and not either do the same thing, get high, or kill myself. We went to see my therapist together a few times. She had gone there with me a few times before all this as well. Eventually, we worked it out that I would come back home. I told her that I would never do that again but if things didn't improve, I would have to leave her. I didn't want it to sound like I was blaming her and I told her this in front of my therapist because I wanted her to understand that I couldn't live with what went on over the previous nine months. I didn't realize at the time but what I did by staying was provide a free pass for her to act on any behavior any time she felt like it. I opened the door for that. I invited it with open arms. It didn't matter what I said about not wanting things to be the way they were, she had been granted a free pass to invade, degrade, and abuse my emotions for the next few years.

Chapter 48. Oh, sometimes I grow so tired, But I know I've got one thing I got to do- *Ramble on, Led Zeppelin*

At the same time all this was happening, I was involved in a lawsuit with Scott. The back-and-forth shit was driving me crazy. His lawyer asked for depositions from a few of us. That didn't get them anywhere except to enrage Scott because he learned that his suppliers all contacted me and were selling to me even after he threatened to cut them off if they did. The fact is, we were doing way more in sales and at a much higher level of profit than him and this was due to our doing business properly. I never purposely sent the wrong items in an order; which Scott did all the time. I didn't lose a single customer in the split and we were selling more than we were when I was working with him. While BJ was driving me crazy at home, Scott was doing his best to push buttons. I was extremely happy with how the business was moving forward, it seemed at the time that I couldn't do anything wrong. Everything we were doing with the business was paying off well.

From the day I started the company, Scott and BJ were the two major causes of stress for me. I was fighting with BJ five out of seven days of most weeks. She worked with me at the office until January of 2001. She would come to the office and go through my computer browsing history looking for instances of porn and she would make it known throughout the office that she was doing so. She would ask about different entries in the business check register assuming they were for some shady reason.

She was earning a lot of money from her sales; she was one of the top sellers in the office. I never asked her to help with any of the bills at home. I would pay everything, and still, within three or four days after payday, she would be hitting me up for money or an advance on her upcoming paycheck. I learned not to ask what she was doing with her money, because that was an invitation to a "you don't love me" fight. I learned to avoid those fights at all costs. In January of 2001 when BJ wanted to stop working because of the pregnancy, I was all for it even though the baby wasn't due for three months. I needed her out of my hair (I HAD hair then). Even her leaving her job, which I was okay with, was the source of a day's long fight. She wanted me to give her full access to the business bank account. I wouldn't dare and I offered to keep at least $500 in the joint account that she could access at any time, which was insulting to her. I wound up giving her a weekly check for $500 a week which was hers exclusively and of course, none of it went towards any of the house bills. I would have gone for access to the joint account if I were her, but she didn't want any accountability for her spending. The $500 was usually gone within two to four days, and of course, if I asked where it went or what was the reason for the need for more before the next $500 check, another fight would happen until she received what she wanted.

Scott would call the office at all hours of the night and leave really strange voicemail messages. I would just save them and give them to my lawyer for our lawsuit. It seemed for a while that this lawsuit would never go to court; they kept asking for more and more information about who we were selling to and how much money we were making.

After everything came out about the massage parlors, Scott found out and called my house leaving voice messages telling BJ I was still doing it. He would name some massage parlors claiming he had pictures of me going into them. He had nothing of the sort because I wasn't doing it. He knew BJ all too well though and was doing this just to mess with her and our marriage. Nothing was off limits to him trying to destroy my life. We were friends for fourteen years. We couldn't work together and because he wasn't making all that money off of my hard work, he set out to ruin my life. Calling my house and leaving those messages was just a hateful, terrible thing to do. I've never forgiven him for that. He wasn't hurting me, he was hurting my family.

It was hard for me to deal with all this, but my therapist helped keep me sane during it. She was definitely a lifesaver during this time. A little more than a month after my daughter Lauren was born, I received my first tax bill after having a local accountant prepare my tax return. I found my next stressor for the next few years, the first year's federal tax bill was $36,000. So here I am at thirty-five years old, a business owner with over one million dollars in annual sales, a newborn baby, and a seven-year-old stepdaughter who needed way more attention than she was receiving. I had a wife who couldn't remain sane for more than three or four days in a row. I had 10 or 12 employees that all knew what was best for the company more than I did and my former friend Scott trying to destroy every aspect of my life. On top of all this now there's a fucking $36,000 federal tax bill. I had all of this to deal with while barely having nineteen months clean. It would be a lot for a normal person to deal with. For me, a 35-year-old who spent the better part of the thirty-three years before this in a whirlwind of destruction and debauchery, it was beyond overwhelming. I had no clue how I was going to survive this all.

Chapter 49. Hell ain't a bad place to be-
ACDC

BJ struggled with her mental and emotional health after what happened. I didn't think we were going to be able to withstand it. While I had no expectations of her letting it go anytime soon and I expected the repercussions to be somewhat painful, I had no idea of what I was in for either. The next few months were insane. First, the baby developed a really bad case of colic; she started crying one day and it didn't stop for three months. While it was going on, BJ, Lindsey and I would walk on eggshells when Lauren was asleep because it was the only time there was quiet in the house. BJ would call me at the office constantly to get me to come home and stay with Lauren so she could go out and get some peace.

Poor Lindsey, was never really happy about getting a sister in the first place because she thought we would stop paying attention to her and then once Lauren was born, all the attention turned towards keeping Lauren calm. Lindsey was discouraged and rightfully so because we were not providing her with the attention she needed. She was only seven and already had suffered through some serious trauma. She went through the worst of her mother's addiction after returning from LA and then after having just a taste of normalcy in her life; all hell broke loose once Lauren was born.

BJ was so unpredictable at this time. At any given time, she could just go off the rails in a rage. It felt like she was trying to control everything I did. If she didn't like or didn't want me to do something, she'd blow a fuse and have an emotional breakdown. She would call me at the office sometimes every thirty minutes and sometimes every thirty seconds. When we went to meetings her eyes were glued on me and whatever I looked at. If I wanted to hang out with my support, she would start by threatening a breakdown because she didn't want me to go anywhere without her. A lot of what my therapist worked on with me helped and I was able to get through those months without being the cause of any more harm.

The lawsuit was draining. Every other week my lawyer would call telling me they were requesting more information. They were attempting to pry deeper and deeper into who we were selling to and what we were selling them. Nothing they did caused us to lose any sales or customers, we were doing better with every passing month. As we grew, I invested more in the company. We went from handwritten invoices to having our custom invoicing software and a computer on every desk. I learned graphics and developed flyers and eventually designed two full-color catalogues of our products.

If all this was happening without the lawsuit and BJ in my life, I'd have probably been the happiest person in the world but that was more of my "magical thinking." My happiness was continuously interrupted by periods of overwhelming stress. We were moving forward so fast. It often felt like my head was going to just spin right off. I would sometimes allow my stress to come out wrongly on my employees, and I would feel bad about my behavior and would do things with them to make up for my poor behavior. We grew together to be a pretty well-run company and most of the fun I had was from the things that went on in the office.

Thankfully, Lauren eventually got past the colic and became a super cute and happy baby. Lindsey still struggled with having a sister. She rightfully felt that we weren't paying enough attention to her. I tried to do things with just her as much as I could. I would walk with her around the four acres our house was on and find pretty spots to take pictures of her or sometimes I would just have her hang out with me in my music studio in the house. She was a really good singer and she loved it when I played guitar for her but in the long run, it wasn't enough. Lindsey struggled to feel like she was part of the family, in part because her last name was different. BJ asked me my thoughts on legally adopting Lindsey. I considered Lindsey to be my daughter. I never called her my "stepdaughter" because, to me, she was my kid. She had a decent relationship with her biological dad so I was unsure about adopting her until I spoke with her about it.

It seemed to be what she wanted. It was awkward and I had no idea how to address this with her dad. I wanted Lindsey to be happy and I didn't want her to feel like she wasn't part of the family. I remembered how I never felt like I was part of my family and how that hurt me terribly. I decided to speak with her father about it. He was very understanding and agreed to allow me to adopt Lindsey. I promised him he would always be part of her life and that he could speak to her and see her anytime he wanted. He was a real man about it, I have respect for what he did for his daughter. I wish there were more people like him in this world.

Problems between BJ and I continued to get worse and there were many times I wanted to leave but there were a few things that held me back from that. I was worried about the kids, that was first. I didn't believe BJ was temperamentally or emotionally fit to raise them as a single parent. I was really scared of the financial ramifications; she had already proven herself to be seriously vindictive and she used that as a silent threat over me continually. I didn't want to be a "weekend" dad either, I wanted to be more than that,

I wanted to be the perfect father, which I know is impossible but still, it's what I wanted at that time.

With all that was going on at the time I almost forgot that I reached two years without using drugs! My support group and my sponsor made sure that I would recognize it though. They all sat in the front row when I shared my story in front of a huge crowd for my second anniversary. I don't think any of those gentlemen realized the positive impact that they had on my life. If it wasn't for them, I would never have achieved two years clean.

Not too long after my second anniversary, I saw an advertisement that The Neville Brothers were playing in Harrisburg. The lead singer is Aaron Neville, my old friend Ivan's father. I loved the band and bought tickets for me, BJ, her sponsor Marty, and my sponsor Paul to all go. The night of the show, we were waiting for Paul to arrive and I was walking around looking for him. We were seeing them at the Harrisburg Forum, which was a really beautiful old-style theater.

I was walking around the back of the venue and I saw some dude about a block away that looked quite a bit like my old friend Ivan. He had his mannerisms too. I walked over there and as I got closer; I was sure it was him. I couldn't believe it! I hadn't seen Ivan in about 8 years! When I approached him, I walked right up to him and shoved him. I knew he wouldn't recognize me at first because I looked so much different than I did when I last saw him eight years before. He looked at me with that look of someone trying to figure out who I was. All it took was for me to say "YO" and he knew right away! He yelled NY MIKE! We hugged for almost a whole minute! It was so nice to see him after all these years and I missed him all the time.

He invited me to come backstage to meet his father and uncles. I backed off and told him I couldn't go backstage. He looked puzzled and asked me why. I told him I was clean for 2 years and I knew all too well what went on backstage. This time he shoved me and said "Yeah, you got two years"? I was expecting him to say anything other than what he said, which was "Well, I got three!" For me to hear those words come from his mouth and to see the look of happiness in his eyes brought tears to my eyes. What a gift it was to see my old friend whom I spent some of the lowest points of my addiction and then find out he was sober just like me! I went backstage with him and he introduced me to his father and pridefully told him I lived with him in NY when he was all fucked up and that I had two years clean!

Ivan was filling in for his uncle who was dealing with health issues. It was so awesome to see him on stage with his father. I caught a lot of the interaction between them. I would see Ivan get his father's attention and then throw in a riff on his keyboard and then I would see his dad smile back at him. It was so heartwarming to see. I remember Ivan telling me when we lived together in NY that his father was very disappointed in him. I was thrilled to see that he was sober and that he was playing in his father's band. This happens to be one of my fondest recovery memories. I am still friends with him. We speak often and whenever he is playing within 100 miles of me I go to see him. Sometimes the gifts of recovery are incomprehensible. I would have never believed this would have happened.

I went to treatment in January of 1999 and at that time I lived in a little 2-bedroom apartment. I had a decent car and made a fairly decent living. By January of 2002, I had a little more than two years clean, a wife and two daughters, my own business, a four-bedroom house with four acres of land, an indoor swimming pool, and 2 very nice cars. Any self-esteem issues that I had were hidden underneath a huge ego. I didn't take the fact that Scott and I got into something at the perfect time into consideration. According to me, 100% of my success was attributed to being a genius.

My family and I were living fairly comfortably. I would buy nice clothes for me and the kids. I renovated the pool and the pool house. I paid off the loan my mother co-signed for, I bought BJ a beautiful Chrysler Sebring convertible, and I owned a super cool Mitsubishi 3000 GT-VR4 that was customized.

After reaching two years clean and my business was one of the larger distributors of body jewelry in the country, I set out to have the company become the biggest in the industry. I started investing in really nicely designed catalogs and sent them out to over 5000 stores. My graphic artist was amazing and he would design the catalogs and advertisements that helped us reach national recognition.

Over the next year, the company almost doubled its sales from the previous year and our sales staff doubled as well. With new staff came new troubles from my wife. I didn't have anything to do with hiring, that was all done by Darlene for office and shipping staff and Paul for salespeople. We happened to hire a few very attractive females for sales and administration and of course, that threw BJ into a tailspin. It was so embarrassing at times, either with her calling repeatedly or showing up and starting a shit show. I would try desperately to keep her calm and let her know there was nothing to fear. I would tell her that I didn't want anyone but her but whenever I tried that I would be called a liar and get accused of fucking the new employees. She'd repeatedly tell me I didn't love her, that the only reason I kept her around was to avoid paying alimony or child support, and other hurtful comments.

One of her newer insults was to call me "Mr. Premier," which meant all I cared about was my image and my business. God forbid one of the new female employees would come to work wearing anything that could even be considered as provocative and for BJ, that could be just showing up wearing shorts. Anytime she saw something like that, I could have expected the next "you don't love me" fight to last at least a few days.

I remember thinking often, or questioning, *how the fuck can life be so amazing on one hand and so discouraging and dismal on the other?* Therapy stopped helping by this time, BJ was out of control. I was getting ready to put an end to it like I promised. I wouldn't do what I did the year before, but I wouldn't live in fear of her behavior. It all came to a head one morning when BJ was on one of her rampages about the female employees at the office. She wanted me to fire them. She said that she would never feel safe with them at the office. By this time, I had been through so much with her over her insecurities over the massage parlor incident or about anything else she wanted changed and I had had enough.

I reached the point that I had said I wasn't engaging in this anymore. I told her she could leave if she expected me to act on every one of her insecure, deranged demands of me. I walked out of the house and to my surprise she followed me out with a huge kitchen knife in her hands. She was screaming at me to fuck her like I wanted to fuck the girls that worked for me or the whores in the massage parlors. She took all her clothes off and was naked in the garage while I was getting in the car. She had a huge kitchen knife in her hand and she was screaming bloody murder. The worst part of this was that both kids were home and heard everything. I was scared to leave her there with the kids but I was more scared of what she would do to either me or herself if I stayed. I drove to the office. My sponsor Paul was there and I told him what happened and told him I was thinking of killing myself. I couldn't live like I was anymore but I also believed she wouldn't let me leave without harming herself.

After talking me out for a drive Paul calmed my nerves a little and talked some sense into me. He said I was right that I couldn't live like this anymore and my fears about BJ harming herself were valid and that we needed to do something. We called BJ's sponsor Marty and told her what happened. We agreed to have an intervention to try and get her some help. We all went to my house and sat down with BJ. I explained that we couldn't live like this anymore, it was becoming dangerous. I told her I wouldn't leave her if she went for a mental health evaluation and if treatment was recommended, that she would accept it and go. Surprisingly she agreed.

We found a nearby partial hospitalization program and she committed to do it. We set it up that Lauren would go to daycare and Lindsey would be in the Latchkey program for kids needing to stay at school until a parent got off work and picked them up. I wanted this to help, I was skeptical but hopeful. I was worried, I was hurt, I was angry, but I still loved her dearly and wanted to keep our family together.

This was the worst of the emotional abuse that I endured from BJ. It's not easy to discuss publicly. It's embarrassing. It's hard for me as a man, to admit that I was a victim in an abusive relationship. The only people I ever spoke about this with were Paul and my therapist. It's often hard to decide what I should or shouldn't include in this book, there are so many things that went on that I've kept out. I feel it's necessary to include this to explain the difficulties of living with someone like my former wife and for people to understand what went into my self-esteem and mental health problems.

Throughout the madness of my everyday life during
this time, the company continued to grow. How I maintained
sanity through it all is a mystery. We were developing into a
well-run business. I give a lot of credit to Darlene. She
became my right hand when it came to running the business.
She did everything right. She always had the company's best
interest in mind, even when that conflicted with what I
believed to be my own personal best interests. I may have
had a few years clean at this point, but I was still a teenager
at heart so I was and am still very thankful for having Darlene
in my life back then. She did everything from hiring
competent staff, developing HR policy, and acquiring
healthcare for the staff. I never imagined owning a business
that was so professionally run.

At the same time, dealing with BJ was still a handful of
heartache. She went to the partial mental health program for
a few weeks and was miraculously cured. She didn't need to
go anymore and was just going to do counseling once a
week. I was truly frightened to death over what she would
do. She wasn't cured. She would still have massive blowouts
over everything. Nothing changed, she still wanted me to fire
most female employees and would still give me shit about
hanging out with friends or my sponsor. Her therapist wasn't
very helpful.

I still loved BJ but was growing ever so tired of dealing with
the never-ending drama she caused. I wasn't ready to leave
her but it was becoming obvious that her behavior wasn't
going to change anytime soon. I started putting most of my

energy into the business. The company was still growing and we were outgrowing our offices. I needed to start looking for a new place of business. I just did anything I could to keep my mind off of the madness at home.

Chapter. 52- But when the lord gets ready, You got to move- *The Rolling Stones*

By January 2003, my company had become one of the largest distributors of body jewelry in the country. The full-page advertisements in every national tattoo publication were helping, along with the tons of sales we were making. I had a team specifically geared towards breaking new accounts and a different team dedicated to reselling customers by calling them every two weeks at the least. We completely outgrew our little offices. I was storing inventory in closet space because our bins would overflow.

By March it was becoming clearly obvious that we were going to have to move the office so I started looking at business rentals in the area. By happenstance, I was getting on the highway very close to my house and I spotted a large "available for lease or sale" sign just past the highway entrance, so I went to take a look. The second that I looked at it I wanted it. It was a 5500 sq. ft. house that was turned into a business. An insurance agency owned it and moved out more than a year before. It was stunning just to look at it. It had a lot of parking and there was a spot that was perfect for UPS to do their pickups and drop-offs. I called Paul and Darlene at the office and told them where I was, which was less than 2 miles away from our current offices. When they showed up they were as amazed as I was. We scheduled a showing and it was all I could think about while we waited to see it.

When we finally met the realtor to view the property, we were in awe of how incredible this place was. It was perfect. It was in a very impressive setting with finely landscaped lawns, a beautiful main room with a huge fireplace, multiple rooms for different parts of the business, and a picture-perfect salesroom. There was a space for a showroom as well, and the topping was what would be my office, which was huge and absolutely beautiful.

I took our whole crew over to see our new place and everyone loved it. They couldn't believe we were going to be working in such a beautiful building. My sales crew got so motivated by it just by seeing the place that our sales numbers were getting even better. I took BJ and the kids to see it and the kids were amazed and loved it. When BJ saw it, her response was just a little different. She cried. I was flabbergasted. I couldn't begin to even try to understand this one. I should have kept my mouth shut. I really should have. Unfortunately, though, I rarely ever did what I should. This wasn't going to be the exception so I stupidly asked. I had to. Another "you don't love me" fight was on the way.

She said she was crying because by having an office like this, I was going to attract women that want to fuck me because I own the company in this building. I could never understand why my success with the business was such a threat to her. It hurt that she failed to recognize that I worked so hard for all this and it wasn't just for me, it was for the family as well. I can't describe what it's like to be on top of the world while at the same time feeling completely drained and defeated. At least this fight didn't go on for days, it was over by the next morning. I gave my current landlord at the office we were in for three years' 60-day notice and prepared for the move.

Chapter 53.= Move on up and keep on wishing, Remember your dream is your only scheme so keep on pushing= *Curtis Mayfield*

Before we moved I bought all new desks and chairs. I had to get the new place wired for a computer network and have the new phone system wired according to how we planned the different sales room desks. I couldn't help but think about how much has changed in a short time. I had less than four years clean. I quit smoking on my third clean anniversary, so I was less than a year without cigarettes. That in and of itself was a miracle, I smoked cigarettes like Keith Richards from the Rolling Stones- one after another, all day long. I still considered myself to be a kid, I felt like one anyway, and here I am planning to furnish and staff a 5500 sq. ft. office. At the same time, I was so sick of the stupid lawsuit with Scott that I took a chance and offered $15,000 to settle it. He jumped on it and like that, it was over. I thought *here's this kid that for 10 years was pretty much homeless in LA. I spent the better part of those years on someone's couch. I slept on the New York subways. I was a drug addict and a criminal. In just three short years I've changed everything and now I am a successful businessman moving into a beautiful huge building!* I was enjoying success, enjoying being a dad, and although our marriage wasn't perfect, I loved BJ and we had our moments when things went well. When she wasn't caught up in fear and insecurity, she was pretty cool. The thing I loved the most was coming home from work and having these two beautiful little girls run into my arms yelling "Daddy" so happy to see me.

It was quite a stunning building. My office took up half of the second floor, it was furnished beautifully, I had a huge U-shaped glass desk with frosted glass tops. I had a beautiful leather sectional couch, and a 55" television. On a clear day, I could see the Susquehanna River from my window! High-speed internet was brand new at that time and we had it throughout the whole building. Each desk had a computer with internet access. We had a new phone system that was automated, so calls were routed to whoever the caller was trying to reach by being prompted by the automated message.

Every year, I would drive to either South Carolina or Ohio to buy fireworks and have a huge blowout on July 4th, and this year I went hog wild! I had between 50 and 60 people at my house. Everyone had filet mignon, chicken, burgers, and hotdogs and I'd put on a huge firework show. Everyone there was completely sober too, no beer, no liquor, no drugs at all! My parents, my brother, and his wife and daughter came out too. I will never forget the look on my mom and dad's faces when they saw the new building. I think it was the second time in my whole life that either one of them told me they were proud of me.

After a few months, I went to Bangkok, Thailand, Shanghai, China and made deals with some manufacturers. I made a deal with the factory in China to list me as a partial owner so I'd save tons of money on international tariffs. I can't lie, I let all this go to my head worse than ever before. I was wearing super expensive clothes. BJ and the kids had everything they wanted and we all were dressed in the best clothes. I felt invincible. I felt like I couldn't do anything wrong. In twelve-step meetings, they often talk about remaining humble but somehow that word was nowhere to be found in any of the dictionaries in my house. How could I be humble when only three years after getting clean I was sitting on top of the world with a business that was considered to be a heavyweight in the industry?

Chapter 54. The roof, the roof, the roof is on fire... *Bloodhound Gang*

I don't know how to explain understandably that it felt like my life was going in two different directions at the same time. As the business grew, my stature in the community grew and at the same time, my life at home was falling apart. I didn't know how to make my wife understand that I loved her. I wanted to have compassion for what she was going through but her level of viciousness would just put me on the defense. She would so often accuse me of not loving her, usually when she didn't get her way and these fights were vicious. Our sex life had completely faded, and of course, that was another reason to argue. I would get accused of cheating because I never wanted to have sex. I would try and explain that I felt like I was constantly protecting myself from her onslaughts of insanity because the things she would say would hurt so bad. I was hurting and defensive and felt that I couldn't allow myself the vulnerability of opening up and having sex or being intimate at all. Any time I tried to explain or defend myself just made things worse and the argument would go back to the massage parlor thing. I had no defense against that so I would just back down and wait for the storms to pass.

At the same time, over the first year in the new building, life was exciting. The business was still going very well and I had around fifty people working for me and everyone was making good money. Everyone was insured and I was happy in the office away from the house. My ego was huge though. When people would see how successful we were they would praise me and say wonderful things about me, about my intelligence, about my business sense, and blah, blah, blah…..

I mean, that shit boosted my ego, as did having access to as much money as I needed for anything I wanted. For a guy who just a few years before was always so broke, always dependent on others, to now be seen as the guy that has everything a man could want felt good. When the outside looks perfect but the inside is a mess, it was easy to allow the words of others to inflate my sense of self-worth. I'd come to learn that my sense of self-worth was fake though; it came from the words of others, not me. Whenever I was feeling down, or exhausted from running such a large company and what was going on at home, I would raise my spirits by buying myself expensive clothes or jewelry. I still didn't understand that polishing the outside doesn't fix the inside.

About one year after moving into the new building, some things started happening that were not expected and definitely cause for concern. The way banks processed checks was starting to change. Up until then, I would write checks to suppliers or for other bills even though the check register was showing a negative balance. A check at that time would take up to three or four weeks to clear the account and there was always a lot of money available in the account. At any time, I would have about forty or fifty thousand dollars in the account and could also have over fifty thousand dollars on the way in from orders that were shipped. We would get the money in our account within three days from the customers receiving their orders. The check register might show that I was maybe ten or fifteen thousand dollars in the red, but it never affected the account because of how fast the money came in.

All of a sudden, the banks started clearing checks a lot faster than usual. Some laws changed and they allowed to use of images of the checks rather than receiving the actual check in the mail so the wait time for a check to clear went from three weeks to three days. Needless to say, I noticed the difference right away because the balance at the bank was no longer so high. There was always money in the account, but not like the forty or fifty thousand that I was used to having in it. Things are always so perfect until they aren't.

Things were never really "so perfect" for me, but I was living a life beyond my wildest dreams. Then for reasons unbeknownst to me, things started going in a different direction. The challenge of keeping the business accounts flowing with cash along with having to deal with a multitude of other problems at the same time was affecting me in what can be called a negative way and by that I mean I started becoming an asshole. A real, true, bona fide asshole to the point that I was mean to people that didn't deserve it. I would get short with staff for stupid reasons like asking a simple question. I would interrupt people in conversations if I felt what they were saying was irrelevant.

Every year up to this point I would file my taxes and my federal tax bills were beyond ridiculous, I would complain to the accountant handling them for me because I didn't understand why the bills were so high. I didn't understand his explanations. He would say that I should be in a different tax bracket and pay a lower percentage but I needed a tax lawyer to help with that. My tax bills were in the area of forty-thousand dollars every year. I would try and pay them off over the following year but would always have leftover outstanding balances. By this time the outstanding federal tax debt was close to fifty thousand dollars.

I started looking for ways to cut spending and learned about a bunch of mistakes we made when we moved into the new building that we were pouring money into for no reason. I also had to let a few people go to save some money each month. I hated to do it; I felt really bad when I let someone go and I would give them a check for $500 on top of their final pay (I was always a bleeding heart).

I was trying to get my sales manager Paul to do more to help raise sales. He was making a fortune because he received a cut of our total sales as part of his deal as manager. He didn't have to make a lot of calls to earn a lot of money because his customers called in regularly. Most of them were huge accounts for the company. I would ask him to work directly with some staff that could have been doing better with some positive direction. It seemed like everything I asked of him was too much. I would show him ways of working with the salespeople to help motivate them to sell more and as usual, he would find a way of doing it without spending time with them.

Paul wanted to turn over a good amount of his customers to the sales staff and then spend the bulk of the day on different sales floors and motivate the staff and for this, he wanted a base salary of $1000 weekly. He wouldn't get commissions on sales but he would still get an override of the sales from everyone under him. At the time I thought that was ridiculous. Maybe I was wrong about this but at the time I was incapable of seeing things differently.

My tax lawyer finally called me to tell me he set up a meeting with the IRS. He didn't provide any information except that he set the meeting. When we met, this lady came to my house and started pointing out things we could sell to start paying them back. She said the company was not bringing in enough yearly income to reach a lower percentage tax bracket and I was liable for the current outstanding debt. I asked the lawyer if this was serious and he stood there like an idiot, speechless. The IRS agent was explaining that interest and penalties were compounding daily and pulling up some outrageous numbers that I would owe after a certain amount of time. By the time the meeting ended, I was freaking out. I listened to his bullshit for months while sending him thousands of dollars every month which could have gone towards the IRS debt. This all happened so fast, and we were still trying to slow the flow of money going out so we could build the bank accounts back up but every day we needed something else or another huge bill was due.

This was beginning to cause me such anxiety that I couldn't sleep. My nerves were shot and I would lose my shit on people that didn't deserve it. A few people decided to quit as a result and they were good sales people so their leaving hurt. I don't blame them though, I was an asshole to them. I got what I deserved. This was a very stressful time and everyone was feeling it.

The shit with Paul reached a boiling point. We decided he would no longer be the sales manager. I raised his commission rate so he wouldn't lose too much money from not receiving his override. I loved Paul, he was with me from the beginning and he was very important to the company but it felt like he was taking advantage of my generosity. I was going through so much with the business, at home, and with the tax situation to take the time to work things out to a better conclusion and I've grown to regret what happened between us. I found myself desperately trying to hold things together while they were falling apart all over the place. I did my best to keep everyone happy but everyone knew that we were in a bad situation. Shit was about to get deep!

Between my fifth clean anniversary in August and my 39th birthday in November of 2004 my world went upside down, right side up, and upside down again. It was a whirlwind three months to put it lightly. My friend Mark from Sales One offered to help out and buy my whole inventory and take over my company. I would be his VP of sales and still run things and receive a 6-figure salary. It was a sweet offer and I was heavily considering it.

At the same time, my tax lawyer and the IRS were negotiating a payment plan for me to pay them the outstanding back taxes owed, but what they offered was ridiculous. At this point, I was somewhat sick of lawyers but I was willing to try anything. I saw this lawyer and within ten minutes she had the answer to fix this whole thing. I could file Chapter 13 bankruptcy and then I would only owe the IRS the remaining debt for the previous three years and pay it off in 3 years interest and penalty-free. Between Mark's offer and talking to this bankruptcy attorney I was starting to feel a lot better about the situation. BJ and I agreed this would help the situation.

I told my staff of Mark's offer and most of the crew were cool with it. Especially when I told them they would be paid a decent salary plus commissions, I paid them commission only. Paul was speculative about it as I knew he would be. His attitude the few months before this was terrible. I had a feeling he was planning on leaving to start his own company. It was a gut feeling. His sales were way down and every time I walked past him he wasn't on the phone selling, he was just staring into space. If I ever tried to guide his sales, he pretty much made it obvious he wasn't listening.

The day after I told the crew, Paul called me at home and quit. It felt terrible that it came to this, I didn't want him to leave. I wanted to work our way past it. I knew he wanted his own company. I was against it because he had most of our best customers on his caseload for years. I tried to talk him out of it but he was adamant. He asked if he were to go into business for himself if I would supply him. I was totally against that. He signed a non-compete contract and I expected him to keep his end of the contract, which was not to have contact with any of his past customers or compete with my company for 90 days and then he could do anything he wanted.

Paul knew I was having troubles so he picked the perfect time for his betrayal. I was going to sue him; he signed a contract. When I went to the office the next day, his computer had been wiped clean. His whole customer database was gone. He had access to the whole company customer database and it was wiped clean from his computer. Luckily it was all backed up on an external hard drive. I called and asked Paul if he did something to his computer and asked why it was wiped clean of everything, even the database. He swore up and down he didn't do anything to it. Unfortunately, I didn't have any hard evidence that he did so there wasn't anything I could do.

I decided to go ahead with filing the bankruptcy. I also decided to accept Mark's offer. The next month entailed Mark and I developing a contract and between us and figure out how much I needed to produce in sales to justify my salary. We worked out how Darlene and the rest of the crew would be paid as well. Doing this made me feel as if a huge weight was taken off my shoulders.

While we were going through the motions of the transition, I was having serious thoughts of leaving BJ. I just felt like she was never really "with me." I always felt that whatever was going on at the time, she always made it about her. I talked with my sponsor Paul about it a few times and he was leaning on the side of me sticking with her to see how things turned out with the transition of the business. I was trying to figure out what was in my best interest. There was so much going on. I had a lawyer drawing up a lawsuit because I was going to sue Paul. I was letting go of my business and joining forces with a much larger company and I was in the beginning stages of filing a Chapter 13 bankruptcy.

Throughout 2004 BJ and I just kind of distanced ourselves from each other. Towards the end of the year, there were a few times I couldn't provide her with her weekly $500, and par for the course, I went through hell until I gave it to her. For years we went without wanting anything. Anything she asked for, she got. Anything the kids wanted we got. Then, the first time I didn't give her the check all I heard was what we didn't have and what the kids were going without. I started to feel like all I was to her was a weekly check and a nice house.

I was super stressed out most nights and couldn't sleep. I'd ask for a massage to help me relax and she'd complain that she didn't want to. I was growing tired of it all. I wasn't an angel throughout this time either. I would come home from the office and just want peace but the kids were excited to see me when I'd get home and I would be an asshole and give BJ money and tell her to go shopping for anything they wanted. Right after my 39th birthday in November, the final straw was broken.

BJ received ten thousand dollars from a car accident she was in a few years back. She asked me how she could help with our situation and she gave me $1000. I asked her to just pay the bills for the house for the month, which came to around $2500. When December rolled in, I received some phone calls from a few people telling me that BJ shared in a meeting about spending every penny of that money without paying one bill. She talked about being scared to tell me. She shared this in a meeting purposely so someone would tell me. I had it at this point. When I confronted her about it, she said she was scared we wouldn't be able to have Christmas with everything that was going on so she did all her Christmas shopping. It was bullshit. She spent a ton of money on clothes for herself along with the Christmas presents she bought.

I was fuming. I just couldn't stop thinking that all I was to her was money. The only time I asked for some help, she just couldn't. It hurt. It felt like she never loved me. My thoughts went back to when she told me to leave after finding out about the massage parlors and she immediately went for the money. Nothing changed at all.

I decided to break up with her after the holidays. I knew she would go after the money and everything else we owned but I didn't care. I felt like I was being strangled and I couldn't breathe. Nothing I ever did was enough and nothing ever came between her and what she wanted. I was devastated. I put up a wall around me over the next few weeks and I wasn't allowing anything or anyone in. I was hurt. I closed my heart. I pretty much acted like everything was normal and went through the motions of the holiday and prepared myself for her wrath because I was done. Nothing but my peace of mind mattered at this point. Just knowing I was going to do this brought me to a peaceful state of mind that I hadn't experienced since she was in Florida. Even though that peace only lasted for a brief moment, it was special.

Chapter 56. Meet the new boss, same as the old boss- *The Who*

The remainder of December and the Christmas holiday went by without incident. We moved out of the old office into a much smaller office and the move went pretty easily except I didn't realize how much stuff I owned. I had to store around twenty-five desks, computers (old-school computers, with huge monitors) filing cabinets, and a ton of other things in my pool house. My bankruptcy was filed and I had a three-year, interest and penalty-free payment plan set up with the IRS. I wound up saving over 60K in current and future IRS debt from this. Everything was falling into place quite nicely until a monkey wrench found its way into the plan, and by that I mean some shit happened that fucked the plan up!

Mark drove down from Connecticut with advanced paychecks for everyone. With that, he brought non-compete contracts, which everyone knew he was bringing. I wasn't signing one, that was worked out in our contract. Then another salesperson was trying to get her weekly salary to be the same as the rest of the sales staff. She was offered a lower salary because her sales were about half the average of everyone else. Mark wasn't going to budge and neither was she. I was trying to show her she would still make a lot more than she was making from me, but she felt slighted and decided to quit too. I signed a one-year contract with Mark and to make the total salary he offered I had to reach two million dollars in annual sales which was possible with her and Chris but completely impossible without them. Mark told me he'd pay for advertising and allow me to hire three more people for sales to make up for losing them. He was a really good guy with a huge heart. My company spent close to a half million dollars with his business and he was quite appreciative of me as well. We had a friendship that went further than that though, we both understood the insane pressure of running our business more than anyone else could ever understand. We were always there as an ear for each other over the years.

Our contract stated that Mark was going to purchase my entire inventory for what I paid for it. I had a ton of money tied up in inventory and I was planning on using that money to pay off the IRS debt so I could get through the bankruptcy faster than the three years in the plan. I had to complete a count of all the inventory first and that was a huge undertaking. It took a long time for me to count and add everything to a spreadsheet.

I had to drive up to Connecticut and go over each item, how many there were, and how much each piece cost. It took over four hours for us to do that. The amount we came up with that I was to be paid for it all was not anywhere near what I paid for it but it would pay Mark back for my outstanding balance that was owed to his company and pay me around 35K in the end. He wanted to pay me over seven months at $5000 per month. I gratefully accepted it. I believed at the time it was enough to cover all my bills and then some, but I didn't take into consideration what was coming next. I broke up with BJ. I thought I knew what was going to come from leaving her. I was way off.

Chapter 58. We're one, but we're not the same... ~ U2

I kept to myself over the two weeks after the holiday. I was angry and hurt by BJ's actions with the money from the accident. I couldn't let it go. We were together for five years, married for four, and I couldn't think of just one time when I felt peaceful. BJ was her usual self. Every time we had one of those four-day-long fights over whether I loved her or not, once we finished, she would believe things would be like they were before the fight and want to act like it never happened. I wasn't capable of doing that. After being called so many vicious names and called a liar, repeatedly, over and over, I was scarred from it all. The anxiety over the bankruptcy, over moving the offices, over debating whether or not to sue Paul was just too much to deal with and I needed a break.

BJ believed I shouldn't have been hurt or angry over the money she spent. It was just like her beliefs that I should get over arguments when they were over and disregard all the ugly hateful things she would say during them. I finally told her I was seriously thinking about leaving her. I said that I needed space to think things through before making a final decision. I asked her if she could stay at her mother's house for a few weeks which she wouldn't do. The fact that I needed space meant nothing. If I wanted space then I'd have to leave.

I rented a hotel room for a few days and then I asked my friend Blaine if I could stay at his house until I decided what I was going to do. Once I left the phone calls from her started. Between the first one in the morning where she was nice, and then by the afternoon when she'd cry and plead for me to change my mind, to the evening where she'd start threatening and cursing. Whatever I wanted didn't matter, it was all about her. Always.

I tried explaining over and over that I needed time to figure things out. I was pleading with her to allow me that. I tried to tell her I hadn't decided anything yet and that her constant calling wasn't helping. Finally, she called me while I was at Blaine's and she told me she went to Domestic Relations and filed for spousal and child support. This was about one week after I left. Within that time, I gave her a shitload of cash, paid for her car to get fixed, and went grocery shopping for the house, spending close to $600 on food and supplies for the house. All that in one week and here she is, telling me she's worried that I won't provide for her and the kids through this.

Needless to say, that made my decision for me. I didn't mean anything to her. The only thing that mattered was the money. I was out. I decided to file for divorce. Looking back now, maybe I should have waited a little longer to make that decision but in my heart, I knew this was going to be the conclusion. It was inevitable. Five solid years of emotional abuse was enough. Five years of walking on eggshells, worrying that at any time, anything I said could trigger one of those four-day-long fights. I was done. Finally. I knew she wasn't going to take it lightly. I knew how vindictive she was but I hoped that she would at some point come to understand that our wants and needs had to come after the common welfare of our children. I should have known to have any sort of hope at this time was foolish. It didn't take long to find out that was evident.

The next few months went by fairly quickly, I tried my best to avoid BJ but I would still have to deal with her from time to time. In March after I filed for divorce I rented a nice house. The rent was affordable and there was enough room for the kids and my little home recording studio. It had a finished basement for the studio and there was a lot of space for all my business materials that came from the old building. My driver's license was suspended for a few years at this point, it started from receiving a six-month suspension in 2002. I got caught driving while suspended a few times and now I was a few months away from finally getting it back. Stupidly, I continued to drive on a suspended license.

We had a custody hearing. BJ got the outcome she wanted. I'd get my kids every other weekend and Wednesday's. I wasn't happy with that but with all the fighting over everything, I gave in to keep her quiet. She was trying to keep everything in the house, even though she didn't pay for any of it. I had my lawyer draw a contract that nothing could be sold or removed until we figured out an equitable distribution. The first thing she did after that was sell my boat. I paid $4000 and she sold it for $750. My lawyer wanted me to sue over it but I had enough of courts, lawyers, and anything that had to do with lawsuits. When it was over I left a house that I lived in for 5 years with almost nothing. There were 3 different sets of living room furniture, I kept the oldest one. I kept one of three big-screen TVs and the dining room table. After 5 years of living in a house that I poured more money than I ever imagined and left with nothing, just to avoid another fight.

My lawyer supposedly ran the numbers and came to an amount of about $2500 per month for alimony and child support. It was a lot, but I would be able to survive it. After the hearing, I received a call from her with terrible news. The settlement that domestic relations came to was much higher, it was a little more than $4100 per month. When I figured out whether or not I could survive on what was left, I barely had enough to cover monthly bills. I had to fight that settlement. She could have held out for up to two years on signing divorce papers which would have provided her $1500 per month in alimony, which before the divorce settlement was called spousal support and that was on top of $2600 per month in child support. Domestic relations gave me a small break and a reprieve from paying any arrears and I had close to thirty days before these funds would be removed from my pay.

As usual, BJ wanted money within two weeks. I told her I wasn't giving her anything until the funds started coming out of my paychecks. Of course, when BJ didn't get what she wanted she'd get vicious and start to threaten me. She said over and over that I knew how mean she could be and that I better give her what she asked for. I had money, but I was tired of her threats and behaviors and refused to give her any money. In turn, she called the police and told them I stole her car and was driving without a license or insurance. I had my car in her name because my license was suspended. The Camp Hill police officer who took her call decided to wait for me by my house. When I pulled up, he pulled me over in front of my house and cited me for driving on a suspended license, and tried to have my truck towed. I provided proof of insurance so he couldn't tow my truck. She called me immediately after and again demanded money, I told her to fuck off and hung up. I never wanted to see or speak to her again after this.

I offered her a lot before she went to domestic relations but she wanted everything. It wasn't just about money, she wanted me to suffer. It solidified my belief that she never loved me. I was just a provider of a lifestyle and nothing more. She threatened me financially a lot after I left by saying, "You better think this through, it's going to cost you a lot." I didn't care anymore, I was finished. My way of coping with all that loss was to at least know I was free. I couldn't bear to live with her anymore regardless of the financial burden. I thought back to what that couple's therapist told me before our wedding. He hit the nail on the head with his prediction. I suffered through five years of emotional abuse and was finally free. Well, at least I thought I was.

Chapter 59. Then you better start swimmin' or you'll sink like a stone, For the times, they are a-changin' *Bob Dylan*

The merger between Mark's company and mine should have been awesome except that Mark and I seemed to be the only people who believed in it. My crew continuously complained about items in their orders getting back ordered because I never did that. I shipped all orders complete. After a few months, it started feeling like a circus. I traveled once a week to different spots in the country to meet with some of our larger customers to ensure they stayed with me after Paul left.

I would be out of the office three days a week sometimes and then come back to complaints. I'd hear shit from Marks staff about my crew, especially from Dennis, the VP of sales. Once he learned what my salary was, he became jealous and tried to mess things up between Mark and me. This guy even had our administrative person, Tara, emailing him about everything I did during the day! This shit was a pain in the ass especially since we were doing awesome in sales. My crew was making more now than they did before the merge. The final straw for me was when Tara left her emails up on her computer one day after she left. I snooped through them and read a bunch of emails between her and Dennis. She reported everything that went on to him. He emailed her saying that once I was gone, he would promote her to run the office. The sales crew wouldn't do anything because they were making so much money that they'd never leave.

The next morning, I had the locks changed at the office early in the morning. When Tara showed up I wouldn't allow her to enter. I told her I was leaving Sales One. Everything at the office remained in my name, the phone, and the internet account, all of it. It didn't take long for the phone to start ringing from Sales One in Connecticut. I told them I would email Mark the news, but the merger was off. We started operating as Premier Body Accents that day, I had plenty of inventory in stock and called some of my old suppliers who were more than happy to have me back as their customer.

Later that evening, Mark called from China. He was pissed. I understood his anger and didn't blame him for feeling that way. I explained my reasoning to him and I emailed him the emails between Dennis and Tara and asked him what he would do if he was me. Even though he was angry, he never lost his composure. He knew everything that I'd been through up to that point with the divorce and the settlement. We ended the call on a positive note.

Mark was always one of the good ones, he didn't have a bad intention in him. I felt sad about the project between us not working. I've questioned this decision many times throughout the years and I've always concluded that I made the right choice. The emails between Dennis and Tara put the nail in the coffin. I hated that things happened the way they did, it should have been everything Mark and I wanted it to be, but unfortunately, it wasn't.

Chapter 60. Now you don't talk so loud, now you don't seem so proud- *Bob Dylan*

When I look back at this period, something I never realized then but I do now is that I seemed to have forgotten who I was and where I came from. My ego was huge. The clothes, cars, jewelry, fancy house, and all that exterior bullshit had become more important than anything. I thought my company could withstand anything because we did so well in the first five years. I was scared shitless of losing everything, but I didn't believe it was possible either.

Around the same time, I noticed that my sponsor Paul wasn't returning calls and whenever we did talk he always seemed to rush me off the phone. My buddy Blaine whom I developed a very close friendship over the time I'd been clean stopped answering my calls too. He also stopped coming to meetings. I started feeling alone. It felt like I had no one in my corner at all. I learned that my sponsor Paul started a body jewelry business and was competing with my business too. He was using my former sales manager Paul as a distributor. For me, that was it. I was devastated. I wanted to confront it, but I also didn't want to lose the relationship with him. He had been through it all with me. He knew times were hard. It felt like being stabbed in the back.

It felt like everything and everyone I had surrounded myself with over the last 6 years dropped me from their lives. Eventually, Paul called me and told me he couldn't sponsor me anymore. Just like that. It felt like everyone who benefitted from being in my little circle left as soon as things got hard, and when they left, they took as much as they could from me with them.

Losing Paul as a sponsor was devastating. I looked at him as a father figure. He was with me through all the highs and lows of my recovery. I couldn't understand why all this was happening. I couldn't understand what I did that was so bad that almost everyone I knew was bailing. They weren't just leaving either, they tried to hurt my company by competing with me and speaking about me in terrible ways from behind my back. All of a sudden it felt like everyone in the recovery community was opening a body jewelry company. I never felt so alone. I didn't want to use drugs or get high, but I often thought I didn't want to live anymore.

Chapter 61. Sometimes salvation is in the eye of the storm- *The Black Crowes*

This was taking a toll on my mental health. I was angry all the time. I was depressed too. I found myself looking up things on the internet about what happens to children if a parent commits suicide. I was planning on harming myself. I was being an asshole to my kids. I stopped being that fun dad and became a dictator. I had no control over anything that was happening.

Lauren was five years old at the time and in kindergarten. One day before taking her to school, we argued and I yelled at her. She said she didn't want to come to my house anymore because I was mean. In a fit of rage, I told her I didn't want her to come over either. That was so mean of me to say. It hurt her and she started crying uncontrollably. That wasn't the real me. I couldn't believe I said that. I felt so bad and wanted Lauren to stop hurting so I stopped and sat next to her and apologized and held her in my arms. How could I be such a terrible person to hurt this beautiful, innocent little girl? I didn't want to be that person. I called a few friends in recovery asking if anyone could suggest a therapist. A friend suggested a place in Harrisburg and I called them and made an appointment.

My first session with my new therapist Kendra was rough. She asked me why I was seeking help and over the hour, I told her all I had been through over the past year. I'm pretty sure her head spun after hearing what I just unloaded on her. She asked what I wanted to get out of therapy. I honestly couldn't answer because I had so many different things happening at once I had no clue where to begin. I told her that I never wanted to be mean to my child again. I told her I didn't know how to deal with the pain of betrayal that I felt from "the two Pauls." They were both the subject of many sessions over the next few years. I told her I wanted to be free from BJ because although I left, she was still a cause for a lot of hell for me. I didn't tell her how much I thought about suicide. That was my secret because if this shit didn't help, and fast, suicide was my next option.

Over the next two years, I started working from home. It helped a lot because my driver's license was suspended. I had a few people working for me during this time and I did a lot of sales myself as well. I was beginning to think that things weren't so bad because I was doing fairly well even though I had huge financial responsibilities. I would often think about rebuilding the business but I also never wanted to go through all that it took to get there.

My therapist was a godsend. I don't know how she put up with me. Week after week I would see her and all I'd talk about was BJ or the business. She would offer suggestions but it was like I didn't even hear her. Her patience with me was astounding. She slowly started the process of helping me see things through eyes other than my own. She would often say, the only way to understand why someone does something is to see it through their eyes. I didn't want to see things through their eyes though, I wanted them to see things through mine. She would often and quite subtly challenge my thinking at times and she had a way of making sense to me from the way she did things.

Although at the time I didn't see it, there were some improvements in my world as a result of therapy. I truly enjoyed seeing Kendra, she was one of the brightest spots in my very dark world. Looking back to that time it's amazing to me that I stayed clean throughout it. Kendra had more of a part in my abstinence during this time than meetings did. She was salvation in the eye of the storm.

Chapter 62. I see your true colors, shining through– *Cyndi Lauper*

Writing this is a lot harder than I ever thought it would be. It sometimes feels like I am reliving all this stuff over. Today, so many years later with almost twenty-four years clean, I am amazed at the amount of perseverance I had at this time. My therapist would often commend me on how I managed to remain abstinent and willing to improve myself in the face of all that happened. I don't know how I didn't see it back then. All I saw was failure, betrayal, desperation, and despair. I guess being in the middle of something makes it hard to see the end or even the edges. I often felt like I was walking through an endless field of weeds. I was constantly working my way through one situation after another.

By the time 2008 rolled in, with almost eight- and one-half years clean and after almost two years of working mostly alone from my house, I wanted to find my way back in the world. After 5 years I finally got my driving privileges restored. I noticed that a local tattoo shop near my house closed down and the spot was available to rent. I called the number and met the landlord and decided to rent the space. It was really small, on the ground floor of a multi-level house. It had a nice front window and awning, and it was on a main street. The rent was affordable. I didn't know what I wanted to do with it at first, it was just nice to go to work rather than wake up and go to my basement. It was nice to see daylight once in a while.

Right after signing the lease, the landlord asked me if I knew a guy named Paul O. He was asking about my first sponsor. When I asked why, he told me that Paul wanted the place too and was telling him not to rent to me because I would fuck him over because I was going through terrible financial problems. I was still hurting over losing him as a sponsor, and now this. I asked myself over and over what could I have possibly done to deserve this from him. It felt as if every time I turned my head, there would be one of "the two Pauls" sticking their shit in my face. Every time something like this happened it became more to discuss in therapy and motivated me to isolate more and more.

I bought some jewelry displays and set the new place up like a jewelry store. I had a large window sign, and one across the awning. I set up 5 desks in the back and my big horseshoe desk up front with the jewelry displays. It looked nice. I put up a help wanted sign and hired a few local kids that were between eighteen and twenty-one and I was teaching them the business and the ins and outs of sales. It wasn't as easy as when I first started, there were many other jewelry distributors out there and there was a lot more competition.

My self-esteem was shot at this time but what I failed to realize was that it was ME that built my company from a small business with two or three salespeople working from an office in my house to a huge fifty-five hundred sq. ft. building with over forty-five people working for me. I was starting from behind this time. Before renting the new storefront, I was paying all my bills on time. It was getting a little harder now though. Because of all the competition, we weren't selling at the huge profits as we were before things fell apart.

The monthly bill that was the hardest to pay, and pay on time was the bankruptcy payment. Child support was the biggest cost and came before everything else and it was a huge drain on the profits. BJ was continuously putting me through hell for one reason or another. The few times that I gave dating a chance wound up being disasters. BJ would find out about and threaten any woman I tried to date. Most of the women were from the recovery community so she would find out from people that we both knew. She'd say things to my kids that made them uncomfortable around anyone I dated. I was divorced from her for a few years and was still dealing with her bullshit insecurities. I wasn't in any way emotionally capable of handling a relationship with a woman at this time but I still tried a few times. I harbored so much anger towards BJ and she so often became the subject of far too many conversations and because of this, the few women I dated quickly found their way out. I had way too much baggage for them.

From the moment I left BJ, she had it in for me. It seemed as if her whole life's focus was to ruin mine. By this point, I didn't want anything to do with her. Leaving her did not in any way help my life improve; it made things a lot worse. I continuously tried to get her to agree to a lower support payment but she wouldn't budge. The bankruptcy court was giving me hell for making late payments all the time. I sought advice from my bankruptcy lawyer, she was the only lawyer I ever had that I trusted.

The few available alternatives she showed me all had pretty horrible outcomes and would make life worse for some time. If I withdrew the Chapter 13 bankruptcy and re-filed it under Chapter 7, the IRS would add all that debt back along with interest and penalties. Both my lawyer and I tried to reason with BJ over the support and told her that if we had to refile under Chapter 7 it would have terrible outcomes for her as well. She still wouldn't budge. If ever there was an example of someone cutting off their nose to spite their face, this one takes the cake. I tried to keep it going for a few months but I finally had to face the inevitable and switch over to chapter 7.

I wish I could blame my ex-wife for everything that was a pain in my ass, but I can't. I own just as much as her in this. I was so unwilling to let go of the mirage of myself being a successful businessman. I was able to handle everything as long as the outside looked fine. The mess inside didn't matter as long as no one could see it. I knew this back then but I was just not willing to face it.

I found an old picture of myself from when I first started the business. I had a backward baseball cap on my head and a t-shirt that said "NY Fucking City." I thought *I wouldn't be caught dead wearing that today.* What happened after that thought was immediate. It was one of those "aha" moments. I felt ashamed of myself. Not for how I looked in the picture, but for who I allowed myself to become.

I had allowed myself to be this judgmental asshole that could judge a book by the cover. Throughout my childhood straight up to my early thirties, I was a goofball. The class clown never really left me. The last years of success and the fear of being seen as unsuccessful dictated the image I allowed the world to see. I hope I'm making sense here. I lost my goofiness to a fear of being seen as a fool, or a loser. I mean, deep inside I felt like a complete failure. I would hide that behind fancy clothes, nice watches, and jewelry. It hit me at that moment. I asked myself "Who had I become?" I realized how important to me it was to look successful. Who the fuck was I to believe that I wouldn't be caught dead in a funny t-shirt and a backward baseball cap?

I was a hot mess back then. I had a new sponsor but I never spoke about the shit underneath it all with him. I was putting forward a bullshit image of myself for fear of people seeing how I felt underneath it all. This became the topic of many discussions with my therapist, and it became one of my biggest struggles because deep inside I wanted to be the goofball again. I wanted to wear the T-shirts and backward baseball caps again. I wanted to believe enough in myself that I didn't need fancy clothes or jewelry to hide my feelings of inadequacy. I had no idea how hard it would be to accomplish that.

After filing bankruptcy under Chapter 7, the letters from the IRS started rolling in like a speeding freight train. They were unstoppable and scary as anything. The debt seemed to have quadrupled. I wasn't making anywhere near enough money to even start paying on this shit. I had a new accountant at this point and he was a saint. He always calmed my fears and made me feel safe. I spoke with him a lot during this time. My accountant was very intelligent and always had very helpful ideas with my best interest in mind. If only he knew how to interrupt the brilliant genius thoughts that always found their way into my mind, maybe I'd have stopped myself before my next ingenious move in my never-ending quest to keep the illusion of my company being successful going.

Although it's hard to admit, my reasoning for keeping the mirage going was so I wouldn't give either of "the two Pauls" the pleasure of seeing me down. They both had their own body jewelry company and each had ventured out and opened tattoo shops as well. It's stupid when I think of it now. I should've just completely forgotten they both ever existed and went on with my life. I just couldn't at that time. Whether you call it ego, pride, or just plain stupid, it was a driving force at the time.

Chapter 63. Don't call it a comeback, I been here for years= *LL Cool J*

When I first opened the store, we did very little retail business. Wholesale sales carried the business. Social media was still somewhat new at this time. Myspace (remember them?) had been around a few years by that point but it was getting to be popular. Social media was awesome back then, especially for small businesses. It was a way to get free advertising and to target specific age groups, genders, and areas all by filtering who you were looking to reach through their search engines. As the friend base on Myspace grew, my retail sales grew.

The building the store was in sucked. Every time it rained, the store would flood. Complaining to the owner wasn't a lot of help. She would send someone to fix the leak and they'd all say the foundation of the building was falling apart and it will continue to happen until it was fixed. I guess the cost of that was astronomical because she wouldn't pay for it. She wouldn't even consider it. By the beginning of summer, the place started to smell pretty bad. Eventually, I found that a wall in the back was covered in black mold. That was all I needed to see to decide to move. The next move was without a doubt the dumbest decision I had made by far. That's not to say there wasn't any potential for success, there was plenty. I just dove headfirst into something that was way over my head.

Harrisburg PA's 2nd St. is in the heart of the downtown area and is somewhat of a mecca for the weekend party scene there. On any given Friday or Saturday night, there could be thousands of young people hopping from one club to another. One day in June, while walking downtown on 2nd St. with a few friends I noticed a cool storefront with a "for rent" sign in the window. Downtown Harrisburg is a pretty cool area, there's something for everyone during the day, and the nights are for the young, wild, and free people to go party crazy. The only thing that downtown didn't have was a tattoo or piercing shop. Immediately I started seeing fireworks, bright lights, dollar signs, and people cheering in my mind. Today, at 57, I've learned to run away when that shit goes off in my head, I wish I had that knowledge back then. Of course, though, I didn't.

I had visions of my company Premier Body Accents' redemption on the world stage. I had visions of the "two Pauls" realizing their terrible mistake of backstabbing me. I truly believed this was going to be the jump start to bring my company back to the national status it once had. I believed the path to ending the bitterness over everything that happened over the last few years was to succeed and show everyone how wrong they were. There were plenty of hurdles to jump over but that was nothing that I hadn't done before, especially when the odds were against me.

I called the agent to check the place out. When I saw the inside, once again I saw what I needed to regain success and relevance. Let's talk about the hurdles though. They were pretty high and very close together, which today would be a screaming brightly lit red flag. Back then they were but a silly challenge placed there for me to crush. The first challenge was the rent. It was four times as much as I was paying at my little store in Lemoyne. Second challenge, I didn't know any tattoo artists that I could get to come work for me. The third and probably biggest challenge was the zoning in that part of the city did not allow tattooing or body piercing. Fourth and final challenge, I didn't have anywhere near the money to do this. As a person who has often thought of himself as a failure, I have no idea where my resolve and belief that I can clear those hurdles came from.

I had a small line of credit that my brother of all people helped me obtain by putting it in his name. I had it for a few years at this point and used it sparingly. I didn't want to fuck it up, nor did I want to cause him financial harm. I went into overdrive selling for a few weeks as well, which helped me raise a good bit of the rent and deposit, and the rest came from the line of credit. I used the social media network Myspace and found a few tattoo artists to work with me so that took care of three hurdles for the time being. Overcoming the zoning issue was a bit harder.

I found out that about one month before this, a tattoo shop opened downtown. How they pulled off this magical feat was amazing. They got past the zoning issue by not using the word "tattoo" in their name. There was zoning for "art galleries" and that's what they called the shop. There was a pretty big thing about the opening of the other shop. They had a televised "ribbon cutting" on the local news with the mayor of the city right there alongside them. My lawyer said they'd be hard-pressed to shut me down because doing so would make the mayor look bad for allowing and being part of the opening of the other shop. That was enough for me to take the chance. The beginning of my redemption was here at last, great God almighty, it's here at last!

It didn't take more than two weeks for a city health inspector to show up with a cease and desist notice. She asked if we were doing tattoos out of the shop and I told her we were. She said we had to stop and handed me the notice. I asked her if she was on her way to the other downtown store to get them to stop too and she seemed to be dumbfounded. She called her office and they asked for me to come to the zoning office.

When I showed up they had the zoning law book out and showed me the law. I again asked if they were shutting the other store down, and I asked, "You know, the shop that was on the news with the mayor at the ribbon cutting?" They asked for my phone and email and told me that for the moment I had to stop, but they'd get back to me about the other store. When I was walking out, I was on my way to the local news television station and was going to make them aware of what was happening. I was ready for this fight.

The very next day I received an email from the Department of Health telling me that I could continue to do tattoos at the store but I couldn't call it a tattoo shop in the window and we had to work by appointment only. My lawyer was right, they didn't want the embarrassment of making the mayor look bad so they caved. For the first time in a long time, I won. It felt really good too! However short-lived, it felt wonderful to not feel like a failure.

Chapter 64. Memories like fingerprints are slowly raising,
Me, you wouldn't recall for I'm not my former-
Pearl Jam

What happened next was something no one could have predicted, but it was devastating. September 29th, 2008, was the most serious financial crisis to hit America since the great depression. It was all over the news how the stock market dropped drastically and some of the nation's largest investment banks and insurance companies all crashed. I had no idea what it all meant at the time, but just hearing about it on the news was scary.

It seemed like the very next day that all movement on 2nd St. stopped. The first month after it happened my wholesale sales dropped over fifty percent. I had thousands of tattoo shop customers buying from my wholesale company and they were all crying the blues about how severely their sales dropped. Before this point, my financial troubles were more from cash flow and lower profits but the sales were always pretty good. Before this, I had to hold off some business debts until the money came in but there was almost always enough on the way in to cover everything. Now, I wasn't selling enough to cover my bills at home or the shop. It was bad but I had no idea how bad it was going to get. I remember thinking that I should get out of the tattoo shop and go back to working from home. What stopped me was my worst enemy, my pride. I was too worried about letting the backstabbers win. I was too worried about looking like a failure.

BJ was a joy to deal with during these times and by that I mean she was the same pain in the ass as always but I heard from her twice as much because I was late on support payments. I knew her well enough to know that she would not have any understanding of the situation. My biggest problem with her was she would always call in front of the kids. They would hear everything. They were told, "I can't afford to take you to the movies because your dad won't pay the child support." When she called in front of them, instead of saying "When can I expect you to pay", she would say, "We're not eating because you're not paying child support", or, "These kids have no clothes because you're not helping". And, instead of realizing that she was doing this purposely and just taking it in stride, I would fall right into the trap and become infuriated and raise my voice and say horrible things to her, loud enough for the kids to hear. My poor kids were in the middle of this shit and I was stupidly playing right into BJ's hands.

With the help of a few of my distributors, we made it through the next few months. It was grueling at times but we made it through to the spring, which was always when tattoo and piercing businesses would get busy again. My mother was really helpful too, she would let me use her credit cards and I would pay them back within a few weeks. I also used the line of credit that my brother helped me get. I wouldn't have survived without all that help.

The shop's sales were improving as well. July was our first anniversary of having the tattoo shop and I wanted to do something big for it. I was going to throw a cool party. I invited a nationally recognized piercer to come out for the party. We were going to attempt a "world record piercing" by doing a multiple-person corset piercing. A corset piercing was done by piercing multiple rings through a woman's back, like a line of six on each side just before the ribcage, and then a ribbon would get pulled and crisscrossed across her back. I had a local hard rock radio station come and broadcast during the event.

The day of the party was lots of fun for everyone. My piercer and our guest piercer worked all day on the multi-person corset piercing and when all was said and done, they had like 18 people tied together through piercings on their sides. I called a few local TV station's news departments and one of them came out for it and it was on TV, live. When the newscaster asked me why I did this, I answered, "You're here filming us live on TV, aren't you?" We all got a laugh out of that and my store got some free TV advertising! We started getting a lot of business after that event. The event paid for itself and helped me with some bills. I wasn't caught up, but I was closer than I'd been in a while which was good enough for me.

It was right around this time that Facebook started getting popular. It was around for a while but it was starting to grow tremendously at this time. It didn't take long and it was bigger than Myspace. Shortly after I signed on, I started finding a lot of old friends were on it too. Once I found a few people from my neighborhood it freaking blew the hell up! In less than a month, I was reconnected with so many people from my past. It was magical! All of a sudden, friends from Middle Village, friends from the NY rock scene, the LA scene, and family from Florida, were all in touch!

One of the best things to happen was on my tenth sober anniversary. I posted about it and people from all over were blown away. I can't say how many people told me they thought I was dead! It was so special for so many people to reconnect at the same time, it truly helped me temporarily forget about a lot of my troubles. It was like the biggest chain reaction ever! I remember spending so much time getting caught up with so many people that I noticed I was staying up hours later than I had in years! It was such a wonderful thing to have happened at the perfect time.

It didn't take long for the bubble to burst though, the owner of the building contacted me and told me he wasn't renewing my lease. My rent was late for like eight months in a row so without telling me, he rented the space to someone else and I had about 30 days to find a new spot. I was pissed off, but for some reason, I wasn't worried. It felt right. I knew I'd find a spot and it would be better than this one. I was looking forward to the change.

Chapter 65. Even though the moment passed me by

I still can't turn away- *The Goo Goo Dolls*

August 10, 2009, I woke up with ten years clean. I never believed I would accomplish something like that. In 1998, over the year before I went to rehab, I remember wanting to stop using and hating myself for not being able to. I remember hangovers so bad that I would vomit after drinking water. I remember the lies I told myself over and over for years and years that I could stop and I knew all too well I couldn't. I remember looking through tears in my eyes as I approached the Woodhaven Blvd. train station because I had nowhere to sleep but the train. I can never forget the look on my father's face after taking my mother's wallet and stealing every penny in it. The one thing I can't remember is ever believing I would get ten years clean.

I wasn't attending a lot of meetings at this time. I allowed my resentments over both "Pauls" to get the best of me so my attendance was down to one or two meetings a week, sometimes less. On my anniversary, I went to a meeting I attended regularly. My sponsor was part of the group and I was supposed to share my recovery story. When I arrived, I was surprised to see both Paul my former sponsor and he was with the other Paul, my former sales manager. Seeing them through me off. They were both reasons for me to attend fewer meetings. I didn't want to see them or have them hear whatever I was dealing with if and when I shared at a meeting. I didn't want to hear what they had to say either. I heard a lot of what they were saying about me through the grapevine, and I was hurt by it. Anyway, I shared my story and shortly after, Paul, my old sponsor spoke he congratulated me on my ten years and spoke as if there was nothing between us.

My mind was spinning, I wanted to ask him why he wasn't sharing any of the bullshit he was saying about me to our mutual friends. I got up and left instead. I didn't want to hear anything from either of them and it bothered me that Paul could talk all this bad shit about me and then congratulate me in a meeting. I had been working hard at letting them both go into oblivion and not giving them any thought at all but seeing them bothered me. I was in my car outside the tattoo shop when I got back, sitting and thinking about the past ten years. I became overwhelmed with gratitude.

I remembered that I had that $100 bill in my wallet from the last day I used. Second Street had its share of homeless people and I found one and handed him the $100 bill. I told him to do what he wanted with it but I also told him if he were to use it on a hotel and dinner instead of drugs and alcohol, he may be able to never pick up another drug and change his life. I wish I knew what he did with it and how things turned out for him. I went home and sat in bed crying for some time. I didn't know why I was crying, but I couldn't stop. How the hell did ten years go by so fast?

I moved the tattoo shop to a nice new building in Lemoyne in September when our lease was up in Harrisburg. The room I used for my office and the wholesale operation had a window overlooking the tattoo room. We painted murals on the walls with really cool tattoo-style art in the waiting room, which also was where we did the retail sales of jewelry and other items. We were finally allowed to call ourselves a tattoo shop, which I believe held us back at the Harrisburg store. Our tattoo business started doing a lot better in this location.

Not long after moving into the new place, I received a phone call from someone whose voice sounded familiar and it turned out to be Brian, the first person I hired to sell jewelry for me when I was in Mt Holly Springs. He was just released from a state prison in North Carolina. He came to the store and got a few tattoos and we hung out a few times.

I made an exception and went to a few meetings with him, hoping he would get back into recovery. Unfortunately, our reunion didn't last too long. Brian started using drugs again and wound up getting arrested again for committing burglaries. I loved this kid, I wish I had more of an influence on him. Over the next few years, I would get letters from him from prison. I don't know why I never answered them but I did happen to keep them all.

Financial issues continued to plague my business and personal life. BJ was a never-ending source of joy over this period. I'd hear what a piece of shit I was from her at least three times a week. It almost felt like I was being strangled. If I paid rent, my distributors went without being paid. If I paid BJ, my rent at home or distributors weren't paid. If I paid the distributors, nobody else got paid. I couldn't win. It's funny to say now, but at that time my sanity came from Facebook. Reconnecting with so many people from my past was awesome and gave me a reason not to dwell on the problems that were going on at the time.

I was friends with one of the local music store owners, Randy "Rockstar" Robertson. Throughout the years I bought all my music gear from him and we developed a cool friendship. His store was going through financial troubles just like me and we would often discuss our problems with each other. It was nice to have his store which was only a few doors away from mine as a little momentary getaway when things at my store were getting on my nerves.

Randy was a really special person once you got past his defenses. He was extremely humorous and it was rare to ever hear him get serious. Underneath that wall of sarcastic humor though was this intelligent, sensitive man with the biggest heart. I'm glad I was privileged enough to see that side of him. Not too long after moving to Lemoyne, I was in his store and he was telling me how he had just started putting a band together with a friend of his. I asked if he had a bass player and I saw the lightbulb ignite above his head and he said "We don't but we do now. Rehearsal is on Sunday at 11 am, don't be late!" I can't tell you how awesome this was. Sundays were becoming my favorite day. We were just doing cover songs, but it felt so good to have a bass in my hands and to cut loose jamming with these guys.

Through Facebook, I reconnected with a lot of people from my past from all over the country. I reconnected with a girl I was close friends with in LA named Kandy. It was cool because we partied a lot together back then and she was sober for 10 years just like me! We had a brief fling but it didn't last, mainly because I wasn't in a position to be involved with anyone intimately. Shortly after that, I met another woman on Facebook who went to Forest Hills High School at the same time I went there. We were talking quite a bit at that time. She was quite beautiful and I was interested in her but again my insecurities about my situation kept me at a distance. I was afraid for anyone to find out how badly I was struggling. Looking back, I guess I just knew I wasn't ready to get close to anyone.

While all this was happening, a childhood friend of mine from Middle Village was putting a neighborhood reunion together. Facebook had put so many of us back in touch and this was a great idea! Catching up with old friends on Facebook became my social life. It may have been just virtual online connections but it was still great to find out how so many of us wound up. So many old friends were surprised to find out that I was sober and a father. I never imagined something like this happening.

I took Denise with me to the neighborhood reunion in June and it was the best time I had in years. To see so many of the kids I grew up with thirty-plus years before was incredible. It was so nice to see so many of my old friends, especially as a sober person. I can only imagine what that night would have been like had I been drinking. I most likely would have made a fool of myself. Most of these people's last memories of me were of some super skinny dude with big hair, makeup, and wild clothes who was usually drunk. It felt good for people to see me as an adult, as a sober person, and with a beautiful woman on my arm. I felt bad though. Denise didn't know anyone there and even though I tried to include her in everything, it felt like she wasn't having as good of a time as me. I'm sure that when we went back to the hotel, Denise was as confused as I was about where our relationship was going. We kissed a lot but it didn't go any further. She wanted it to but for whatever reason, I couldn't. My mind was racing and my insecurities seemed to be screaming at me. After the drive home the next day, I was sure there wasn't anything real between us.

I dated a few girls since leaving BJ five years before, but none of the relationships were serious. I was very insecure and at the same time, I was scared of being involved with someone intimately. I'm sure Denise was able to notice that. A few days after the reunion Denise messaged me that she didn't want to continue with our relationship. I was okay with it; I wasn't sure what I wanted and didn't want to hurt her from my indecision.

This was such a crazy time for me. The business was having lots of ups and downs. Somehow, although barely, we managed to stay above water. I'd get behind on bills but then there would be a few really good sales days, and some days that the tattoo shop did well and I'd squeak my way through another month. My relationship with my kids was a rollercoaster ride. Lindsey wanted to spend her time with her friends rather than me on the weekends. I had trouble understanding why she didn't want to hang with Lauren and me. We would argue a lot. Lauren and I were close but it was hard for me to keep her occupied on the weekends when she was with me because I was also dealing with the shop. I would try and do something with her every time she was with me. I'd take her to see movies or try and find something we could do together, but she wanted Lindsey to be with us too.

A lot of the talks with my therapist were about what was going on. These poor kids were always in the middle between their mother and me and with all they heard about me from BJ, I'm sure they didn't know how to feel about me. I wish that I was more capable of dealing with that situation properly. I wish they never had to deal with all they were dealing with. I wish I had a more understanding father at that time. I sometimes feel like I failed them back then.

Donna and I were speaking more and more, usually through text messages throughout the days and nights. I started the day texting her and ended the night the same way. We were both battling our demons at the same time and it was nice to have someone to talk with and feel heard. It felt like I could hear and help her as well. There was quite a special connection between us. We laughed a lot. I remember feeling like I had never felt so in touch with a woman as I did with Donna. Whenever the notification sound of a new text message came from my iPhone, I lit up! We eventually met up in NY around Thanksgiving and went to Little Italy and had dinner together and spent the rest of the night walking around and talking. It was nice. I don't remember ever feeling so comfortable around anyone. I didn't even feel the urge to lie about anything which even at that point was strange for me. For whatever reason though, I was okay with just being me when I was around her.

Chapter 67. Mother will she tear your little boy apart.... Pink Floyd

2010 came and went faster than you can blink your eye. After texting and talking on the phone for months, Donna was coming over to my house on New Year's Eve going into 2011. Back when I was getting high, hooking up with women was so easy because I was only in it for the sex. Rarely were feelings ever involved, just pure lust. Unlike many of my friends, I didn't get into relationships unless I needed a place to stay and when I did so, it never ended well. I was usually sent packing after a month or two. The two serious relationships I had in my life both ended with my heart being broken so I learned how to protect myself from that ever happening again. I would stay wasted and not allow myself to have feelings for anyone. My marriage wasn't much different even though I was sober for it. Even though I left her, I was heartbroken over the whole experience, and leaving only made it worse because she wanted to destroy my life. Now here I am with eleven years clean, six years after the divorce, with very strong feelings towards this person and she was coming to spend the next few nights with me at my house. I was literally petrified!

I made a really huge anti-pasta salad that was loaded with goodies. For someone that might be 5"1" tall and may have weighed 100 pounds, that little Sicilian girl could eat!! While we were eating, I felt the need to be totally honest with her because she trusted me enough to tell me about her situation so I told her about cheating on BJ and going to massage parlors. I was scared to tell her because I was afraid of being judged but she was really understanding. God, what a relief. Shortly after, we kissed for the first time. Everything felt so perfect with her. It just felt like it was meant to be. I remember not wanting her to leave when she did. After she left, I felt really lucky. I allowed myself to experience true happiness; something that I hadn't felt in a long time.

I started seeing a lot more of her. She would drive to PA on weekends and I drove to NY occasionally too. Being with Donna felt really good. She was very easy to talk with, we had similar interests and our intellects matched perfectly. She was aware of my financial problems and would try to get me to stop paying for us when we went out together but it just wasn't in me to split a bill or God forbid, have her pay. The business was getting a lot harder to manage, and the wholesale side was suffering. There was so much competition and I wasn't calling nearly as many customers as I needed to because I did everything myself while also managing the tattoo shop. I was stressed out quite a bit and Donna knew it. I tried not to act worried in front of her, but she knew. I don't think she understood how whenever I was with her, she took my mind off of the rest of the world.

A crack appeared when I bought her flowers for her birthday. She called after receiving them and instead of saying something nice, instead of recognizing that she meant so much that I would do that despite having financial troubles, she got mad that I spent the money. I understood that she knew I was struggling financially but it still hurt when she did that. If it had happened with anyone else it would have bounced off me, but not with her. I was falling for her and didn't expect that reaction, I guess that's what made it hurt.

The next few months were a nightmare. My mother fell at home and broke her hip. My father wasn't home at the time and she was there by herself and was unable to lift herself up. Eventually, my dad came home from wherever he was and called an ambulance. My mom was hospitalized. She needed surgery and I came up for it. My dad was having health problems too. He had heart problems for a few years and he had a pacemaker with a defibrillator placed in his chest. I started going up to NY almost every weekend and sometimes during the week as well. After my mother's surgery, she was placed in rehab to try and get her up and walking. There was so much happening at once.

My wholesale business suffered tremendously and it was getting harder to pay my bills at home as well as for the business. Red flags were going up in my relationship with Donna. It seemed like I couldn't make her laugh anymore, we stopped flirting through text messages and our phone conversations were getting shorter as well.

My mother's mental health became an issue, she was always somewhat narcissistic but it was much worse and she was almost impossible to deal with. She was convinced that we were all against her. She would accuse my brother, his wife, and me of loving my father more than we loved her. She was driving my father crazy, she would yell for him and expect him to jump and be there immediately.

With all this happening, I was constantly stressed. It felt like I was getting hit from all directions. There were times that I looked to Donna for comfort but almost always felt worse after speaking to her. I was losing hope. It felt like everything could fall apart at any time. I don't know how but I managed to put another anniversary party together for the store. I had five local bands, including the band I was in with Randy lined up to play in the parking lot across the street. I had a few award-winning guest artists lined up to come out and work with us all day. We were offering $10.00 skull tattoos for a few hours. I had a guitar raffle and we gave some 10-year-old kid a really nice Jackson guitar that I bought at Randy's store. When Donna and I pulled up in the morning, I was shocked to see about 200 people waiting for us to open. It turned out to be a great day, everyone made a ton of money and I made enough to pay for the bands and the company we rented the stage and sound system from and to get myself temporarily out of debt for a week or two. I was pleasantly surprised at how successful the day went. Playing the gig with our band was so much fun too. It was so hot out that day that I thought I was going to die from heat exhaustion, but I made it through the whole show. We played in front of about 200 people and everyone was telling us how good we were.

I wish the success of the day would've been enough to turn things around but it wasn't. Within one week, two of my artists gave notice that they were leaving to open their own shop, and within a few days after that, I received word from my bank that a customer bounced a huge $3400 check. This customer worked for one of my company's biggest accounts but he left them to start his own company. He placed a huge order with me and after receiving it he declared bankruptcy. I was out all the money without any chance of getting reimbursed. That was it for me. I was done. I didn't even give it thought. I announced the closing of the tattoo shop and arranged for a few different companies to ship my wholesale orders for me. I was done owning a company and a tattoo shop. I didn't even accept their two-week notice, I just closed down immediately. It took less than two weeks to sell everything from the store and all my music equipment. I had to quit playing in the band with Randy while I arranged to start working from home. I was a mess. I felt less than two inches tall.

In the whirlwind of closing the business, I had defaulted on the line of credit my brother set up for me and a loan that my mother took out for me. When I told my parents, they were very understanding and loving towards me. They knew I was dying inside from the embarrassment. Things went a little differently when I told my brother. He was angry and rightfully so. He said a lot of really hurtful things that really dug deep into my heart. He accused me of taking advantage of our elderly parents and a lot of other things with no purpose other than to inflict pain. He called me neglectful which pissed me off. It felt like he had no clue what I went through trying to hold that business together for so many years. I answered him with the definition of the word neglect with my argument of why I felt I wasn't. His answer was so hurtful. He said "Really? I need some idiot with a GED to tell me what something means?" That shit hurt, terribly. My whole life I tried to get this fucking guy to see me. I always wanted him to accept me and to be my big brother. I became defensive at some point and wound up telling him I never wanted to talk to him again. All this took place before I was able to just sit down and let all that happened sink in.

When I finally took that time, it was overwhelmingly devastating. I didn't want to face anyone. My kids were really supportive but I couldn't face them. I tried reaching out to Donna and I guess it just wasn't the right time to lean on her. Her daughter was leaving for college at the time and she was dealing with that. She eventually sent a text after we had some words between us and said she didn't want to see me anymore, she wanted to go back to being friends. Honestly, although it hurt terribly, it needed to happen. I knew it wasn't working out between Donna and me but I couldn't end it. For the first time since getting clean, I felt completely alone. I couldn't face anyone. The only thing I felt I had going for me was that I didn't even think about using a drug. I was without hope, I had to have something to grab ahold of, and my sobriety was all I had. I temporarily deactivated all social media accounts; I turned my phone off and hid in my house for a week. The only people I spoke with were me girls, my sponsor Bob, my therapist, and Randy. Randy was probably the only person who was able to cheer me up, even if it was only for a moment, he always helped me feel better.

Chapter 68. I get knocked down, but I get up again...*Chumbawamba*

All this was getting harder to deal with. I wasn't having trouble staying clean, thank God, but I was a complete mess. Once again, I felt like the world's biggest failure. I was behind on all my bills at home. I closed the business owing a lot of distributors' money. I sold all my music equipment except for my acoustic guitar. I just felt like I was losing everything and everyone. I wanted to die. I told myself over and over that I would never be able to face anyone and that I would never be able to put things back together. I was ready to just give up. I guess deep inside I wanted things to get better so I called my therapist and set up an appointment with her. I hated the thought of going back to therapy even though it was always helpful. I guess there was also a part of me that didn't want to get better so I would have an excuse for suicide or getting high at some point.

I changed sponsors a year before and my Sponsor Bob was the only friend I felt I had. He was very loving and understanding towards me and my situation. I first met Bob when I had a few weeks clean. Bob was an elder in the recovery community, he had more sober time than anyone, I think at that point when I met him he had around twenty-five years of continuous sobriety.

After a few weeks of negotiations with a few different distributors, I decided to have my old friend Mark's company ship my sales. It was a gamble, I was worried about how his staff would be towards me, even though Mark and I remained friends after what happened a few years back, I knew his other employees hated me. I knew that dealing with his accounting staff was going to suck, his CFO never forgave me for what happened. I knew he would never accept responsibility for his part in it.

It felt like BJ used this as an opportunity to further divide me from the girls. She was bitching about child support as usual, in front of the kids and saying things like "Your kids are worried you're going to let them down for Christmas." I can't say what was going through her mind but it certainly felt like she used this situation to hurt me and to make it seem like I deserved all this for leaving her.

While all this was happening my mother and father were really going through hell with health issues. My father was having troubles with his heart, he'd been to the hospital a few times and I would go to their house to stay with my mom while he was hospitalized. I tried so hard to get through to my mom that everyone wasn't against her. We all just wanted what was best for her and my father. We had some wonderful conversations during these times and while it was rare, it felt like she would let her guard down when it was just the two of us. She just couldn't maintain though and would get back on her soap box and start complaining that no one cared for her.

A few weeks after splitting up Donna wanted to talk about the split. We never had the chance to talk about it after. I had so many things happen at once, it felt like my life was a complete disaster and I had no idea what was next. I went to see her after visiting my mother and father and we had dinner at her house. I really didn't know what she wanted to talk about she made it clear when she broke up with me that she didn't want to continue. We were talking at dinner and she asked me how I felt about what happened. I told her it came as a surprise. I felt her starting to distance herself from me a few weeks before and instead of letting the cards fall where they may I tried to hold on. I guess in doing so I pushed her away and that made her want to end it. That wasn't at all what I wanted. She asked if I believed that for us to move forward, it should've felt like we were growing closer. I thought we were but she said that wasn't how she felt. I didn't know why she felt the need to drag me through it again. I was going to spend the night but I couldn't sleep and felt uncomfortable at her house so I left at like 4 am to come back to PA.

After being home for a few days, I talked to my sponsor Bob about everything and he suggested that I start taking college classes and work towards getting out of sales to start working in the field of addiction recovery. I had thought about starting college a few weeks before closing the business and applied to a school that turned me down, so I gave up on the idea. After talking to him I started thinking about it and for whatever reason thought it might be a good idea. I mean, here I am, 46 years old, a failure of a businessman, broke as a joke, single and alone, what did I have to lose?

By far, this was the hardest time I ever had since getting clean in 1999. Towards the end of 2011, I started looking into different college programs to see what would be best for me. My sponsor suggested Albright College in Reading PA. They had an accelerated degree program where I could earn a bachelor's degree in four years and only have class one night a week. Figuring out the path I was going to take in college was the only thing I did that took my mind off feeling like a failure. I wanted to work in some kind of human services position, as a counselor or something along those lines. Albright offered a bachelor's degree in applied psychology/organizational behavior in their accelerated degree program. I decided to go for it. I completed the online application for student loans and was approved. I completed the admission essay and applications for Albright and was accepted. I was about to be a forty-six-year-old college kid starting in January!

I was working from home for Marks company. I struck a deal with them for a decent commission. Mark was truly a great friend; he was such a special person with a huge heart and an understanding of people that was far beyond what most people could ever dream of having. I believe it was why he was so successful. I was in pitiful financial shape. I was deeply in debt and late on all my bills and was running out of the money I had from selling everything in the tattoo shop and all of my music gear. The company paid its sales staff a salary plus a monthly commission. I was an independent contractor so I didn't receive a salary but my commission structure was a lot higher.

They wanted to pay me once a month but I just couldn't live that way. I had daily access to money for eleven years of being in business and I needed to be paid at least once a week. Of course, Mark's accounting staff was completely against this and refused. I went to Mark with it and he made it happen. That was the first nail in the coffin between the accounting staff and me. The original CFO, Elliott was still there and still had a grudge against me so he did whatever he could to make my life hell. I hated people like him, these little pseudo-tough guys who think they can treat anyone however they feel. I met Elliott in person, he would NEVER talk to me in person the way he did on the phone. He was a little twerp with a control fetish. It took everything I had to keep from putting him in his place. I'm not one to keep my mouth shut but I had to. I needed this company to ship my sales and pay me.

I was still reeling from the loss of the business. I was still hurting over Donna as well. This was the first time I was ever in a relationship that ended while still being connected through social media. It was hard for me to see her communicate with men on Facebook. Usually, when a relationship ends, both parties go their own way. Social media changed that dynamic. 2011 was a disaster. I wanted to put it all behind me and move forward. I wanted to stop thinking about suicide. I wanted to stop hating myself. Guilt and shame were controlling my every decision and I needed to get out of the funk. I didn't know how to. My counselor and my sponsor sure had their hands full with me. Besides my parents, they were the only two people I spoke with.

Chapter 70. Learning to walk again... *The Foo Fighters*

I made it through the holiday. I was able to get the kids some presents and spend part of the holiday with them and part with my parents. My mom and dad were both really surprised to learn I was going to college. They were both really struggling with health issues. My mom was getting harder to deal with every day and she was wearing my father down. He needed to recuperate from his heart problems. I did my best to be a loving son. I tried to be understanding with my mother, but it definitely wasn't easy. My brother and I both tried explaining to her that our dad needed rest and that he couldn't take care of her like he used to.

She was approved for in-home help but she kept refusing it. My brother lived around the corner from them, and he was taking care of their finances and other needs. We weren't really on speaking terms but if he reached out for help with them I would always come up there. I was able to work from their house since I worked from home. I was about to start school, I had no idea what I was in for and I was petrified.

Albright's accelerated degree program was perfect for me. I needed to start from the beginning since I didn't have any college credits. The degree start program was one class per week, and the semesters were seven weeks long. They shortened the regular semester time by seven weeks by giving us a ton of homework. My first class was Psychology of Gender and we were given a homework assignment the first week. We were to review an empirical journal article. I never heard of a journal article before and didn't know what the word empirical meant. I was ready to quit!

I had a friend who was currently at Penn State University for her master's degree and she met with me and explained what I needed to do. She had a way of explaining it that made it easy for me. I did the assignment and received my first grade, an A! I don't think I ever received an A in high school so I was really happy about it. At a time when everything hurt, when I was in no way over losing the business or Donna, this A meant the world to me. It was the only justification I had that showed me I wasn't a complete failure.

I was under direction from my sponsor Bob to start going to 12-step meetings again. I really didn't want to. I was really embarrassed and worried about what everyone who knew what happened thought of me. Between him and my therapist Kendra, I was getting help to rebuild my confidence and my spirit. I never told either of them about the suicidal ideations but I did often talk about how sad I was. They had completely different modes of helping me. Bob was all about picking myself up, dusting myself off, and getting back on the horse. My therapist was more about getting me to start the healing process through meditation and therapy. I didn't want to lose any more relationships so I followed Bob's direction and started attending a few meetings every week. I didn't speak much in the meetings; I didn't talk to anyone either. I just wasn't ready to.

I was talking with Bob on the phone one day and giving him my usual whining session about poor me, how my life was over, how rotten I had it, blah blah blah... After a few minutes, he said "You need to shut the fuck up." I didn't think I heard him correctly and asked him to say it again. Again, he said, "You need to shut the fuck up." Until this time, Bob had a very sympathetic ear and always would listen and then give me some kind of spiritual motivational talk. Not this time though. When I asked him why he was being an ass to me he said, "You whine and complain about how terrible your life is, your so concentrated on what you lost that you don't realize how well off you are!"

This was not the comforting talk I was expecting, not at all. I tried arguing but to no avail. He was tired of the bullshit and not going to listen to any more of it. During the argument, he asked me a really silly question that took me by surprise. He asked, "How many blue cars did you see today?" I said "What?" "What the fuck does blue cars have to do with any of this Bob?" He told me to shut up and answer him. I was getting tired of being told to shut up but I finally answered him and said I didn't know. He said I didn't know because I wasn't looking. I was getting pissed by this time, but he kept going. He said, "If I ask you to tell me how many blue cars you see tomorrow you should be able to answer me right?" I was kind of dumbfounded at this point. I finally said, "Whatever Bob, if you tell me that looking for blue cars tomorrow is going to somehow help me, I will spend the whole day looking for blue cars and tell you how many I saw." His response floored me. He said "I don't want you to look for blue cars tomorrow, I want you to look and find where God is working in your life. You seem to have forgotten where you came from and are walking around moping like it's the end of the world when you actually have it better than most."

I mean, come on, really? Why the fuck do I have to look and find where God is in my life? How the fuck is that going to help? Finally, I gave in. I promised to call him with the answer the next day. Honestly, though, I was pissed. That wasn't what I felt I needed. I needed someone to hold my hand and tell me everything would be okay. This shit hurt my damn feelings. I need a new sponsor. Anytime someone confronted me with the truth, I needed to replace them but I always managed to come to my senses when it came to Bob. The fucker was always right. I hated that. I woke up the next morning and with a pen and paper, I started writing about where God was in my life. To my surprise, I found God in way more places than I imagined. I had a home, a car, a cat, and two kids that may not have liked me so much but if I stay the course and continue to be their father and not a friend, they'll realize the truth at some point. I was in college and doing well.

Maybe I wasn't so bad off after all. I didn't want to call him and tell him this. I wanted to make believe I was sick and couldn't talk. Unfortunately, he called me. I caved and told him what I came to find about God in my life. He said, "Good, now go to a meeting every day and talk about that, not how terrible your life is." He didn't know that even though I was going to meetings, I was keeping my mouth shut. I felt foolish after talking to him so I told him. I was under a new direction to share at every meeting. God damn it, I hated his ass.

I went to a meeting the next day but I was telling myself, I'm not listening to him. I'm keeping my mouth shut. Fuck him. Some young kid was sharing, he'd been coming to meetings for a few months. He didn't have a sponsor or talk to many people and he just used the other day after having about two months clean. He started saying some really stupid shit about relapse being healthy or something along those lines. After he shared, I opened my mouth. Without trying to humiliate him I let him know he was sick and stupid at this point and he needed to get a sponsor and listen to him. After the meeting, I walked up to him and gave him my number, and poked him in the chest. I told him I was going to sponsor him until he found one or decided to stay with me. So after not coming to meetings for years and then coming around for a month or so but not talking at all, here I go and rip some knucklehead a new asshole and tell him I am going to sponsor his sick and stupid ass. I didn't want to sponsor anyone! What the fuck was I doing? What is wrong with me? I called Bob to tell him what happened, and he already knew. The 12-step grapevine (it's something like a gossip page in the recovery community) was fully functional!

I wish I could say that everything changed from that point, but it didn't. I was a mess for some time. I didn't give up though, I kept going to meetings and therapy. A few months after this, I learned that my father's sister, my Aunt Lee was dying. She had severe health problems for years, especially since her husband passed away. Over the years that I didn't speak to my parents, she was always there for me. She always accepted my calls, she never judged, and always listened. She lived in Florida but she was in New Jersey at my cousin's house at the time. I went to see her and spent a good part of the day there. After that, I went to my parents' house to visit them. When I arrived there, to my surprise, they were both giving me shit for visiting my aunt. I tried to explain she was dying, but they were having none of it. How can I go and see her when I rarely see my parents who both are dealing with health problems? I went to see them at least two times a month but still, not good enough. Also, for the first time in years, they were bringing up things I did while in my addiction. I knew this was the work of my mother and she got my dad all riled up about it as well. I knew there was no getting through at that point so I left before saying something I would later regret.

When I saw my therapist later that week, I brought up what happened. We somehow got to talking about my adolescence and I showed her a picture of me in my junior high school yard. She immediately picked up on my poor posture and the look on my face. I had explained to her how hard it was growing up at that time. I talked about the bullies, about my fear of asking girls on dates, my drug use, and about being punished pretty much about ninety percent of the time. I could tell the wheels in her head were spinning. She mentioned that I am still looking for my parents' approval. I tried to play it off with bravado and said I don't need anyone's approval. She wasn't buying what I was selling though, she was smarter than that. She then asked me to look at the picture and then hit me with the bomb question. She asked, "If this kid was in this room with us right now, what do you think he'd need to hear from you? What would you say to him?"

I had been seeing this therapist for about six years at this point. I never cried in front of her. We had a great relationship and she was always very helpful to me. Until now. I didn't need this. I tried to get out of it by saying our time was up (it wasn't) but she asked me again. I was looking at the picture and I was shaking. I felt my eyes fill with tears. I tried to stop them but couldn't. At that moment I became a twelve-year-old kid right in front of her. I was crying uncontrollably. All this anger that I held on to for years came flooding back. I couldn't stop crying. I couldn't speak. I tried but I couldn't get the words out. I wanted to say that I would tell him he was loved and deserved to be loved. I wanted to tell him he was good. I would tell him he wasn't the kid his parents and friends told him he was. I wanted to tell him it wasn't his fault that his brother never stuck up for him. I couldn't say a word though. I just sat in the chair in her office crying uncontrollably. I don't think either of us expected that response. Our time was up and I had to leave. She gave me a really warm hug and gave me her cell phone number and told me to call or text if I needed her. She told me to talk to that kid every day and tell him what he needed to hear. I told myself on the way out that I never wanted to see her or that fucking picture ever again.

Over the next week, all I could do was cry. When I texted Kendra, I asked why this was happening and all she could say was because it had to happen. I've been holding on to it all my life and it was time to let it go. *Let what go? How did she know this? What the fuck did she do to me?* When I talked to Bob about it, he said she touched something in me that opened it up, and that it needed to be opened. *What the fuck was he talking about? Why is everyone saying this fucking shit needs to happen? There was nothing good about it. It fucking hurt, I felt physically sick. Why the fuck can't I stop crying?* I was raw, I never felt so exposed in my life and it exhausted me. After about a week I finally stopped crying. I made a few attempts to talk to the kid in the picture but it felt stupid. I wrote a letter to my teenage self instead. I don't know why but it felt better that way.

My financial troubles were far from over. My car was repossessed in August. I was working hard to stop the self-defeating, self-loathing thinking but things kept happening that continued to keep me from moving forward. Luckily, I had a friend who let me use his car and sold it to me fairly cheaply. I was able to pay for it with a refund from my student loans. Things were slowly improving, and those student loan refunds came in handy, even though I knew all too well at some point they were going to bite me in the ass, but for the time being, they were necessary for my survival.

In September I learned of a job opening at a halfway house for men who recently completed rehab. I interviewed for it and was hired. It was a nighttime house manager position and all I did between midnight and 8 am was check every room once an hour, check the refrigerator and freezer temperatures, and in the morning hand out meds. I loved the hours, I didn't start selling on the phone at home until around 1:00 pm, so I would have time to sleep in the day. Classes at school were between 6 and 8:00 pm. I was free to do my homework while I was working at the halfway house as long as I made the rounds at the appropriate times. As soon as I started and had the opportunity to talk with some of the clients when they couldn't sleep, I knew that I could work in this field. The pay sucked, it was $9.43 per hour, but I was earning something during hours that I would normally be sleeping so I was happy with it.

I made it through 2012 with a 3.8 GPA and a new job that could lead to a new career. It most likely was the longest year of my life. At the beginning of the year, I didn't believe I would get through it alive. I was seriously suicidal, so making it through was a miracle.

Chapter 71. Carry on my wayward son...- *Kansas*

Early in the new year, my friend Dona called to tell me the organization she worked with was hiring for a new position. It was a "recovery specialist" position. A recovery specialist worked with people who were new to recovery and were either just released from jail or completed a residential rehab. The specialist would help the newcomer to recovery achieve their early recovery goals, help the person get on their feet, and find a pathway to recovery that works for them.

The organization, the RASE project, was started by a woman I knew from the local twelve-step community, her name was Denise. I took a shot and interviewed for the position. When I walked in I was surprised because Paul, my first sponsor was in the room with Denise. I had no idea he would be there, so just imagine what a shock it was to see him! He was running that program for the RASE project. I thought the interview went well although I felt some of the questions Denise asked me were maybe a bit personal and inappropriate. She asked some questions touching on my love life, she was inquiring if I ever dated women that were new to recovery. I answered truthfully even though I thought it was none of her business. When I learned that they hired someone else I wasn't bothered about it. Denise asking all those personal questions and having Paul as a supervisor somewhat turned me off about working there.

A few weeks later Dona called to tell me there was another position open at the agency in a different program. It was for a care of services coordinator in their medically assisted treatment program. It was working with clients who were trying to get off opiates and heroin with the help of medication and treatment. When I asked about what Denise would say, Dona assured me Denise wouldn't get in my way. I also asked about Paul, Dona was aware of the bad blood between him and me. She told me he wasn't involved in that part of the program. She said the job paid 30K per year and it was mine if I wanted it. I wasn't making great money in jewelry sales but I would be able to continue doing it while having this job. I would just call customers after I came home from working at the RASE project and, I would still work a few nights a week at the halfway house. I accepted the position. Dona told me she believed I would do really well at it, and that they needed people with my recovery experience to help these people. I was looking forward to starting.

I started in January 2013, which also saw the start of my second year at Albright College. The job was relatively easy, but I was kind of thrown into the jungle without proper training. I took it upon myself to develop a training guide for the MAT program. I listed what should be done from start to finish when processing a new client. I described the proper way to begin a client chart and how to report meetings with the client. It took about two months to complete as I was learning the process myself as well. I learned pretty quickly that my experience as a person in recovery helped guide the clients through their process.

I enjoyed working with the clients. It was hard at first because my pathway is the twelve-step path, which is a program of complete abstinence. I've always known about methadone and suboxone programs but I was taught that they were the wrong path. Once I started working in the program though, it made more sense to me. I never questioned the twelve-step path, but it does leave a void for those who can't maintain a program of complete abstinence. It was fairly easy for me to tell the difference between the clients who truly wanted help and the people who were just looking to not experience withdrawal. It didn't matter though; we were to help all clients regardless of their desired outcome from the program. Unfortunately, within a few months after I started Dona accepted a position where her knowledge and skills would be put to better use. I was sad to see her go, she was the most helpful to me out of everyone in the agency.

At the same time, things between the kids and me were a little crazy. Lindsey never wanted to spend time with me and I took it personally. We were constantly fighting and I hated that. I wanted to be a different parent than mine were to me and I had no clue how to make things better. Lauren was going through problems of her own. She was having trouble in school and they requested we take her for a psychiatric evaluation. I found out that Lauren was missing a lot of school. She would stay up all night on her phone and then not be able to wake up for school. I told her mother a million times to take the phone and internet away and to be a parent and exert some rules and boundaries but she would never do anything I asked of her. It seemed like she would do the opposite purposely. We took Lauren to a psychiatrist, she was diagnosed with ADHD and "Oppositional Defiance Disorder", which could lead to much worse problems if not addressed. The psychiatrist agreed that Lauren should not miss school, so BJ's answer was to look for another psychiatrist. When we met with the administrative staff at Laurens school, they would say the same thing, but to no avail.

Things like this happened often between BJ and me when it came to parenting our kids. I wasn't perfect but I did know how some things should've been handled. I felt that the only reason BJ ignored my input was because she didn't want me to be relevant to my kids. At the time this was devastating. I remember how I would get really sad when Lauren would stay with me. She would get so defiant and it was because her mother told her that she didn't have to listen to me. She told Lauren that I was abusive and trying to control her. This started a pattern of Lauren always trying to get out of staying with me on my weekends. The impact this had on my self-esteem was debilitating.

BJ would tell Lauren that I didn't care about what she was going through and that I only wanted her to do what I told her to. Through this type of triangulation, I was becoming less and less relevant in both of my kids' lives. This killed me inside. I knew all along that BJ was not above using the kids as weapons to get them to take her side. She eventually told them about the massage parlors. I was so embarrassed when Lindsey told me. Lindsey and I went through times when we were very close and times when we were at each other's throats. She learned early on how to use the bad blood between her mother and me to her advantage. We stopped speaking for a few months after I threatened to beat her boyfriend up. Throughout all this, I was still entertaining thoughts of suicide. I felt so alone, even though I had Bob, my parents, and my therapist. I have no idea how but I managed to maintain really good grades at school and to move forward in my new career.

When July rolled around, I was hired for a job I had applied for 6 months earlier. Alternative Rehab Communities (ARC) was an organization that owned several residential placement houses for adjudicated teenagers. My sponsor Bob was a cofounder of the agency. He worked there for 31 years before retiring in 2006. I was going to be an assistant counselor in their facility that was slated for kids with substance use problems. I gave notice to the halfway house and prepared to work even more hours while dealing with serious problems with my kids and my ex and while continuing to work towards my bachelor's degree. While it felt like my world was still falling apart, I failed to see that it was actually falling into place. I was so used to things being fucked up; I lost the capability to see anything positive.

One thing that happened did turn out to be really positive. My friend Brian was released from prison. He showed up without warning at my house. I was very happy to see him, it was a few years since I last saw him. He seemed a bit different this time. I could tell that he was clean. He looked quite healthy. He told me he had been clean for about three years and was ready to start the recovery process. He asked me to be his sponsor. Before I agreed, I pulled out all the letters he wrote from prison and showed him how many times he would say he was ready to change before this and I asked if he was serious this time. He showed me a book that he had written over the last three years in prison which made me really proud of him. He promised he wanted to recover and asked me to sponsor him again. I agreed.

Having someone trust me enough to speak to me about his problems helped me feel like I had some worth. Brian would become an important part of my recovery after this. We developed a really tight friendship and were always there for each other. I don't believe he'll ever know how my becoming his sponsor helped me so much. I was still stuck in the belief that I was a failure and sponsoring him helped me start believing more in myself. I still believed I was a failure but sponsoring him helped me gain self-confidence.

Chapter 72. Lay your weary head to rest, don't you cry no more... *Kansas*

In May 2014, I moved out of the house I lived in for nine years. I couldn't afford it, even while working three jobs. My landlords were the sweetest people ever; they were always helpful and understanding. They went above and beyond when it came to helping me but I needed to move out. I hated it, but I hated dealing with the financial hardship and being late on rent and bills more. I moved to a very small two-bedroom apartment in Wormleysburg, it had a beautiful view of the capital and the Susquehanna River.

The apartment I was moving to sucked. It didn't have a bathtub, just a stand-up shower. There was only one electric outlet on the kitchen counter. I had to take the middle leaf off my dining room table for it to fit in the kitchen. I tried to have a positive outlook but I couldn't get past leaving my house for this little place. I saw having to move out of a house that I could no longer afford as another failure but in reality, it showed personal growth on my part. I just couldn't see it that way at the time.

I was working full time at the RASE project and I was also working around thirty-two hours a week at ARC. I would return my body jewelry customers' calls and fax jewelry orders to Sales One a few times a day. I couldn't understand how I was still broke all the time. My attitude was pretty crappy at this time; I needed to get a better outlook. I loved both jobs and I truly enjoyed the work but they both sucked when it came to earning a living wage. I constantly struggled with the fact that I was earning so much less than I used to earn. It was hard living on such a limited income. I still had a hard time accepting the fact that I was no longer living the lifestyle I'd grown accustomed to for years after getting clean.

Lindsey and I finally found some common ground and started rebuilding our relationship. She was working full-time and asked to move in with me because her mother had been evicted from three houses in the past two years. I was giving BJ about $400 per month in child support and she had a pretty decent-paying job as a contract counselor for a local outpatient substance use treatment organization. School started back up for Lauren and she was already missing a ton of school. It didn't matter who told BJ she needed to get Lauren to school, she kept looking for excuses rather than getting Lauren the help she needed. I was beginning to think I needed to get custody of Lauren. I started to think that BJ may have been using drugs but I couldn't prove it and both kids said they didn't know, but they believed she wasn't.

It's hard to describe what was going on with me in the early days of my new career. I loved working with people with substance use disorders and really liked working with kids at the residential placement facility but my emotional health was not good at that time. I never truly got over losing the business and Donna. I was constantly stressed out about what was happening with my daughter Lauren. My parents' health was another stressor. There were plenty of positive things taking place but I was unable to experience pleasure and I was finally starting to notice that.

I talked extensively with my therapist about this and she was trying her best to help me through it. While I didn't realize it at the time, I wasn't the easiest client to deal with. There were answers to my problems often staring me in the face. My therapist was trying to steer me toward them but I was blinded by self-pity. My sponsor was probably experiencing the same frustration as Kendra but he was just very consistent with the same message. He'd say the same thing every time. "Mike, you're on the right path. You're in school, you're working a lot and getting a lot of experience in a new field which you will do really well in. Just keep walking forward." My thick stubborn Sicilian head wouldn't allow them to be right though. In my mind, I was a loser, a failure, and a terrible parent. Poor me.

It wasn't until I was working at ARC with teenage juvenile delinquents that I noticed I could make a difference in someone's life. Most of the kids there had no interest in recovery, they just wanted to do their time and go home. Every once in a while, though, I'd notice a kid paying attention to what I would say in group sessions. I could see he had an interest in what I was saying. It was hard for the kids to speak about recovery or changing behaviors in a group setting. It was too important for their stature within the house for them to talk seriously about changing behaviors.

I was allowed to drive some kids home for their weekend passes after a few months of working there. I picked a kid up after his home pass and drove him back to the facility one night. He lived pretty far away so we had a lot of time to talk. I could tell he felt more comfortable talking when there wasn't a bunch of kids from the facility around. He spoke about his drug use and how much trouble he would get in because of it. He asked questions about stopping using, twelve-step groups and other recovery-oriented topics. I shared my experience with him. He was really interested in what we were discussing, which was obvious by the way he listened and the questions he asked. When I got back to the facility I was about to get off and he was heading upstairs to the bedrooms, he turned and said, "Thank you, Mr. Mike, you're the best thing to happen to me since I came here." While I was driving home I realized I was smiling. I remember thinking that it was a long time since I had a smile like that.

My sponsor Bob co-founded the agency and worked there for thirty-one years before retiring. I don't think anyone worked with and understood those kids better than him. I told him about driving that kid home and the talk we had, and then what he said before he went upstairs. Bob said he believed I have something special in me that very few of the counselors have, which is the ability to have those kids identify with me. He said they could tell I was the real thing and not someone just collecting a check once a week. I remember thinking he was blowing smoke up my ass, but I also felt really good about what he said. I can't explain how much I needed to have what happened that day to happen. After almost a year in the field, that was the very first truly rewarding experience and it felt so good to experience it.

Brian and I had grown very close during this time. He was like a little brother to me, and the fact that I had to be an example for him helped keep my spirits up. He didn't know but he was helping me more than I could ever have helped him. There's a statement in Narcotics Anonymous literature that says, "The therapeutic value of one addict helping another is without parallel". Rarely has there ever been a truer statement.

Throughout 2014 I continued working two jobs and still doing sales once in a while. The school year went pretty easily. I was maintaining a pretty high GPA. Most of the year went by as if I were on autopilot. I had to go to NY a few times to help my parents, my father had to go to the hospital a few times for heart problems and I would spend time with my mom because she couldn't be alone.

If you've ever heard the expression "when it rains, it pours", that was happening in my life in real-time. I received a call from my brother telling me our dad had a heart attack and was in the hospital. He asked if I could come and spend time with my mother till my dad got home. I drove to NY and spent about three days there with my mom. When my dad came home doctors were saying he needed to rest, his heart was operating at around thirty-five percent of where it should be.

My mom started acting crazy and saying out loud, "God help me, he's going to die before me." She was crying and making it all about her. My brother came by before I left and told her that she had to have a live-in assistant because our dad needed to rest. My mom fought this but my brother was adamant. He threatened to place her in a nursing home. I felt so bad for both her and my dad. My mom was in panic mode and I couldn't help her. Both my parents were struggling with health issues, my dad had heart problems on and off for years, my mom had emphysema for years and after she broke her hip, she seemed to have given up. She rarely left her bed and never left the house. I'd never felt so powerless in my life. I drove home in tears.

I may have been home for two days when I received a call from my brother as I was getting out of my car before work. He told me our mother was unresponsive this morning and my father called for an ambulance and they came and revived her. I asked him a ton of questions that he couldn't answer. He only said I should prepare myself for the worst. Later that day, I received a call from my mother's house and when I picked up, all I heard was my mother crying and saying something like "keep your promise" over and over. It sounded like my father was struggling trying to get away from her and I heard him repeatedly say the word "stop". I was trying to speak to them but neither of them would answer me. I hung up and called my brother to tell him what happened. I asked him to go there and see what was going on but he just seemed nonchalant. He said he'd go there in a while or something. I knew something was wrong and kept trying to call them but they didn't answer.

I called my brother and asked him to call the police to do a wellness check. I couldn't believe how he was so offhand, he just kept saying that it was probably nothing or something to that effect. The next morning my brother called at almost the same time as the day before and broke the news, that our mother was unresponsive again but this time they couldn't revive her. She was dead. I don't remember saying goodbye, I don't remember hanging up, all I remember was everything around me started spinning. I closed my eyes and tried taking a few deep breaths but everything was still spinning. I needed to get to my father so I drove to NY through a terrible storm. I needed to breathe. I continued to tell myself that I couldn't make this about me, it had to be about my father. They were married for fifty-three years. When I got to their house, I saw my father's face, I realized how much I loved him and just held him in my arms and cried with him.

My mother remained true to her nature until the end. She didn't want a funeral or a service of any kind and as usual, we didn't respect that wish. In retrospect, maybe she felt alone so often because we never listened to her. We had a very small service at the funeral home where she was to be cremated. I didn't know how to feel about her passing. On one hand, my mother was miserable her last few years because she was a very independent woman her whole life and in the end, she was dependent on everyone. In her mind, nobody met her needs. I understand that. I regret never telling her that I understand. I didn't have to agree with her to understand.

The song Blackbird by the Beatles always reminded me of my mother. To me, she had broken wings. She never realized her potential. She was always emotionally flawed, she would lose her temper fairly easily, usually when she didn't get her way. She was a lot like BJ in that regard but she didn't cause the chaos like BJ would. She had a need to control everything which would cause major problems between her and me in my adolescence, and also between her and my dad throughout their marriage.

She grew up with no control over her life or where she lived. Her mother died when she was six and her father left her right after that, rarely to ever be seen again. She grew up moving between her aunt's and her grandmother's houses. She talked about never feeling like she was good enough for either of them. She excelled in school and skipped two grades yet never received any recognition from either. I guess that's the reason she needed to be in control as an adult.

I adored her when I was a toddler but once she went back to work when I was five years old everything changed. She would get so frustrated and scream at me when I struggled with homework assignments and then later on in my teens when she tried unsuccessfully to get me to be home on time or to stay out of trouble in school. Unfortunately, we never really came to terms with my adolescence. I blamed her for a lot of my problems during that time but she never took accountability. I will always be grateful that we repaired our relationship and that she was around to see me clean and as a parent. I've never been able to come to terms with how she passed away though. She always felt that she was alone and unloved. I tried desperately to show her that we all loved her, but she wouldn't acknowledge it.

What bothered me the most was that my mom died believing she was alone. In my heart, I believe she took her life by stopping her medication after my father returned from the hospital. My brother threatened to place her in a nursing home that day. I think about what happened the day before she passed when I received the phone call from her house and I think maybe they were arguing about her doing that. I'll never know for sure but I believe it with all my heart.

I had to turn my attention to my dad. He was in poor health and now he had to face living alone. I was afraid of him living alone, but my brother and I were both hopeful that would do better without my mom driving him crazy, which she did until the day she died. The day after my mom passed I took my father to one of his favorite places in Queens, Lenny's Clam Bar in Howard Beach. He had his favorite dish, muscles in the sweet sauce, and a dozen raw clams.

Back at his house I prepared his medicine for the next month and promised to come back and do that each month. I went home after about four days and the drive home was horrible. There were a few times on the way home that I had to pull over because I'd lost my shit. I'd just start crying without warning and I was screaming in my car yelling at God. I didn't understand what his will for me was. I didn't understand why I had to go through all this shit by myself. I was mad that my mother and I never really cleared up a lot of our issues. It sucks knowing that the answer to unanswered questions will never be revealed.

How the hell does someone go back to working two jobs and being a college student after this? At this point it felt like I'd never be free from the grief that losing my mother brought. I was constantly worried about my father living alone. I'd call him every day to check on him. He was always sad. I felt terrible for him, I knew he loved my mother. I knew he was hurting, I just didn't know how to make him feel better. The Christmas holiday was coming in a few weeks and I didn't want to celebrate. I didn't want to do anything but sleep.

I took Lindsey and Lauren with me to NY the day after Christmas so we could hang out with my dad. We took him out to eat and spent most of the day with him. He was always really good to my kids and even though he was hurting inside, he was happy to see them. It was a really nice day. My mother's birthday was on December 30th and I was just really sad. When the kids and I drove home from NY, we stopped in Middle Village and picked up a few Sicilian pizzas from Rosa's pizza which was around the corner from the house I grew up in. My kids absolutely loved Rosa's and it was a ritual to bring some home anytime we visited NY. My kids came over on New Year's Day and we had the pizza together.

Shortly after going back to work I was fired from the RASE project for a pretty stupid reason. I didn't fight it, I welcomed it. I was able to collect unemployment benefits which I never did before and to continue working at ARC while having time to work on schoolwork. I'm thankful for the opportunity the RASE project provided me. It was pretty easy to get over getting fired though, I liked the extra time at home.

Six months after losing my job at the RASE project, I received a call from someone from Gaudenzia asking me to interview for a counselor position at a rehab in Harrisburg called Siena House. It was a rehab that housed and treated men in the criminal justice system that are on parole and gave their parole officer a urine that was positive for drugs. Gaudenzia owned the rehab that I went to 15 years before and I was always grateful for them. I couldn't wait to interview.

Shortly after leaving the RASE project, I moved from that crappy apartment in Wormleysburg. my lease was up and I hated it there. My new apartment wasn't much better but it had a lot more room. The six-month break from working after getting fired by the RASE project was so necessary. I never before felt as strong a connection to God as I did during this time. I lost close to thirty-eight pounds after changing my lifestyle and eating very healthily while going to the gym every day. I felt my spirit coming back to life over these six months.

I knew losing the business took a toll on me, but I didn't realize how much until I started feeling better about it and just basically feeling physically better as well. I was going to NA meetings with my friend Brian fairly regularly. I think having some desperately needed time at home and going to meetings had a profound impact on my mental and emotional health. My life was about to undertake a pretty huge change with a new job and I believe the break from working helped me start a healing process that I didn't even realize I needed.

I interviewed for the position at Siena House and was offered a position as a counselor assistant. I would become a counselor 1 (1st level counselor position) after graduating with my bachelor's degree, which was about a year away. A counselor assistant does exactly what a counselor does but they're not supposed to have more than six clients on their caseload. I almost didn't accept the position because the pay sucked but I felt that since Gaudenzia saved my life all those years ago, I owed them so I accepted it. I had no idea that doing this would change my life forever. I had no idea what I was in for either.

I found out on my first day that the dude who was my counselor at Common Ground, Jim, ran the halfway house upstairs from the rehab. It was so awesome to see him. I looked a lot different so he didn't recognize me at first. When I introduced myself to him I asked if he remembered me and what he said was awesome. He said, "Mike, I very rarely remember clients, especially from so long ago, but you, you're one of those clients that are impossible to forget." My first day at Siena house was crazy, I didn't do anything but watch a few group sessions and sit in on an individual session that a counselor had with a client. I had to read all these policy and procedure books for the first ten days but I was allowed to take breaks from them and sit in on groups if I wanted. The first group I watched was a circus. The clients were not happy, they all complained about the staff and their fucked-up parole officers. I guess I have to explain how the place worked so you can have a better understanding of what it was like to work there during my first few weeks.

Siena House was a rehab strictly for men on parole from state prison. Their parole officer would send them to treatment if they tested positive for drugs. No clients ever came to Siena house willingly; they were all mandated by parole. Almost every time a client was brought in, he came in kicking and screaming. Their parole officers would tell them it's a thirty-day program but in reality, their treatment could last up to ninety days depending on the client's progress. They would totally freak out after hearing that. They all had the same story too, "I only used *once*, or my parole officer has it in for me" and "I don't need treatment!" Almost every client would be resistant to the program over their first week. Siena House was a "therapeutic community" (TC) rehab. They're not super easy programs to go through. Common Ground was a TC, and I had a hard time when I went through it and I went willingly!

Once I completed the ten days of reading, I was assigned two clients and had to also run 1 group every day. I had no idea what I was doing and asked all the other counselors what I should do which would always bring a laugh and then they'd say, "You need to figure that out yourself." It didn't take long for me to start questioning if this was for me. In the beginning, I would run the group sessions according to the curriculum word for word.

The clients would always try and veer off the subject and complain about the facility and the staff. I had no idea how to handle that and I would invite an argument that would end up with all the clients pissed off at me or the other way around. I remember thinking back to when I was in treatment to try and think how the staff handled the clients and sometimes I'd get a better understanding of how to deal with things a little better after remembering.

As the weeks went by, I became much better at handling tough situations. Bob was really helpful with this. He would always tell me to lean on my personal experiences. I would often self-disclose little pieces of my own story which would garner credibility among the clients. It was easier for them to talk to a person in recovery than a counselor with just an education. I started getting my own groove there while learning the ropes of being a counselor in a therapeutic community. I had my own schtick after a while and I started getting along well with the clients.

I was gaining valuable experience working for ARC and Siena House. Both places had the potential to be really volatile at times and working through times like that is the best to learn and gain experience. I was supposed to get promoted to full-time at ARC after I left the RASE project but I took the job at Siena House and stayed on part-time at ARC. I loved working there. The kids were sometimes a bit much to deal with but once they realized that I was not going to allow certain behaviors they would usually fall in line.

I need to go back in time to tell this story, but it's an important part of my journey. Before I took the job at Siena House, I was working around 32 hours a week for ARC, that was the most hours a part-time employee could work in a week. I developed some really good relationships with some of the kids and staff there. This one kid Darren and I developed a pretty strong bond between us. He was younger than most of the kids there, he was only 15. He was really tall and a great basketball player and he was definitely a leader. He had the respect of all the kids in the house. I would drive him home on his weekend passes. A few times he came back and tested positive for marijuana, and he would get consequences. He often lost the privilege of going home and he would have to write some essays and work more hours. I talked with him a lot about addiction and recovery. He didn't think he was an addict but he would continue to use despite negative consequences, which is actually the definition of addiction. I worked there through his whole time in placement and when he finally got the approval to go home, I was there for his last night.

I was about to clock out, and I pulled him aside to say goodbye to him. He didn't want to look bad in front of the other kids in the house so he kind of blew me off. I was a little hurt but I understood why he would do that. Anyway, I was in the next room getting my jacket and about to clock out and I heard someone ask to "cross-over", which meant a kid wanted to leave the room. To do that he'd need to ask for permission and have staff walk him over. No kids were ever allowed to be by themselves anywhere in the facility except the bathroom. The counselor that was working with me that night opened the door and asked me to wait a minute and then Darren came in and without saying a word he grabbed me with the biggest hug I ever had. He said he was sorry and said goodbye to me. I had to hide my face because I was in tears. From that point, I never questioned if I made the right career choice. I knew this was my calling.

I often gave the same answer every time a client at Siena House would ask me how I was doing. I would say, "I'm always wonderful, I slept on subway trains and woke up in a bed today." I started doing that when I was at the RASE project. Back when I started in this field, I was not a happy person. I was stuck in bitter resentment over losing my business. When I started working at ARC, there was a counselor that I gained a lot of respect for. His name was Demone. We could not have been more different. He was African American and from the inner city. He was a basketball player and probably fifteen years younger than me. We really didn't have anything in common. He was an excellent counselor though. He was respected by the kids in the house and the staff as well. He taught me a lot over the time that I worked there. There was one thing about him that drove me crazy though. Whenever I asked him how he was he would get this goofy smile on his face and say "Awe you know, I'm always good". After a while, it started to piss me off. How can someone be "always good"? It's just not possible to be "always good." We all have bad days. I worked with the same kids he did and they would get on my nerves regularly. How the hell was he always good? I wanted to be "always good" but that really seemed impossible.

One day I told myself I was getting to the bottom of this. I need to confront him about this because he was full of shit and I was going to show him. I asked him "dude, how the hell are you always good, it's just not possible to be 'always good'"? He got that goofy smile on his face again and his answer pissed me the hell off. He said, "I'm always good because my mood is always my choice." I thought *really Demone? REALLY?* I told him you can't choose your mood, especially if someone gets you mad. People always ruin my mood, how the fuck are you immune to that shit? He answered that "no one can ruin your mood unless you allow them to."

I went home and thought about what he said. I thought about it all the time. It bothered me that I couldn't get it. I remember bringing it up to my therapist and she told me he was right. I was so mad, I thought *fuck her, I am going to fire her stupid ass*! But I kept thinking about it. I guess at some point I got it though but I can't remember exactly when. I remember working at the RASE project and a coworker asked how I was and I said "I'm always wonderful". I remember asking myself "Where the hell did that come from?" She said you can't always be wonderful Mike, that's impossible. I answered her exactly how Demone answered me, I got a goofy smile and told her my mood was my choice. She walked away thinking I was nuts or something and she may have told me to fuck off or something to that effect.

After a few weeks of always telling the clients at Siena house I was always wonderful they cornered me and confronted me. "Mr. Mike, you can't expect us to believe that you're always wonderful. It's just not possible". Again, I felt myself make this stupid ass goofy smile and explained how my mood is my choice. They weren't buying it. They tried their best to break me but I wouldn't allow it.

About six months after I started working at Siena House, I saw one of the clients who was there when I began my job walking out of the facility. He moved upstairs to the halfway house after completing treatment. I was happy to see him and I stopped and asked him how he was and wouldn't you know it, he got that god damned goofy ass smile on his face that I knew all too well and told me he was "always wonderful" and said, "thanks, Mr. Mike!" I had to stop and give him a hug. Then I had to let what just happened to sink in. I realized that this shit really does work! As I started walking away, I noticed I was crying. When that young man said he was "always wonderful" it brought me to a level of happiness I don't think I've ever felt before except maybe when that kid Darren hugged me at ARC. I realized that how we present ourselves can have a positive effect on others if we just decide to choose our mood. I took it as a powerful lesson that I could learn from anyone, even a black dude from the inner city who was probably fifteen years younger than me. I'm forever grateful that I met and had the opportunity to work with Demone. He'll probably never know how his goofy smile had such a positive effect on my daily outlook on life and my career.

Chapter 75. Oh, dear dad, can you see me now, I am myself, like you, somehow...*Pearl Jam, Release*

I visited my father every week over the summer and fall of 2015. We placed him in rehab shortly after my mother passed away. He wasn't eating well and he wasn't taking his meds properly so he was hospitalized again. We were looking into getting him into an assisted living facility, but shortly after he was approved to leave the rehab he fell and broke his hip. Every time I visited him he seemed to be really sad. He couldn't hide it.

I was with him one night and I became overwhelmed with grief. I had already made amends to him and my mother in my 9th step but for whatever reason the guilt hit me like a ton of bricks that night. I started crying and telling him how sorry I was for my behavior when I was a teenager and for all the hell I put him and my mother through. He kind of laughed and told me to go home and said all that was so far in the past and I should let it go. I couldn't though, I don't know why it hit me as it did but I was really feeling it. I called Bob when I was about halfway home and told him what happened. I was hoping he would have something to say that would make me feel better but his response floored me. It was a knockout punch. He said in a raised voice that I just unloaded my guilt on a dying man so I could feel less guilty. He told me to turn around and go back and instead of apologizing and seeking forgiveness, I should ask him what it was like for him while I was living that way.

I was never so pissed off at Bob as I was when he said that. I mean, that shit stung. I felt like a damn idiot. I was trying to think about who I was going to ask to sponsor me after I fired Bob as I turned around and drove back to Long Island. I made it back to my dad in about an hour and I walked back into his room. He was sleeping but he woke up when I walked in. He was mad and he asked, "What the fuck do you want, why did you come back?" I held his hand and asked him what it was like for him all those years I was fucked up. He squeezed my hand and said it was hard, he could never figure out why I hated myself and him and my mom so much. He also said he would get scared when he heard an ambulance because he thought I might be in it dying from an overdose. He then told me that he hadn't felt any anger towards me for years because I turned my life around and he was proud of the man I had become. He was proud when he saw me with my kids and he thought I was a much better parent than him. Then he said, "Now get the fuck out of here, I want to go back to sleep. I was dreaming about Gina Lollabrigida and you fucked it up!" I didn't want to let go of his hand and I fought the tears from coming. I don't think we ever connected like we did in that moment. As I was driving back home again I realized I wasn't mad at Bob anymore.

I visited him a few more times after that and each time I saw him he seemed sadder. He lost a lot of weight, he pretty much stopped eating. He told me he saw my mother's grandmother in a dream and I thought at the time that it probably wasn't a dream. He was always pleasant when I visited but I could tell he didn't want to be here anymore. I was getting ready to drive to NY after work one night and my phone rang, it was a Long Island area code so I answered and it was the physician from the rehab. He told me my father passed away in his sleep. I suddenly felt something like wind go right through me. I can't explain it any other way, but I'm sure it was my father's spirit that came to visit me one last time.

The doctor told me he tried to reach my brother but couldn't so he called me. I thanked him and hung up. I had to pull over and I started to cry. I was going to miss my dad more than anything. I was relieved too. I knew he didn't want to be here anymore and I was happy he made it out without suffering. I was actually going up there to tell him that he could let go of whatever he was holding on to and that I'd understand if he did. I called my brother and told him, then I drove home and cried myself to sleep.

I went to NY the next morning and spent the next night at my brother's house. We arranged for a viewing at the funeral home around the corner from my parent's house. The viewing was nice, my cousin came up from Florida with her sister from New Jersey. Some of my friends from Middle Village showed up too. Donna stayed with me the whole time. We had maintained a really nice friendship over the last few years. She was with me when we dropped his ashes at the same spot in the ocean where we dropped my mom's ashes about a year before. They died within eleven months of each other. I had no idea how to live the rest of my life without them.

Chapter 76. Lean on me, when you're not strong and I'll be your friend- *Bill Withers*

I was an emotional mess when I got home from NY. By the grace of God, I never once felt like getting high after my mom or my dad passed away. It never crossed my mind. I was sad, but I needed to get back to my job. The first anniversary of my mother's passing was coming up, she died two days before Thanksgiving. I didn't want to celebrate any holidays and when I spoke to Bob about it, he once again ruined my plan by telling me that the holidays weren't about me; they were about my kids. I was really getting sick and tired of him being right all the damn time, but he was right. I asked the kids what they wanted to do for Thanksgiving and they wanted me to cook lasagna with of my homemade sauce and meatballs. It was always their favorite and we had a wonderful day together.

I didn't even bother telling Bob that I didn't want to celebrate Christmas or New Year's, I knew what the fuck he was going to say. My brother called me two days before Christmas and told me after paying him back from the line of credit I defaulted on, I was going to get about twenty thousand dollars from my parents' insurance. I made him repeat what he said like four times because I didn't believe what I heard. I had no idea my parents had life insurance and

I never expected to receive anything. It was a total surprise. I was so happy that my brother finally got his money back, it had been about four years since I closed the business and defaulted on the loan. We rarely spoke after our last fight and I may have held a grudge, but I always felt guilty about that loan.

The money from my parents made it possible for me to get music equipment again. All I had for the past four years was an acoustic guitar. I put away a chunk of the money for my kids and bought myself the equipment to have a little home recording studio. My girls and I had the most wonderful Christmas together. I did something different that year, I took them out shopping and handed them each $300 and told them to spend it any way they wanted to. I surprised Lindsey with her share, she turned 21 in February and I knew it would blow her away! Lauren was to get hers after graduating high school and turning eighteen, but I gave her a $500 advance on it which was the most money she ever had at one time in her life. I asked them to thank their grandparents in a prayer.

I went back to work at both jobs after the holidays and my classes at Albright started back up. I had almost 2 years to graduate, but there was a way I could knock about six months off that by passing two CLEP tests. After three years of school, all I could think about was getting it over and done with. I had to do my TC training for Gaudenzia, every staff member has to take that training. It was two weeks of training in which everyone taking it had to spend two weeks being a client in a TC and learning what it's like to go through treatment. The fact that I was a Guadenzia graduate and completed treatment back in 1999 meant nothing, I had to do the training.

There were about thirteen of us when it started and we all made our way through it as a team. One of the trainers was the director at Siena House, and through some of the treatment exercises we did, she was able to tell that I was holding on to a lot of pain. How the hell did she know that? In one of our talks, she said the reason I am such a good counselor is how I draw from my pain to have the strength to withstand our clients and that my strength comes directly from that pain. Her name is Kristina, and she will most likely never know how much what she said meant to me. Unfortunately, she also told me that she was leaving Siena house and there would be a new director when I returned.

When I returned to the facility with my newfound knowledge, I was ready to whip the joint into shape. We had a new program director, Natasha, and she debriefed me on the TC training and talked to me about my position. She told me that Gaudenzia believed I had strong leadership qualities and she asked me to work with the two new counselors that were recently hired. She wanted them to turn in their paperwork to me, and I should either approve and sign off or give it back to them to fix. It felt good to have my work recognized and to be given this opportunity while I was still a counselor assistant. She introduced me to our new clinical supervisor Kasha, and told me to have her help me with any questions I may have about overseeing these two new counselors.

The biggest problems in the rehab were drugs in the facility, smoking in the bathroom, and the use of cell phones.

Clients were not allowed to have cell phones while in treatment and smoking cigarettes was not allowed in the facility. We allowed between four and six smoke breaks between 8am and 6pm and they were allowed a few after those hours. Our clients were obviously not rule followers, I mean, they were all convicted felons with substance use disorders, so not following rules is expected. Some of them were really savvy criminals and found ways to bring drugs and cell phones into the facility. We had to regularly monitor the bathroom and the clients when they were in their rooms. We spent almost as much time tracking down contraband as we did providing treatment. It was a constant cat-and-mouse game but it was necessary. We didn't want anyone to die from using drugs in the facility and cell phones were used to set up drug drop-offs.

I took on the responsibility of security for the facility which was supposed to be the job of the house managers but with the number of clients turning in hot (positive for substances) urine screens and cell phones I would find, it was obvious they needed help. It was easy to catch cell phone use, especially for me because I knew how their minds worked. I'm cut from the same cloth! Usually, when the clients went out for a smoke break if one or two clients stayed behind and didn't go it was almost always to hide in their room or the bathroom to sneak a call. Getting caught with a cell phone would usually get the client kicked out of the rehab because of the danger that posed to the community. Using a cell phone could put the whole community at risk depending on the drugs they had smuggled in. So, on and on went the cat and mouse game. It drove all the staff crazy but it also had a benefit, we were growing together as a team. I really loved working there, however crazy it got, it felt good to not go through it alone and to have a team we all could rely on.

I continued to work at ARC part-time, usually between twenty-eight and thirty-two hours a week. I loved it there but things were starting to change little by little. The director that hired me had retired and the new director was a really cool guy, but his approach was much different. Before he came we ran a very tight house. With him, it was starting to run a bit more laid back, which gave the kids a belief that they could get away with some behaviors that were forbidden. The counseling staff had more to deal with as a result and the kids we receiving more consequences.

Some counselors were quite strict and they kept to the structure and curriculum and rules, and then there was the more relaxed staff. These counselors made life harder for us, the kids would get confused because some staff would allow behaviors that other staff wouldn't. It seemed like we were working against each other and it was often frustrating. These kids weren't angels. Some of them committed violent offenses and a lot of them were involved in gangs.

I can't deny that things were improving. I stopped having suicidal ideations and spent more time focusing on my future rather than the past. That's not to say that certain resentments stopped popping up, but I was able to deal with them better. My biggest concern at this time was Lauren. There was so much going on with her and I felt like I was forced out of relevance by the actions of her mother. It bothered me constantly and I wanted things to change. Our original custody agreement was still in place, I was supposed to have Lauren every other weekend and on Wednesdays. It rarely happened and things needed to change.

Chapter 77. Bad luck, Blue eyes, Goodbye- *The Black Crowes*

I would love to say that BJ and I were able to put the past behind us and work things out so we could co-parent together as a team, but I'd be full of baloney if I said that. The shit was about to hit the fan. BJ was evicted from her third house in as many years and took Lauren and moved in with her mother, at least that's what I was told.

Lindsey called me shortly after her mom moved and told me that her mother lost all of her snoopy decorations and stuffed animals. I bought her one for her high school graduation which was her favorite and she also got a lot of them from past birthday and holiday presents. Lindsey has been obsessed with Snoopy since early childhood. Evidently, her mom stored some stuff from the house in the garage and never went back for it after being evicted so the landlord wound up throwing it all out. The bulk of BJ's and the kid's belongings were in storage.

Shortly after that, Lindsey called me and she was absolutely livid. BJ put her electric bill in Lindsey's name without her permission and ran a bill that was over $4000. I was so pissed off about this but there wasn't anything I could do. Lindsey also told me that her mom was drinking alcohol and she was tired of hiding it from me. I knew it. I was trying to get to the bottom of what the hell was going on for over two years. I know BJ, there is no way in hell that she can drink alcohol without using drugs. When I confronted her about it, she denied everything. She tried to tell me Lindsey was lying because she was mad but I knew BJ was full of shit. Lindsey was staying with me on and off for a few years and she wouldn't lie to me. We managed to put all our past problems behind us and we grew really close. What happened next is still hard to believe.

Lindsey went to work one day and left her laptop on and open in my kitchen. I looked at it and noticed Lauren's Facebook page was open. I looked at her messages and what I read almost caused a heart attack. There were a bunch of messages between Lauren and her friends talking about buying weed, Xanax, and other drugs. Then after checking a few more messages, I learned Lauren was living with some boy Nick and his family. His mother and sister were both heroin/opiate addicts. I knew Lauren smoked weed but I had no idea what else she was involved in. I was so shocked and upset I thought I was going to kill BJ. I called Bob first and he told me I needed to file an emergency lawsuit for custody. While I was in the process of doing that, the next morning I parked a block away from BJ's mother's house and waited to see if Lauren left for school. I eventually called the school and they said she wasn't there yet and that she hadn't been in for a few days. I called BJ and confronted her. I asked her why Lauren wasn't in school. She was in the middle of telling me Lauren was sick when I received a call back from the school and they said Lauren just showed up and a man named Nick dropped her off. I clicked back to the other line and asked BJ, "So, Lauren is sick and in bed?" She said she was. I told her the school just called and told me that a man named Nick just dropped Lauren off. I told her I knew Lauren was living at her friend Nick's house and that it was Nick's father who took Lauren to school. BJ tried feeding me some bullshit. I just told her to go fuck herself and that I was suing for emergency custody and hung up. I just caught her in the biggest lie ever.

I borrowed some money from my cousin to have a lawyer draw up the petition and she did a really good job on it. The emergency petition was approved and our first hearing was in less than a month. It was in March of 2016. A question I often asked myself was "Why the hell is all this happening"? It was a question that was never answered.

It felt like things could never just go on an even run for me. Things could be okay in one area and have complete chaos in another. I can't say how many times I heard that counselor's voice, the dude we saw before BJ and I were married and he told me not to marry BJ. I heard that line repeatedly, over and over and if I was actually able to give myself a swift kick in the ass, I would have.

Chapter 78. But I'll live on and I'll be strong, 'cause it's just not my cross to bear- *The Allman Brothers*

I prepared for the hearing for days. I printed copies of all three of BJ's evictions. I printed copies of all the messages from Lauren's Facebook messenger. There was text after text of Lauren telling friends that she was living with Nick. There were messages about buying opiate pills for Nick's mother and other damning evidence that Lauren was neglected by her mother. I had a serious claim that I should have custody.

On the day of the hearing I was ready. I went over everything I wanted to present as my argument, I had copies of all the evidence so I could provide the judge and BJ copies. I had bulleted talking points. I guess the only thing I wasn't prepared for was the depth of the level BJ was willing to reach with her lies. After swearing us in the judge allowed me to present the case. I first discussed the three evictions in three years, BJ actually objected and accused me of lying, so I presented the evidence of printed court documents proving I was telling the truth. I told them about catching BJ red-handed lying to me about where Lauren was.

When it was BJ's turn to testify, she accused me of lying about everything, but my evidence proved I wasn't. When it became obvious that the judge wasn't buying her bullshit, she played the card she held up her sleeve. She lied and accused me of physically abusing her while we were married. She went as far as accusing me of abusing both kids emotionally and she said I physically abused Lindsey as well. I was so pissed at her for this. I told the judge she was lying. The judge took Lauren to another room to talk with her. When he came back he ordered that I be investigated by the county Children and Youth Service Commission. It seemed he knew she was lying. He said in his temporary decision that every accusation of abuse has to be investigated whether they're believed to be true or not. He also temporarily removed the standing custody order. I couldn't see Lauren without supervision pending the outcome of the investigation. He also made it clear that Lauren was not to be at Nick's house for any reason and that Lauren needed to attend school every day. He set a date for almost two months for the second hearing and put in an order for Children and Youth Services to investigate BJ's claims of abuse.

I always knew BJ could be vindictive and vicious. I've dealt with her trying by any means necessary to get her way. I knew her goal in life was to ruin mine because she needed to get back at me for leaving. I knew all this. I thought I was prepared for anything, but to be accused of being an abusive parent was far beyond anything I expected. I never put a hand on BJ or Lindsey. Lauren stopped getting spankings when she was four. I never called the kids a bad name. I never purposely harmed them. BJ went way below the belt on this.

Thoughts of suicide were running rampantly through my head; then the thoughts became plans and then I got scared. As a counselor, I knew that when a person's suicidal ideations turned into plans, they were in danger. I went to Bob and my therapist Kendra and told them everything. Of course, both had polar opposite thoughts and advice on what I should do.

The next day, I woke up and realized that I no longer wanted to take my own life. I had been considering suicide as a form of revenge against BJ for everything she had done to me over the years. However, I came to the realization that seeking revenge was not a good enough reason to end my life. I remembered the third and eleventh steps of Narcotics Anonymous, which urges members to surrender their will to a higher power and seek guidance through prayer and meditation. I decided to follow God's will and trust in his plan for my life.

Every time in my life when I faced a challenge from someone, I always believed myself to be such a piece of shit that I should just give in. I was always wrong anyway. Chronic low self-esteem plagued me most of my life. This time was different. My thoughts were telling me that I wasn't wrong this time. I wasn't the bad guy. BJ has done so much wrong to me and created so much misery in the fifteen years I've known her that I was finally ready to fight back. I wasn't going to give in this time. She wasn't getting away with this. Not this time. I've had enough.

Children and Youth sent two agents to interview me and I answered every question they asked. I could tell they believed me. Everything I told them was making perfect sense. I was a responsible parent and BJ wasn't. It was so much easier for Lauren to live with BJ because she got away with everything there and I would always hold her accountable for her behaviors.

The investigation found no evidence of abuse. However, the judge's decision granted me only one more day of custody every other weekend. Lauren was ordered to stay away from Nick and attend school every day. I knew BJ wouldn't be able to get Lauren to school every day. Though I felt defeated, I held on to hope that BJ would either become a better parent or we would be back in front of the judge.

Chapter 79. We can be heroes, just for one day... = *David Bowie*

One day in April I came home from work and there was a large package on my steps. I brought it to my apartment and opened it and I was surprised to see my cap and gown for graduation! I took the CLEP tests and passed and was granted permission to walk at graduation in May. I was in my last two classes which were over in June. After four and a half years this was actually going to happen.

On May 22, 2016, I walked across the stage at Albright College and received my bachelor's degree. Me. The failure. Me, the loser that destroyed a multi-million-dollar company. Me, the "idiot with a GED" was now a college graduate with a 3.8 GPA and a bachelor's degree. Never in my life would I have believed I would achieve this. So many friends congratulated me on Facebook that it was overwhelming. I often used Facebook as a diary and didn't realize that so many people followed my journey from closing my business to graduating college. The only thing that bothered me was my parents weren't there to experience it with me. It was awesome to have Lindsey, her boyfriend Brandon, and Lauren were with me. It felt so good to finally not feel like a failure to them. I don't think they ever believed me to be a failure, but I felt like one since closing the business. I didn't feel like a failure that day though.

It was so long since I felt I was on top of the world that I forgot how good it felt. I went to work on Monday morning and my coworkers all applauded for me and had a huge cake waiting for me as well. My boss called me into her office to congratulate me and let me know she approved a

$7000 raise on my yearly salary and promoted me to the position of counselor 1! (counselor 1 is the 1st level of being a clinical counselor). I wanted the moment to last forever.

I resigned from my position at ARC. I had three jobs while I was in college at Albright. I never had time for myself. I decided to go for a master's degree in social work at Temple University and classes were starting in September. I wanted the summer off. I didn't want to go back to school but a lot of people told me a bachelor's degree can only take me so far and if I wanted to be a licensed counselor I'd need a master's degree in either clinical counseling, psychology, or social work. I was literally exhausted after finishing school at Albright. I made a promise to myself to stay out of intimate relationships when I started at Albright which was necessary but hard to keep. The Temple University MSW program was supposed to be three years and I'd have to keep that promise going. I didn't want anything to get in the way of completing the MSW degree program and an intimate relationship would definitely take my mind off school.

I was getting Lauren every other weekend and we were having a lot of problems getting along. She would want to spend the night at friends' houses but when I asked to speak to their parents before allowing that she would get super angry and sometimes completely flip out. Her mother would never check, so she was not used to any kind of responsible parenting. She pushed the limits on everything. Her bedroom looked like a tornado hit it. I would ask her to straighten it out but she never did. I would not allow her to go out until it was straightened out which would infuriate her and she would get vicious. She would often tell me she hated me and said other really hurtful things when she didn't get what she wanted. She was a lot like her mother in that regard. I had struggles with Lindsey at that age but they were nowhere near what Lauren put me through. Her behavior made me immediately think about the verbal abuse I gave my parents which helped me understand what they were going through with me when I was her age.

Lindsey and I became very close during this time. She was angry at her mother for basically stealing her identity and severely damaging her credit by not paying that electric bill and letting it get as high as it did. BJ had no way of paying it back so Lindsey started making payments on it. I felt so bad, I wished I had the money to pay for it but I never had money. I always wanted to be a hero to my kids and always fell short. I promised myself that I was going to change that and find a way to be their hero.

In September 2016, Lindsey dropped a bomb on me and told me that she and Brandon, and two other friends were going to move to Colorado. Marijuana was legal for recreational purposes there and she was going there and then spending a few years traveling the country with her boyfriend and their friends. I didn't want her to go, but there was no way I could stop her or talk her out of it. I also really did want her to go and have the experience of a lifetime. Not wanting her to go was my selfish side and I let go of that and was just really happy for her.

Before they took off on their adventure, I had to be a dad and lay down the law for them and by that I mean, I was going to tell them what they had to do even though I knew they weren't going to do any of it! I told Lindsey I wanted at least three Facetime calls every week and I wanted her to promise that if they happened to get in any trouble she should not be afraid to call. I would not get mad and I would do my best to help. *(those were the words I wished my parents or my brother had told me when I left for LA when I was 21 years old)* I was honestly so excited for her, I loved that she was doing this. Nothing was exciting about growing up in PA and this was her chance to cut loose.

Chapter 80. Because the hook brings you back... *- Blues Traveler*

The start of the school year for Lauren brought no surprises. She started missing school from the beginning. Any attempts to talk to BJ about it were met with resistance to do anything about it. BJ was incapable of making anything about anyone other than her. Her newest thing was that she had been diagnosed with some terrible disease that was making her lose weight, messing with her teeth and her physical health. She kind of sounded like me when I was telling everyone I had health issues that were causing me to lose weight back in the days of smoking crack. I tried to get as much information from Lauren as I could, it seemed like she wasn't being honest and I had a sense that she was feeling some guilt over it.

I started classes at Temple University's Harrisburg campus in September 2016. I could tell right away it was going to be a lot harder than Albright. The semesters were fourteen weeks long. The syllabus for each class outlined all the assignments and readings. It was pretty overwhelming. I was used to one class, once a week and now I'd be in two classes a week. Both classes required a ton of reading and written papers that were twice as long as what I had at Albright. My first few classes went really well; the professors were awesome and made me feel much more comfortable about the classes. I mean, I was still in partial shock over getting a damn bachelor's degree and now I'm in a fucking master's degree program. I remember thinking "People like me don't have master's degrees", but that is exactly how the mind of an addict works.

I took BJ back to court a few times and each time it seemed like it was becoming more apparent to the judge that BJ was full of shit. He eventually threatened to send BJ to jail if she continued to lie. Our last time in court the judge was fed up. He put the fear of God into BJ by sentencing her to six months in the county jail but was suspending the sentence for thirty days and if she complied with his orders, he would suspend the sentence permanently. The only thing he didn't do was give me custody. I was getting quite frustrated but was powerless over the judge and his decisions so I was stuck letting the cards fall where they may.

Lindsey returned home in late April, and the shit hit the fan on her first day back. BJ came and picked them up. She was taking Lindsey to return a trailer, and then back to my place. I was under the belief that they were all going to rent a house and live together. When they returned to my place, I could tell something wasn't right just by the look on their faces. Lindsey came to my bedroom and said we needed to talk and it was important. I had no idea what was going on but the look on their faces said it wasn't good. What they told me floored me and rocked me to my core.

BJ was high when she picked them up. They didn't know for sure what she was on, but they suspected it to be crack. Lindsey told me that BJ was asking them if they had any weed and if they wanted to get some beer and liquor and hang out for a few hours. Lindsey told me she had to drive because her mom's driving was terrible. If that wasn't enough, I learned Lauren knew about it for months and never told me. I was mad, but I also understood her position so I kept my anger under wraps. Lindsey told Lauren she needed to tell me the truth about everything.

I didn't know what to think. What I had just heard helped the last five years make sense. I was furious. I called BJ and informed her that Lauren would be staying with me. I also told her that I wouldn't involve children and youth services if she went to rehab. Additionally, I mentioned that if she went to rehab and attended 12-step meetings, we could discuss Lauren moving back in with her. However, she couldn't stay with her until she had at least six months of sobriety. The new plan was for Lindsey, her boyfriend Brandon, and their Pitbull Loki to stay with me, Lauren, and our dog Nancy. All of us, in my little 2-bedroom apartment.

I initially promised not to tell Children and Youth about this, but I later discovered more information. I was at home with Lindsey, and she informed me that BJ was also smoking marijuana with Lauren. Lauren was using the threat of revealing everything to me to bribe her mother into allowing her to do whatever she wanted. BJ used to work as a substance use counselor but is now smoking weed with our sixteen-year-old daughter. I was furious because I had endured five years of emotional abuse from her during our marriage and eleven years of her trying to ruin my life and relationship with my children. And now, she had participated in corrupting our adolescent child. I confronted her about it over the phone, but she initially denied it. However, when I told her that I had heard about it from both Lindsey and Lauren, she eventually admitted to it.

Chapter 81. Can I sail through the changing ocean tides? Can I handle the seasons of my life? — *Stevie Nicks, Fleetwood Mac*

I placed the call to Children and Youth Services and told them what I learned. They were at my house within a few hours. They questioned Lauren and she was truthful with them. BJ was not allowed to see Lauren without supervision. BJ's mother was approved to supervise visits. I was against this but pretty much powerless, there wasn't anyone else who could supervise the visits. BJ was looking into a few rehabs but was hesitant. I refiled for emergency custody of Lauren due to the circumstances.

Lauren was enrolled in cyber school, but due to BJ's lack of diligence, Lauren failed to complete most of the year's work. When a child is in cyber school, the parents are supposed to go over their work. The school explained that the parents needed to commit to over an hour each day to help the child. BJ did nothing, she accepted Laurens's bullshit about completing her work without checking. There was less than one month of school left for the year and I had the summer to decide what to do.

I watched powerlessly as Lauren went from being the sweetest, most loving child into a troubled teenager with serious emotional issues. I knew deep down she was hurting, but she wouldn't allow me in. In some way, she was damaged to the point of losing trust in almost everyone. She had been in therapy a few times. She was in an adolescent partial hospitalization program at Pennsylvania Psychiatric Institute a few times as well. The first few times I came in weekly for family sessions. BJ would only show up for family sessions once or twice. When she did, she would do her usual dance to avoid any responsibility for what was going on in Lauren's life.

Children and Youth Services sent an agent over once a week to check on Lauren. Dealing with her through this was not easy. She was so set in her ways; she basically had no real adult supervision for years and now she's dealing with me and CYS again. When I first tried to get custody and BJ accused me of being abusive, Lauren believed that it was true because BJ would tell her that. Any time I tried to be responsible BJ would call me abusive. Lauren told the CYS workers how I was as a parent and it was them that told her that I was not abusive, that I was trying my best to be a responsible parent. I truly believe that part of the reason Lauren was so messed up was because of the confusion caused by the different parenting she received from BJ and me. She heard every terrible thing BJ had to say about me for years and whether she eventually started to believe it or not, she definitely learned how to use the differences between us to her advantage. Lauren would tell the CYS agents that I was too strict and that she wanted to move back with her mother. That wasn't possible at this time is what she was told by CYS and if I had my way, she would never go back to living with her mother.

Lauren's high school wouldn't take her back because she lived with me and I was in a different school district. I had to get Lauren enrolled in a school near me. She had not passed from ninth to tenth grade yet and she was supposed to be starting her third year. She wanted me to give her permission to drop out, which I wouldn't. We had a therapeutic support specialist for her, and CYS set it up. I was doing my best to motivate her about starting school but in her defense, I understood perfectly that she was scared to start in a new school where she didn't know anyone.

Between the time in late April or early May when I found out everything and Lauren came to live with me through late fall, BJ was still involved with Lauren and would still get in the way of my trying to responsibly raise her. There were a few times when she would take Lauren to the mall even though it was forbidden by CYS for her to be alone with her. I would call CYS and tell them and they would put it on me to get Lauren back. Instead of them confronting BJ about breaking the rules, they wanted me to enforce them. They threatened me with declaring Lauren dependent if I didn't. So again, I had to be the bad guy, the one trying to get in the way of Lauren and her mom. By this time, I looked at CYS as a joke. They weren't in any way helpful to the situation. Lauren would complain to her mom often, and of course, instead of trying to help, BJ would just tell her she couldn't wait for Lauren to come back to living with her. I couldn't have been more relieved when BJ finally went to treatment.

The next few months were crazy. It was becoming harder and harder to get Lauren to school. If she did go, she stayed in the counselor's office and wouldn't go to class. We fought constantly. She would get so mad she'd tell me she hated me and wished I was dead. Her therapeutic support specialist was very helpful to me, but she couldn't help Lauren either. It felt hopeless. The fights between us over going to school were killing us both. She would get so vicious that I would lock myself in my room to get away from the verbal abuse. I began missing work a lot because of the daily fight to get her to school. To me, it was becoming a losing battle but Lauren was under the direction of the court and CYS to finish school. She would cry so hard it would tear me apart. There were times that I recognized that I felt exactly how I felt when I was married and going through the "you don't love me" fights with her mother.

Lauren learned that if she kept pushing to get her way and never gave up, her mother would finally fold. I came from a different cloth though, I never gave in. Lauren would get so worked up after a while she would find herself unable to calm herself. I would explain that she needed help and offer it either through the partial program she went through a few times or we can look for other help. The one thing I wouldn't do was continually allow her to miss school and let her do as she pleased during the day by hanging out with friends when she was supposed to be in school. Her mother did that for years and its why things are the way they are now. If she was going to miss school, we needed to find help so she could attend classes.

After BJ completed treatment Lauren wanted to return to living with her but CYS wouldn't allow it. Laurens' behavior became more erratic. She would beg and plead to stay home from school, then she would give in and have me drive her, and then ½ way there want me to take her back because she forgot something. She started doing this every day until it came to a head. She began threatening to harm herself. She had self-harmed herself by cutting in the past and I would never look at a threat as a bluff. I offered to take her to Pennsylvania Psychiatric Institute or crisis intervention at the local hospital. After trying to get me to go back and forth again, I wound up taking her to crisis intervention. She admitted to threatening to harm herself so that permitted me to have her hospitalized for a few days. I continually asked her to let me take her to PPI but she had reached a point where I couldn't talk her down. We were in the hospital for over twelve hours waiting on an ambulance to take her to a mental health institution called The Meadows. I reached a point where I was ready to give up and take her home after waiting so long but in a very rare moment of clarity, Lauren told me to just wait there with her till the ambulance came. They finally showed up after midnight and took her. I ran home and packed some of her clothes and drove to the facility. When I dropped the clothes off they wouldn't let me see her. They said it was in her best interest not to see me and that I could call the next day.

Lauren called me early the next morning begging me to come get her. She said that this place wasn't for her because it was for seriously mentally ill patients. I wanted to cry. I just wanted this child to get some help. I didn't want her to be in a place with dangerously mentally disturbed kids but I didn't want us to return to the same level of dysfunction that we were in. I promised I'd come get her but before we left together, she needed to sign an agreement to go to PPI for an evaluation. We went to PPI the same day, and their evaluation recommended she go to their partial hospitalization program again. She accepted their recommendation and I was quite thankful for that. I was hoping that we would at least be on a better path.

Lindsey was my rock throughout this time. We went through a tough phase during her late teenage years, but as she turned eighteen, she started seeing things differently. She realized that I was more stable than her mother. I still remember the most profound statement she ever made. She said, "I used to believe you were the biggest jerk and you used to make me really mad. But now I know you always loved me, and I appreciate you for never changing." She gave me so much hope when I started to believe that maybe there wasn't any when it came to Lauren. I loved both kids so much, all I ever wanted was to be their father and for us to be a real family. I didn't want us to have the relationship I had with my parents. Lindsey's support helped me believe that was possible.

When Lauren was in PPI's partial program, I would go there for family sessions and they were helping. Through their help I came to realize it wasn't only Lauren that needed to change, I learned I needed to let go of some things as well. We were able to communicate a lot better with a third party.

I felt more confident about the possibility of our relationship improving after her participation in their program. When she completed the program there were some coping strategies that were agreed upon between us to help prevent things from escalating to a boiling point. Right before Lauren was to return to her new school, their counselor called with some news that they found an alternative school for Lauren, it was especially for kids with emotional problems like Lauren. Lauren agreed to go there and I couldn't have been happier or more hopeful.

I knew Lauren smoked weed; I was against it but was powerless over it. I needed all the help I could get with her and I welcomed the new MST (Multi-Systemic) therapist Children and Youth provided for us. Laurens upcoming summer vacation frightened me. I was really worried about how and if we would get through it okay.

Chapter 82. You got to lose to know how to win- *Aerosmith, Dream On*

Earlier in March, I received a letter from the state of PA telling me that I was selected to interview for a job at a state prison. I had applied on the state employment website for a substance use counselor position. The prison was pretty far away, about seventy-five miles, but the increase in pay and benefits that included a pension made it worth the drive. I went on the interview and was confident that they would hire me, which they did. I was to start in April. There was a bunch of onboarding things to do before starting. I had to obtain clearances with the state police, FBI and child abuse. I knew that wouldn't be a problem, I had to get them for Gaudenzia too.

I received a call from someone from the prison making me aware that I had a warrant for my arrest from back in 1994 in NYC and that I needed to clear it up. Once he told me what it was for, I remembered exactly what happened. I went to visit my Aunt Rose and she surprised me with $300 in cash. I told her a few weeks before that I thought I needed glasses and before I left her house she gave me the money for them. I tried to refuse it. I told her I didn't need glasses but she wouldn't take no for an answer. I was living with Ivan Neville in NY at the time and we were really fucked up back then. We smoked crack all the time. It was when he was recording his second album.

As soon as I left my aunt's house the dope fiend in me took over. I ran to the subway station because I wanted to get home to tell Ivan and his wife about having all that cash. When I got to the train station, my stupid ass thought it was wise to hop over the turnstile rather than stand in line to get a token. I didn't notice the police were right there and they caught me in the act. They asked me why I did it and I made up a lie and also showed them the card my brother gave me to show police if I ever got in trouble. They were about to let me go without a ticket but they searched me first. They found the $300 in my pocket which pissed them off. The cop asked "how can you have $300 and be so stupid to hop the turnstile? I had no answer so they said "we were about to let you go but now you can go fuck yourself, were taking you in". It was pretty stupid of me to do that. I went to the police station with them, in handcuffs, and sat there for a few hours until they gave me the ticket and let me go.

So now in 2018, after twenty-four years, I have to go face a fucking judge about this stupid warrant. I took off work and drove to Queens to take care of it. While I was in the courtroom, I started to panic. The judge was sending people to jail for warrants that were less than one year old and here I am with one from twenty-four years ago! I was literally shitting myself. When it was finally my turn, I went in front of the judge and he asked what this was about. The prosecutor told him and proceeded to tell him that they don't even write tickets for that offense anymore.

The judge kept looking at his desk and then looked at me. He did that quite a few times. Finally, he asked, "where have you been for the last twenty-four years Mr. Genna?" I told him I was a homeless drug addict back then and I've since cleaned up and was sober for nineteen years. I also told him I was clearing this warrant up for a job as a drug and alcohol counselor in a state prison. He started looking at his desk again, saying nothing, just looking at me then his desk. Then he asked "do you have any idea of how you looked back then?" I said I can only imagine. He invited me up to his bench and showed me the picture the police took when they arrested me.

I looked horrible, my hair was long and all over the place and my skin was pale and thin with my eyes sunk deep in my face. It was shocking to see. The judge then said "Mr. Genna, you're a miracle, I am proud to see you here as a person in recovery and doing the right thing." He then told me he would adjourn the case and drop the charge if I didn't get in any trouble within the next ten days. He said that was least amount of time for an adjournment with contemplation of dismissal allowed by NY state law. I was so appreciative of him and I asked if I could hug him, which he actually allowed. I can't explain how good it felt for me to hear that from a judge. He let me take a picture of the photo on his desk so I can have the memory. Finally, before I left, he shook my hand and told me to keep up the good work. I drove the whole way home smiling from ear to ear.

My last day at Siena house was harder than I thought it would be. I really loved it there and I will always believe in what my coworkers and I did over the three years I was there. I spent a few hours just talking about recovery with a few of the clients and it was really special. For once, I got to be just me, not Mr. Mike the counselor, not the hard ass that called everyone out on their behaviors, not the douche that caught clients on their illegally brought in cell phones. Just me. Mike Genna, the person in long term recovery.

When it was time to clock out, I made my usual final round of the facility while most of the clients were outside on their smoke break and wouldn't you know it, I caught a knucklehead on a cell phone. I could have let it go, but that just wasn't in my heart. There was no way I could ever live with myself after all I preached about changing behaviors to let that go. I took the phone and wrote the infraction documenting the rule that the client broke. The dude tried his absolute best to manipulate the situation in his favor. He tried playing on my guilt, he tried getting angry and finally gave in and accepted the fact that behaviors have consequences. When I walked out the door and past the clients out on the porch smoking, they all wished me well. Some of the guys gave hugs, and then, walking to my car one dude yelled out, "Mr. Mike, always stay wonderful"! What a perfect ending. I held back the tears until I got in my car and drove off.

Chapter 83. I watched you suffer a dull aching pain, then you decided to show me the same... ~ *The Rolling Stones, Wild Horses*

I started working at the prison in April of 2018. The seventy-five-mile drive there was hellacious. My hours were 8:00 am to 4:30 pm. I left my house every morning at 6:00 am and would get there by around 7:40 am. Driving home took a little longer sometimes. I eventually found a way home that was easier than taking the highway and it had some overwhelming views which was perfect to help ease the stress of a day working in a prison therapeutic community.

I was away from home for twelve hours, which made keeping tabs on Lauren next to impossible. I asked her mother to help but of course, she didn't. Lauren wanted to move back with her mom but she couldn't. CYS wouldn't approve it. BJ was driving the CYS people crazy with her avoidance of providing urine samples for drug testing. They gave her a break and allowed her to see Lauren without supervision, which I didn't agree with. I mean, just a few months ago she was smoking weed with Lauren and smoking crack while living with her mother and she was already pulling dope-fiend behaviors when it came to providing urine screens. I didn't believe that she was staying clean.

Lauren pushed the limits of my sanity as far as she could. She wanted the lifestyle of an adult while she was only seventeen. It was still a fight if she wanted to stay at a friend's house. I wouldn't allow it unless I spoke with a parent. There was a night over the summer that she stayed at a friend's house and they snuck out and went to some boy's house and took acid. Lauren called me around 2:00am begging me not to get mad at her. She said she was high on acid and having a bad trip and wanted me to come get her. I wanted to lose my shit but I held my temper and picked her and her friend up. Her friend was two years younger than Lauren and when I called this kid's father he was absolutely useless. This kid was fifteen and sneaking out to go to boy's houses and taking drugs. I really wanted to slap some sense across the guy's mug, but again, I had to be the responsible one so I of course refrained.

Lauren continued to push harder and harder throughout the summer. It culminated when I grounded her for a day, and she went to her mom's instead of staying at my house. As usual, BJ broke her word to me and allowed Lauren to go out even though she was grounded, and Lauren decided to push the envelope again. She didn't come home on time, she wouldn't answer her phone or return calls. BJ claimed not to know where Lauren was or who she was with which turned out to be another lie but I wouldn't find out until a few days later. Lauren stayed out the whole night and continued to the next day.

I was in contact with some of her friends and after twenty-four hours I called the police and gave them all the information I had. I was worried sick about her. I posted on her Facebook for her to contact me. Some of her friends contacted me with some ideas of who she was with and I called and gave the police that information. Finally, at about 1:00am the second night she was out, I received a call from the police that they located her and had her at the station. I went and got her and the only thing she said was that she hated my guts.

The next day I came home from work and she wasn't home again even though she was grounded. Something had to change. School was going to start very soon and I wouldn't be around to get her up and ready for the bus that picked her up. We met with the MST counselor a few times while this was going on. I was really getting tired of dealing with Lauren's lack of respect and her terrible attitude towards me. The next few weeks were a blur, so much happened in such a short time. I wound up dropping out of the semester at Temple. I needed to be there for Lauren and with all that was happening and I wouldn't have been able to do schoolwork anyway. I don't even know how to explain all that went on but I'll give it my best shot.

One-night Lauren was with friends in a hotel room and they were supposedly making a lot of noise and someone called the police. After the police showed up I received a call from them requesting me to come get my daughter. She received a citation. The police found marijuana, a scale, and drug paraphernalia in the room. She was underage to be in a hotel without an adult and she wasn't compliant with the police. She received citations for a few things, but they gave her a break and didn't charge her with possession. Her friend Maddie was with her, this was the fifteen-year-old who was in the boy's house when Lauren called me while high on acid.

When we went to court for the hearing, the police officer was a gentleman who was trying to talk with them and made an offer to reduce the charges further. Lauren and Maddie were being assholes to him, so he recharged them for the original offense. A new hearing date was set.

The one thing I wasn't going to do was allow Lauren any luxuries while she was behaving so terribly. I was paying for her phone and called Verizon and had her service turned off. I told Lauren when her behavior improved I would turn it back on. I also changed the password on my wireless internet so she couldn't sign on. I grounded her for the night and went into my room. She kept bugging me to let her out. She decided to leave anyway. I told her I was calling the police. She still left. She came back in a few hours and started demanding I turn her phone back on. I wouldn't. She was screaming and crying that she wanted to call her mother but I wouldn't let her use the phone until her behavior changed. She wouldn't give up, she began pounding and kicking on my door and screaming at me as loud as she could. I was trying to hold my door shut but she kept it up.

I decided to leave the house and pushed my way past her and walked out. I got in my car and tried to drive away but she wouldn't let go of the door handle. I turned the car ignition off and walked away. I couldn't believe this was happening. I called the counselor and told her I was going to call BJ to come get Lauren for the night because this was becoming dangerous. Lauren was following me down the street and I kept trying to walk away from her. I called her mother and told her to come get her and tried to explain what was happening. Lauren approached me and tried to grab the phone from me and as I tried to turn away, she put her arms around my neck and spit in my face. I was in total disbelief at this point. I was in shock. I grabbed her jacket collar and pushed her down off me pretty aggressively and started walking away. I called BJ and told her that Lauren was not allowed at my house anymore and she should come get her. I wasn't allowing her to step foot in my house. I went into the house and started putting her belongings in bags and clearing out her room. Lauren accused me of picking her up by the throat and throwing her down to the street, which I didn't do.

She called the police and they showed up within minutes. I explained to the officer that Lauren wasn't in her right mind, that she wasn't taking her depression meds properly, and that she was in an extremely manic state. The policeman listened to her and then checked her throat and neck. There were absolutely no marks on her and he told her there weren't any signs of her being picked up the way she explained. Her jacket showed signs of how I grabbed her by it just like I explained and he believed me.

She became verbally abusive towards the officer. He was handling himself really well despite her behavior. She eventually became so out of control he threatened to arrest her. Thankfully, BJ showed up. I asked the officer not to arrest her and explained I would call CYS in the morning and report what happened. He agreed not to arrest her and stayed there while I packed the rest of Lauren's stuff and she left with her mother. I called Melissa and told her what happened and we talked for a while. She did really well at calming me down.

The next morning, I took off work and called CYS and told them what happened. They had to investigate it and promised to keep in touch with me throughout the process. I called the police to speak with the officer that came to my house but he wasn't available. They were contemplating charges against Lauren which I begged them not to bring. I explained she was emotionally challenged and that she's been through a lot. I was still a little scared about the CYS investigation. I couldn't believe Lauren would tell such a lie that could possibly cause me to lose my job or worse, get me arrested.

The CYS investigation was over fairly quick. They spoke with Melissa and the police officer who came to my house that night and concluded that I didn't try in any way to harm Lauren. I was relieved when I heard that. I still needed to deal with what happened. I called my therapist and she took me in on short notice. She was always super helpful to me. When we talked, we went through the whole week. She was really understanding and assured me that I did the best I could. I was having trouble accepting that though. I knew that I was nothing like I was when I was using but I still struggled to believe I wasn't a bad person, especially when a situation like this or similar to it happened. I am forever grateful for Kendra and her gentle, loving approach to treatment. I have no clue how I'd have wound up if I didn't have her as a therapist.

I was really hurt by Lauren's actions. Lauren called me acting as if nothing happened and asked if she could come over to see the dog. I wanted to tell her to fuck off, but instead, I just told her that what happened really hurt and I need time to heal from it. I told her I wanted to straighten things out between us and that I loved her but I also needed some space from her. I could hear in her voice that she knew she really messed up but she couldn't bring herself to apologize or even accept responsibility for her behavior. As usual, she argued that I should let her come over. I stood my ground. I usually had a hard time with confrontation, years and years of being the bad guy conditioned me to always believe I was wrong. Something was changing though, after going through what happened I wouldn't allow those thoughts to cloud my understanding and I was able to accept that this time I wasn't the bad guy.

Chapter 84. I Shed a tear 'cause I'm missin' you, I'm still alright to smile=*Guns n Roses, Patience*

It didn't take more than two minutes for BJ to start hitting me up for child support. It didn't matter that I had full custody for eighteen months without receiving one penny from her. It didn't matter that she was living with her mother and had no bills because her mother paid for everything. It didn't matter that it was obvious she was still using. She was adamant that she needed $400 every month to survive with Lauren staying there. Lauren would turn eighteen in less than six months so I just paid it. At that point, I'd have paid anything to not hear BJ's voice so I figured I got off easy.

I maintained contact with CYS because I was worried about Lauren leaving school and that BJ was using while Lauren was living there with her. Without telling me officially, they hinted around enough that I could figure out that BJ was still avoiding providing urine samples, so I knew she was using. I also maintained contact with Lauren's school, they were always helpful to me. They made me aware that Lauren started missing school almost immediately after leaving my house. It almost felt like they were pressuring me to take Lauren back, but there was no way I would. Lauren was still holding on to the lie that I choked her and she was still vicious if she didn't get her way.

This situation really helped me see what I put my parents through for so many years. Lauren was exactly like her mother in the way that she could speak to me as if nothing happened ten minutes after saying some of the meanest things to me. I realized that she wasn't only like her mother. I did the same fucking thing to my parents. I was very confused during all this. I was seriously angry with Lauren, but I missed her a lot too. I didn't want to go years without seeing or speaking to her like I did with my parents, but I didn't want to sweep what she did under the rug either. I wanted her to take accountability for her behaviors.

When I realized that I put my parents through the same or worse than what Lauren was putting me through, I also realized that I wasn't the only person going through hell. So was Lauren. I understood that I was just as incapable of taking accountability for my behaviors as Lauren when I was her age. This was another of those "aha" moments. I remember the time my therapist asked me what I would've told myself when I was a teenager in the picture I showed her. I realized how much was missing in my life at that time and understood that Lauren was missing the same things.

Being in recovery and working through the 12 steps has provided me with the wonderful gift of seeing my part in things either in the moment or shortly after. Doing this allowed me to think about what I needed from my parents but didn't receive as a teenager and understand that whatever was missing for me was exactly what I needed to provide for Lauren now. When this finally dawned on me I was able to change my approach with Lauren. I learned that Lauren most likely needed something she never experienced. She needed someone to understand her. I wanted to repair things with Lauren and be there to help her with what she needed and to show her I understood what she was going through. For the longest time, I believed Lauren needed structure and direction more than anything. I finally understood how much more than that she needed and I was also finally willing to see things through her eyes.

After a few weeks of continued meetings with Melissa, we started speaking about the night she spit on me and though she never fully took accountability for it, she did at least admit she was out of control because she wasn't taking her meds correctly. Having Melissa there to help us was awesome. I may not have agreed with her way of doing things all the time but she did have a way of helping me accept things that I'd have never before accepted. It felt good to see an improvement in my relationship with Lauren.

I started to find my groove at the prison after a few weeks of being in the TC (Therapeutic Community), which is a residential rehab inside the walls of the prison. Inmates who received a recommendation for that level of treatment care would live in the TC unit for four months and work their way through the program. The inmates could tell fairly quickly that I was the real thing. In the TC unit, I did the same as I did in Siena House. I called out all negative behaviors. I never missed an opportunity to pull someone up and address their issues. I did this all without ever being mean, judging, or condescending. My experience at Siena House provided me with the tools I needed to succeed in the prison TC. It was kind of like going from the minor league to the big league.

One day I noticed the dude whose phone I took and I wrote him up my last day at Siena House. This guy was fucking scary. He was at least 6'5" and weighed at least 350 pounds. His head and face were covered in tattoos. I was immediately scared that if he saw me he would try and hurt me. I don't know how or why, but I somehow gained the courage to walk towards him and tap his shoulder. He looked at me like he wanted me dead. He said with a deep raised tone of voice, MR MIKE! I started looking for guards, because I thought this huge dude with tattoos all over his head and face was going to kill me, and he said, "Man, I was so fucking mad at you that night, you could've let me off, it was your last fucking day", I then I heard myself praying in my head *hail Mary, full of grace*, and then he said, "but I had a lot of time to think about everything you said at Siena House, and I wished I would have listened to you, I'm tired of this life and I want help". I thought *Wait, what?* I stopped the prayer in my head and asked him to repeat himself because I couldn't believe what I just heard. He said it again and extended his hand to shake mine. I wanted to stay and talk with him but I had to go to the bathroom before I shit my pants!

I had to think about what had happened when I got back to my office because it was truly quite profound. I had been working in the field for about five years at this point and was finally realizing that doing this saved my life. After the business collapsed, I was mentally and emotionally sick. I didn't want to live. I fantasized about dying. I fantasized about my funeral. My spirit was defeated worse than when I was getting high. I realized though that I hadn't thought about killing myself or dying in a long time. I didn't *want* to die. While things were nowhere near perfect, I was enjoying living.

I thought about everything that's happened since starting in this field. I remembered the kid who hugged me at ARC before he was successfully discharged and the other kid who told me I was the best thing to happen to him since he got there. I thought about the dude at Siena House with the goofy assed smile that told me he was "always wonderful". I couldn't forget the countless former clients from ARC, the RASE project, and Siena House who reached out and found me on Facebook to tell me the effect I had on their lives and recovery. And now the huge tattoo-headed guy that I just spoke to. All this, every little bit of it, has helped me become the man I always wished to be. Honestly though, I was always that man; I just never realized it until this.

On my drive home from the prison, there was a spot at the top of a hill that once reached, a majestic view of the mountains and the Susquehanna River appeared below. I could only see it for like three seconds and then the road veered the other way. When I reached the spot that day, I parked and just sat there staring. I hadn't really or meaningfully prayed in a long time, but I prayed. I remembered Bob making me tell him where God was in my life when I was all caught up in my misery and realized he was with me right now. I laid there in the grass for about 15 minutes counting blue cars and then some no-toothed dude holding a fucking rake, with the most nasal voice I ever heard asked me "What the hell are you doing here?" I told him I was just looking at God's gift of a beautiful view. He then asked, "You're not a crackhead or something like that are you?" I smiled and wished him a wonderful day and drove home with a different view of the world than I've ever had. I actually drove nice and slowly. I never drive slowly.

Chapter 85. In this theatre that I call my soul, I always play the starring role... *The Police*

Looking back at my experience up to this point I started to recognize how I had a positive effect on some of the people I'd worked with over the years. What happened with the tattoo-headed guy at the prison shortly before I left the job had such a profound effect on me. I realized how my experience from going to treatment and maintaining sobriety for all these years could profoundly affect people trying to recover from the same disease I had. Because of this, I started having a more positive outlook on life. I realized that changing my career path and pursuing education were the best decisions I could have made, and the resulting outcomes had a significant impact on my current state of mind. When my business fell apart, my decisions were made out of desperation. I was frantically trying to keep my sinking ship afloat; I was more concerned with saving face than with saving my ass from the financial, emotional, and social problems I was facing. The transition from a state of desperation to a place where I was able to make confident decisions was the result of years of therapy with Kendra and guidance from Bob.

After re-enrolling back in classes at Temple I accepted an opportunity to start an internship at Siena House where I was previously employed. I was going to develop a new reentry program that could bring better outcomes to the clients after completing treatment. Unfortunately, the Department of Corrections denied my request to do the internship with Siena House because it appeared to be a conflict of interest because Siena House was contracted by the DOC. I decided to leave my job at the prison to pursue an internship. I knew in my heart that the program I would develop would help more people maintain sobriety and work their way out of the prison system. I made this decision before having another job lined up. I had no idea what was ahead of me but I wasn't worried at all. I worked hard to get where I was and I knew things would work out. This was most likely the first time in my life that I made a choice based on self-confidence and without fear.

During my time working with inmates in both the TC and outpatient departments, I formed strong relationships with some of them. On my last day, while overseeing a 12-step meeting, the inmates requested that I share my recovery story with them. Although it was frowned upon by the DOC for staff to do so, I accepted their request humbly since it was my last day. I shared my recovery story with a roomful of incarcerated men, and it felt good to be myself in the meeting. I understand why prison staff do not speak about their personal lives to inmates. In some cases, inmates can manipulate staff using the information they learn about them. However, it was nice to make a connection between myself and the inmates. In my experience, prison inmates are not always treated as humans, and incarceration can be a terrible experience. I am happy that I was able to provide these men with a chance to feel a little more human by allowing them into my world, even if only for that one moment.

Luckily, I had a lot of friends in the field and not two days after turning in my resignation, a friend told me about an outpatient program on the street that was looking for a counselor. I emailed the clinical director and had a job waiting for me as soon as my two weeks were up. I had to think for a minute, things like that don't happen to people like me, or so I thought. I always do that, I fail to give myself the credit I deserve. Actually, things like that do happen to people like me. It was about time I realized that.

I worked hard to get to where I am today. I went through four and a half years of college while working three jobs. I gained a lot of knowledge and experience through this work and became really good at being a counselor. I am proud of my accomplishments and try to acknowledge them regularly. At one point, I realized that I was changing for the better, and when I shared this with Bob, he was very supportive. He said, "Mike, you're becoming the man you always wanted to be." It felt so good to hear him say that.

Chapter 86. You dropped a bomb on me... *The Gap Band*

Lindsey and Brandon found an apartment in Harrisburg and I's see them regularly. I'd stop by their apartment if I was close and she'd do the same and they would come by for my Sunday dinners. When I first left BJ, my relationship with the kids often went through struggles. I was always so stressed out over the business or their mother that I wasn't always fully there for them. These days, I was enjoying what I had with both of them. It was nice to finally not worry about it.

Lindsey was doing well at this time; she found a job she loved and was in her little apartment with her boyfriend Brandon. He surprised her with an engagement ring and asked her to marry him. I was so happy for her when she told me. I knew she wanted to be married for a while and she was super excited that he asked! Before getting sober, I never believed I would walk my daughter down the wedding aisle to her waiting soon-to-be husband. After Lindsey told me about accepting his proposal, I happily looked forward to doing that.

Lindsey and Brandon did all their wedding arrangements on their own and found the venue for it as well. They were getting married on October 4, 2019. We were all pretty excited for her. I was really proud of them for getting their wedding arranged completely on their own. Since Lindsey left high school, she has been the most responsible of us all. She got her own car and was approved for her first loan because she paid all her bills on time and always had good jobs. We had developed a really cool relationship since she left school. We became really good friends and grew a lot closer over the past few years. I have to say how amazing it is when I would see Lindsey do or say things that came from me. For example, I never tell someone I'll be there in ten minutes, for whatever reason I picked up this habit of saying "I'll be there in seven minutes." I will never forget the first time I heard Lindsey on the phone with a friend and say "I'll be there in seven minutes!" I brought it to her attention and we shared a laugh about it.

Chapter 87. People get ready, there's a train coming... ~ *The Impressions*

I began working as an independent contractor for an outpatient agency right after leaving my job at the prison. As a contractor, I would be responsible for my taxes and health insurance. Although the job paid well, I was only paid for the time I spent with clients, either in a group or an individual session. I was advised to start the paperwork for the client chart during the session, but I found it difficult to do so because I got too involved in the session. I believed that this would not be fair to the client, as it might make them feel neglected. Being a contractor, I was able to set my schedule, which made my internship easier. My primary focus was on the internship because I believed it would be beneficial to many clients.

The day of Lindsey's wedding arrived quicker than expected. It was surreal to realize that she had grown up so fast. Regardless of her age, I always saw her as the cute five-year-old kid that I fell in love with the moment I met her. I had an idea for a speech/toast I was supposed to give. When Lindsey was between five and seven years old, I would read her a book called "Dinosaur's Banquet" about a dinosaur who loved his blanket. I would get really into the reading, and I was very animated while reading it to her, which made her laugh and laugh. I read that book every single night for years. I thought that as a wedding present, I would find the book, narrate the story about reading it to Lindsey as a young child, and give it to Lindsey and Brandon as a gift (hint!) so that when they had their first child, they could experience the same joy that I did when I read it to Lindsey. It turned out to be a wonderful idea and brought Lindsey to the brink of tears.

Upon returning home, I found myself in a serene state of mind. The little girl that I met and fell in love with twenty years ago has now grown into a full-fledged adult. Time seemed to have flown by so quickly. I was overjoyed for her and realized that I was also happy for myself. I was able to enjoy the relationship with both girls in the exact way that I always wanted. It felt like an accomplishment after years of struggling to be relevant. I was proud to have made it this far. It's something that I never thought would be possible just a few years ago.

I started my internship a few days before the semester even began. I began writing about how the program should work and was surprised at how quickly the ideas came to me. I had the outline of how the program should run in just a few days. I shared my thoughts with three former coworkers, and their input was invaluable. These ladies, each with their own unique and wonderful qualities, had all played a role in making me the counselor I am today. It felt great to be back at Siena House, a place where I had always loved working.

To convince the Department of Corrections and parole board to agree to my program, I needed to prove its effectiveness. I presented evidence from various aftercare programs that provided resources to ex-offenders and parolees. This evidence showed that individuals who were provided with community resources to help them adjust to life outside of prison were far less likely to relapse into drug use or criminal behavior. I also presented the program guidelines which showed that we were selective about who we allowed to participate. To ensure accountability, the program only accepted individuals who met certain criteria. During the meeting with the DOC and parole board, I was accompanied by the director and clinical supervisor of Siena House, which made it an easy sell. They agreed to a pilot program at first, which made me ecstatic.

As time moved forward I started to believe that everything promised to me from the outpatient agency I was contracting for was not happening as they promised. I was not getting the number of clients I needed to survive financially. I was told I'd have close to thirty clients within a month, I was there two months and wasn't close to that yet. I was running a group a few days a week, which helped but I wasn't where I needed to be yet. Also, I was told most clients show up for their assessments, but that was not true, it was like half would show and I would have to play phone tag or chase people to get them to come in for their appointments. When a client didn't show up, guess who didn't get paid?

By the end of the year, I realized that I wasn't into my job at the outpatient facility. I liked everyone there, and working with the clients as well. I also believe that because I was doing my internship at Siena House, I missed it there and that weighed on my lack of love for outpatient. The director of Siena House offered me a full-time position as a counselor 3, the highest level of counselor in the agency, but the pay was terrible compared to what I made at the prison and the outpatient facility as well so I declined the offer.

Right after the new year, I saw an ad that Gaudenzia was hiring for a program director for Common Ground, where I actually went to rehab. The thought of coming back to the program where I received treatment twenty years later as a director would be amazing. I interviewed for the position and the dude that interviewed with sounded like he was really interested in me. I was super excited about the possibility although I knew that I just barely met the criteria for the position and I was sure people more qualified would apply.

The director of Siena House called me shortly after interviewing at Common Ground and gave a better offer of employment with a higher salary than previously offered. He said I could do my internship hours during work hours too, which would save me 16 hours every week so I jumped on it. I felt bad that I was leaving the other job so I offered to stay on part-time for ten hours a week since I would be saving so many hours from my internship. Shortly after accepting the position I learned that the director position at Common Ground was filled by someone with way more experience than I had. I wasn't mad at all, I considered Siena House to be home.

I decided that with this change in jobs, I needed another change and decided to move from my crappy apartment to something a little nicer. I found a townhouse in New Cumberland and fell in love with it. I definitely couldn't afford it, but that didn't matter, I'd make it work. I had been driving for UBER part time and I thought I wouldn't have to do it anymore but if I wanted this townhouse I would need to continue. I was so ready for the upcoming changes, I loved Siena House, and I was optimistic about completing my internship. What I didn't know was, what was coming over the next month was something that not only rocked MY world, but it rocked the whole world. No one was prepared for it.

Chapter 88. Helter Skelter, it's coming down fast- *The Beatles*

I moved into my new townhouse on February 1, 2020. I started working at Siena House on Monday, 2 days after moving, my house was still completely disorganized. I started the 2nd half of my first internship in January and by the time I started, I had every part of the new program I was developing figured out. All I had to do now was to line up all of the ancillary resources that the program participants would need for their re-entry. I was honestly tired of school but I was getting closer to completing it.

Lauren surprised me shortly after I moved into the townhouse, she said living with her mother and grandmother was becoming unbearable. She said her mother was using again and she was out of control. She asked if she could move in with me, and, if her boyfriend could move in too. Did she not know that I'm Sicilian? Did she not know I was a man? I had to check her forehead to see if she was delirious from a fever or something. What in the Kentucky fried crack rock was she thinking?!?! What man in his right mind would allow his nineteen-year-old daughter and her boyfriend to live with him? She had to be crazy! A responsible Sicilian father would never allow a boy to live in his house with his daughter, especially if they weren't married!

So after they moved in I had to lay the rules down and they were non-negotiable (you see what I did there?). The number one most important rule without a doubt was there were never to be any noises coming out of that room. None whatsoever. If I heard noises, the boyfriend was getting beat up. The second rule was that I was not cleaning up after anyone. If I had to clean after anyone but myself, the boyfriend was getting beat up. The third rule was no drugs or alcohol in the house. Ever. Again, if any drug use or drinking went on in the house, the boyfriend was getting beat up. By the time I was done handing out all my orders, Lauren's poor boyfriend needed therapy.

Of course, I'm kidding, a little, but I had to check myself to see if I was doing this because I wanted Lauren to like me or if I truly believed I could trust her. After examining my motives, I came to understand that I did trust Lauren. She had come so far over the past year and more than just trusting her, I was proud of her. We spoke a few times about what went on when she lived with me, the fights, and her stubbornness, and she accepted responsibility for her behaviors and meaningfully apologized. It felt good to know I could trust her.

Things at Siena house were completely out of line with how it was when I previously worked there. I was the only counselor utilizing the basic rules which had the entire population of clients pissed off at me. I was changing their routines and they were not happy with some of the things I was trying to put back in place. I was attempting to put things back in place but all I was doing was pissing everyone off. It seemed as if the director had no idea what he was doing. The director and Beverly were both okay with my attempt to get the place to run like a TC is supposed to run, but they weren't supportive when I faced backlash from the clients in the community.

The saying "when it rains it pours" came back into play at this time. We started hearing news that a deadly virus was killing people in China. We didn't know anything about it except it affected people's lungs and it was deadly. When the first case of it hit America, the person who had it died within days of it. Suddenly, this virus was all over the news. In an instant, cases were popping up all over the country and people were dying from it. In all my fifty-four years I've never experienced anything like this. We were being told to distance ourselves by at least six feet from others. There was talk of needing to wear masks for protection. We were being told not to leave our house except for supplies and food. Then some things that were regularly available became impossible to find, like freaking toilet paper. I mean, people were preparing for the end of the world and buying all the damn toilet paper, someone please make that make sense to me! Once the sports games were canceled, the state governments were placing "shelter in place" orders in the communities, and only essential workers should leave their houses. Myself and the rest of Siena house staff were considered as essential workers so we were allowed to leave our homes.

If someone came in contact in any way with the virus, they were to quarantine for at least 15 days. Even if you weren't sure that you were in contact, you still had to quarantine. I found out about this the hard way. We had a client start complaining of chest pains, coughing loudly, and saying he had all the symptoms of this virus which now had a name, COVID-19. We took him to the emergency room, and they checked him out and then ordered him to quarantine for 15 days, no one could go in or out of his room. My boss asked me to escort this guy back to his room. I wore a mask and stayed like ten feet from this guy, who was purposely coughing in my direction. I was horrified and scared to death so I told my boss what happened and went home. I called the hospital and asked if I could get tested or something, but tests were not yet available.

I was told to quarantine at home for fifteen days and report any changes in my health to them. So now I'm off work without any paid time off because I just started at this facility. I had to be home for fifteen days. When I didn't get sick after like five days I knew I didn't have it but I still was not allowed to leave until the fifteen days were up. I later learned the dude who went to the emergency room wasn't sick, he was faking it. I still couldn't go back! A lot of the clients were using this to try and get out of the facility, but parole wasn't allowing it, nor were they coming into our building so we were basically on our own without their support.

When I returned to work after the fifteen-day quarantine, things were crazier than usual at Sienna House. Clients found out that parole wasn't coming to the facility for any reason and they started sneaking out the windows at night and bringing synthetic marijuana (K2) and suboxone into the facility. Normally, if anyone absconded, even if they returned, they would be removed and parole would come and take them back to jail. The same would happen for anyone caught with drugs. During Covid though, we were not allowed to release clients even if they broke cardinal rules. Usually, if a cardinal rule was broken it meant automatic unsuccessful discharge. Parole expected us to keep these people at the facility while they were doing these things. After a few more weeks we completely lost control of the facility. Our director was doing nothing to stop it. If it were me I would have removed anyone bringing drugs in because the safety and sanctity of our clients comes first. It wouldn't have mattered to me what parole wanted. There were clients there that truly wanted to get better and they were having a hard time because there were other clients using drugs in the bathrooms. Parole forcing us to house people who were a danger to the community was too much for me to handle. There were also clients trying to use the pandemic as a way out of treatment. They would call anyone who would listen stating their lives were in danger because the facility had no protection from the virus. Because of the pandemic, my part-time job at the outpatient agency informed me that I was being let go. I couldn't have been happier.

The last straw for me at Siena house was the day we caught five men in the bathroom using K2 (Synthetic Marijuana) in the bathroom. They were so fucked up they couldn't speak and they were walking around like zombies. We wound up calling for ambulances. The next day, our director brought in hamburgers and hotdogs and brought the grill out on the front porch, and had a surprise barbecue. All clients were allowed to attend, even the five that were taken out in ambulances the day before! I returned from lunch and the director asked me to escort five or six guys to the bathroom, which I did. When they didn't come back to my door within five minutes to go back outside, I went and checked the bathrooms and of course, they were smoking K2. They didn't even try to hide it.

I continually asked the director and his boss to do something about what was happening and all I got back were stupid excuses. I told my clinical supervisor that I had to leave, what was happening was too much for me to deal with. After I left I called the central office to discuss what was going on. I went over the chain of communication because the two people above me were the people I was complaining about. The regional director took the information from me and thanked me, but also reminded me to utilize the chain of communication. She knew I couldn't, but she said it anyway. The next day when I came back to work I was called to the division director's office upstairs and he told me I was getting written up for abandoning my post. He asked who I spoke to about what was happening at the facility and I wouldn't tell him. He continued to try to get me to tell him. He threatened my job and I told him to fire me. I wasn't quitting and I wasn't telling him anything. He had no idea of who he was dealing with when it came to me. I told him nothing and wasn't fired.

My boss, the program director, had a meeting with all of us, and more than a few people questioned him about rewarding the clients while they were using drugs in the facility. He tried making the situation about me. He was pissed off that I went over his head and complained. He and I argued in front of the whole staff. I knew I wouldn't get anywhere, he was an idiot and I was planning on leaving once I found a new job. I was disappointed with the way Siena House turned out. When I last worked there, we were all aligned and had the facility running better than ever.

With all this going on, I managed to have everything lined up to start my new reentry program. When I told the director, he told me that he was not going to let me start the program. He tried telling me that we didn't have full approval from the DOC. He was at the meeting with parole and the Department of Corrections and he knew it was approved. He was retaliating because I complained to the central office about his negligence.

I was scared that if I didn't get the program started my two semesters of internships were going to waste. I wanted to start this program. I worked very hard at putting it together and now this dumbass director was blocking it.

What finally happened was the agency heads called an all-staff meeting for one week later. At that meeting, we were all informed that Gaudenzia was closing Siena House for good. They were blaming the pandemic. We were told that we would receive one-month severance pay and that our insurance would be canceled the day we closed. So it didn't really matter about the program. I spent close to a year developing this and it wasn't going to start. I was also out of a job.

So much was going on at this point with the pandemic, it was like living in another world. Everything was closed. The streets were empty. The stock markets were crashing. Businesses were closing down for good. People were scared to death of getting the virus. On the news, they showed hospitals filled to the maximum with people dying in the hospital halls. They were storing bodies in trailers outside the hospitals. The death toll kept climbing. Thousands of people were dying. The unemployment rate was at levels not seen since the great depression. Twelve-step meetings were moved to online chatrooms. There weren't any meetings to attend in person. Without a doubt, this was the most extraordinary thing I've ever experienced. The news programs were calling it a once-in-a-century pandemic. All I knew was I didn't want to get it so I was glad when we were let go at Siena house. I had no idea how long the lockdown would last. I had one month of pay coming and then I'd have to collect unemployment.

It took a while for my unemployment to kick in so I was grateful for the severance pay I received. Between July and November 2020, all businesses were on lockdown. People stayed home most of the time and when they went out they wore masks to protect them against the COVID-19 virus. The death toll never stopped rising. The whole world was completely upside down. The country was in a war against itself over politics.

I started my third internship in late August, it was at a nursing home. Nursing homes were hit the hardest by the pandemic. My job was to help residents in the nursing home place Facetime calls to their families since visitors weren't allowed in the facility. I had to wear full personal protective equipment from head to toe. I would be on the Covid ward many times throughout the day. Sometimes the Facetime calls made me so sad because some families were saying goodbye to their parents or grandparents knowing they wouldn't get the chance to visit. I had this semester and then one more to complete until I graduated. It was taking so long that it seemed like I would never get there.

I went on a few job interviews, and a few organizations made offers but I wouldn't survive on the salary they offered so I declined them. I was finally hired in November by an organization that was a provider of medically assisted treatment medication for people addicted to opiates and heroin. I was hired as a lead counselor, which is a supervisory position just under the clinical supervisor. I was taking an online class as well. By the end of the semester, I passed the internship and barely passed the class with a C+. I've never received a grade that low before. The new semester was starting in January, I had two classes and then one class and a final internship and I'd be done.

One day in January, while we were in the middle of a staff meeting, I started to feel some kind of tickle in my throat. I couldn't get rid of it. I felt okay and didn't feel any fever or any other signs of being sick. When I arrived home that changed though, I started getting chills and felt achy. I immediately went to the closest hospital and had a Covid test. They said it would be a day or two for the results. I was able to sleep that night and woke up feeling somewhat normal but I had to take off work until I received the results from the test. Later that evening, I started feeling it. I had uncontrollable coughing, a terrible headache, and chills. I couldn't sleep at all and it felt dreadful. I received the results in an email stating I was positive for Covid. At this point, a little less than one year after it started, America was experiencing over twenty-five thousand deaths from Covid every week. I was scared to death. I never felt this sick before, not even in the very worst throws of withdrawal. This was bad, I thought I was in a lot of trouble.

I had to have medicine delivered, and an oxygen sensor that measured the oxygen in my bloodstream. Lauren and her boyfriend moved out to their own place a few months earlier so I wasn't worried about infecting anyone. I was worried about surviving it though. The first few nights were unreal. So much was happening at once. I couldn't sleep, my fever was always around 103 or a little higher. I had diarrhea so bad that after two days it started burning terribly. My mouth would be really dry and if I took a sip of water or Gatorade, immediately after swallowing it my mouth would be dry again. I was very sick.

After about a week of contracting Covid-19, I became eligible for monoclonal antibody treatment. The treatment was done through an infusion at the hospital. Although the doctors said that I should start feeling better soon, I felt like I was getting worse every day. On the tenth day, there was a real scare as my blood oxygen level fell to 80%, which was below the recommended level of 90%. I contacted a friend who is a respiratory therapist, and she advised me to call an ambulance immediately. However, I was too scared to call an ambulance as I didn't want to die alone in a hospital with a tube down my throat. By the grace of God, my oxygen level went back up to 90% after about fifteen minutes. I believe that a medication that I was taking for rheumatoid arthritis, Prednisone, saved my life. Even though it's a powerful steroid that could cause severe side effects, I was fortunate enough not to experience any side effects.

I wound up missing fifteen days of work. I had double pneumonia after which kept me out for another week. I was supposed to start classes the week prior but I was too sick. It was really hard sitting through the classes when they were online, but it seemed to be so much harder when I was sick. I wasn't able to concentrate, I wasn't comprehending any of it. It took a long time to adjust after it as well. It's hard to explain but I didn't seem to have things together. I was having lots of trouble concentrating on anything.

I heard on the news that many survivors were experiencing the same thing as me. They called it "Long Covid". I was struggling to keep up with my studies, failing both classes. Even the assignments I managed to complete received failing grades. I spoke to my school advisor and explained everything to her. She suggested I take a leave of absence, but I didn't want to. I was so close to finishing school and didn't want to miss a whole year. However, I realized I wouldn't be able to get through the classes in my current state, so I took the leave of absence. It was heartbreaking, but I refused to let depression win. As I began recovering and getting out of the house more, I started attending online NA meetings. I didn't realize it at the time, but I was improving in many ways, not just from COVID-19. Looking back, it's clear to me now.

Chapter 90. I know all your graces
Someday will flower;
In a sweet sun shower= *Chris Cornell*

I had some negative consequences to deal with when I returned to work. Although I was supposed to have completed my probationary period, the director informed me that they were extending it for two more months. However, I had only missed three weeks, not two months. I appealed the extension and was able to complete my probation in just three weeks.

A lot of the clients did not want to attend their counseling or group requirements. Most of them believed they were just fine and that the medication was keeping them sober so they didn't need treatment. It didn't matter that it was required by the state that they do. We would place a hold on their medication so they had to see their counselor before receiving their dose if their attendance was a problem. Doing this would get some of them angry and they would either act out, yell, or do whatever they felt was necessary to get them past this and get them their dose. It was like a cat-and-mouse game sometimes. It was stressful at times, especially when the clinical supervisor was berating staff if their counseling hours were short, even though it wasn't their fault. I was the supervisor just under her, and her negativity allowed me to build positive, solid relationships with the counselors.

I learned my lesson from being the strict, overbearing boss when I had my business. I had many years of reflection after losing my business and accepted that I had a major part in what happened. The never-ending stress I went through back then contributed to my being an asshole to my staff. I understood that I was the reason that a lot of important people left the job. I also learned a lot from my education at Albright about the importance of inclusion, positive motivation, and being open-minded to people who worked under me. I can't remember how many times I kept someone from quitting because they were angry with our clinical supervisor. It's amazing how just doing a few little things can motivate staff to do a great job.

I reached a point where I had enough. I applied for and accepted a position with Pennsylvania Psychiatric Institute's MAT program. It was a step backward from leaving a management position to being a counselor, but I didn't care. I couldn't be around that Clinical Supervisor anymore. I put in three weeks' notice on a Thursday and was told they would let me go the next day, Friday, which was fine with me. I collected unemployment for three weeks and had a mini vacation.

While all this was happening, BJ was struggling to maintain sobriety. This was going on for the better part of two years. My kids would tell me about some of the things that were going on. I was saddened to hear about it. There has not been anyone in this world that's hurt me worse than BJ but she was my kids' mother and somewhere inside I still had love for her. BJ was living at her mother's house for a few years by this point, and from what I heard she was lying and stealing her way out of that house.

My kids would tell me how her bedroom was gross and that she'd smoke crack and hide in it for days without coming out. I knew all too well how horrible it is to live like that. The memories are vivid. Even now. I can never forget being so high and paranoid that I would hide out in a closet in my bedroom holding a gun tightly in my hands. I always believed that someone was coming to get me. Hearing that BJ was living like that saddened me. I never wanted things to turn out that way for her.

Lauren called me one day and told me her mom was going to the hospital by ambulance because she was claiming to be sick. I told Lauren I'd pick her up and follow the ambulance to the hospital. Lindsey was with us too. When I got there, they were loading BJ in the ambulance. I knew right away that she was going through withdrawal and going to the hospital seeking meds to curb it. She looked horrible. My girls were worried sick. Even though they were saying how tired they were of this, I knew they were hurting and they wanted their mom to be okay.

I felt an urge to write a letter to BJ, even though I wasn't sure why. I wanted her to know that she could move past her current situation. Her kids loved and needed their mother back, not the person she had become. I reminded her of the person she used to be when she was an important figure in the recovery community and helped so many people. BJ decided to go to treatment after reading my letter, and I was relieved, although still skeptical. She called me a few days later to let me know that she was on her way to rehab and thanked me for the letter, which had helped her decide to get clean. A week later, I received a letter from BJ in the mail. She apologized for our past and thanked me for not giving up on her. I felt hopeful, but also unsure about whether she was sincere.

It's funny how certain things happen in such an order that's just too hard to believe they are a coincidence. One day I was in PennDOT getting my car registered and I ran into my former sales manager Paul. He said hello to me and I nodded and kept walking. I hadn't even thought about him in years. He sent me a text within thirty minutes that said he wanted me to know that he doesn't hold any resentment against me and wishes for me to be successful. I wanted to message back and tell him I don't give a fucking rat's ass whether he had resentments or not. Like, for real, why should I care? I called Bob and told him about it and what I wanted to do, and he told me not to allow that person any space in my head whatsoever. I thought about it for a few minutes and agreed, deleted the text, and forgot about his existence until writing this.

I started working at Pennsylvania Psychiatric Institute and immediately loved it there. The hospital is a collaboration between Penn State Hershey and UPMC. The MAT program was run more professionally than any other organization I ever worked for. I developed relationships with my clients and was able to provide them with more than I have been able to in the past simply because at PPI, my only job was to be a counselor. They had people there doing the intakes, insurance billing, social work, and other community resources. Not having any of those responsibilities allowed us to concentrate solely on the client's needs and the behaviors and attitudes behind their addiction.

I love being a counselor. I never was and never will be a "by the book" counselor. I invest heavily in building a relationship with the clients. I don't paint pictures of rainbows or grassy fields with flowers that give false hope. Addiction is way too deadly a disease and I believe to help someone in treatment it's best to be completely honest with them. These days the insurance agencies, the policy makers, and politicians have stripped so much away from the arsenal a substance use counselor once had.

I won't deviate or go against any state or federal policy, but I also won't sit by and watch a client kill themselves by trying to bullshit their way through treatment. I will always tell it like it is. I will always call bullshit when I see it. I will always tell a client when they are destroying their life by holding on to the attitude and way of thinking that got them where they are in the first place. I don't mean that there is only one way to provide treatment, different clients need different modalities for sure. To have the courage to face someone's addiction head-on to show them how their thinking is the main problem is always the best way to gain trust and credibility. My counselor Jim from when I was in Common Ground for treatment called me out every time I was full of shit. He was relentless in provoking my feelings and helping me get to the exact nature and roots of my problems. Unexpectedly, after nine months at PPI, Gaudenzia called me to offer me a lead counselor position in their adolescent outpatient program and I accepted their offer. I believed I owed it to Gaudenzia for saving my life.

I loved PPI, the money sucked (as it did everywhere), but the organization was without a doubt the most professional program I ever worked for. I wanted to stay there so I asked if they would meet what Gaudenzia offered me, which was around $8000 more per year than they were paying. My boss told me they couldn't meet that but I would get more when I completed my degree. It was a hard decision but I accepted the offer. I definitely still had a bad taste in my mouth after my last episode with Gaudenzia at Siena House, but I will always love the agency that saved my life and I looked forward to returning.

Temple allowed me to use my job at PPI for my final internship semester and now I had to ask them if I could change that to my new job with Gaudenzia. Luckily, the school allowed it and I was on my way to completing my degree. I had one class and the internship which was basically to report on my current job and I would be done. Finally.

The previous two years went by so fast, like a storm. Some amazing things happened, I would say the most important was how well I was getting along with my kids. We were getting close. Both of them would sometimes call me for advice, which was incredible. For years I would try to guide them and they would never do anything I told them. Now they're calling me to see how I am, sometimes asking how they should deal with certain situations and they would come over for Sunday dinners without me even asking them to.

I remember reflecting on how difficult it was to deal with the aftermath of losing my business. I recalled the challenges I faced in raising my two daughters during their teenage years, as well as the chaotic times I experienced with BJ. It was then that I realized I was finally living the life I had always wanted. Although I didn't have a lot of money or the luxurious lifestyle I had when my business was thriving, I was happy. I enjoyed being alive. There was a time when I had lost hope and didn't want to live anymore, but now I was truly appreciating life on my own. I used to rely on Bob to show me that life wasn't all bad, but now I was able to see it for myself.

Chapter 91. Shine sun, over my life= *Ivan Neville*

I went to work at Gaudenzia's Harrisburg outpatient office to set up and start their adolescent outpatient program. My boss handed me a folder with a few referrals from juvenile probation of Dauphin County and a few from the Harrisburg school district. I wasn't shown how to do anything, I was left alone to get these kids in for their initial assessment and make recommendations for a level of care. My first three appointments were with girls between fourteen and sixteen years old. One was a referral from her school and the other two were on juvenile probation. The kids on probation turned in a positive urine to the probation officer and were required to complete the outpatient program and the kids referred from school only needed an assessment and a level of care recommendation if there was one.

When I was at ARC, the kids were often violent and sometimes substance abusers. Most of them only messed with marijuana and some went harder and used Percocet or Xanax. Our main focus with them was their behaviors and thinking. They lived at the residence between 6 months and a year and once in a great while a kid would be sentenced to more than a year, but that was rare. We spent between eight and twelve hours each day with these kids, we developed relationships with them and spent a lot of time helping them recognize how their thinking and behaviors led to incarceration and drug use. Everything we did was based on the development of a positive relationship with them.

At this outpatient facility, the kids were usually on probation for getting caught with marijuana at school or other minor law violations. Some of them were hardcore users and some were just occasional users. The kids from the inner city of Harrisburg were usually boys, in gangs, and were fairly hardcore weed smokers. They would usually be in our highest level of care and come twice a week for group sessions and once a week for an individual session. The kids from the suburbs were an even mix of girls and boys. These kids would mostly smoke weed on weekends and maybe one or two days of the week before or after school and didn't need such intense treatment and would just have one individual session per week.

I was basically in charge of putting the whole adolescent program together, which is something I loved doing. It was challenging because I'd never done anything of that magnitude before and I was pretty much on my own. I had a supervisor that I could call any time, she was helpful when I was able to get ahold of her. There were quite a few challenges. I needed to figure out how to set up groups for each level of care, even though most of the kids from the suburbs didn't meet the criteria for the intensive groups, so I also had to develop a group curriculum for a lower, less intensive level of care. I came to find I liked the challenge of developing the program more than I liked working with the kids. I hoped that once I put everything together, the agency would let me hire a counselor and promote me to be the director of adolescent outpatient programming. My boss made it seem like we were heading in the right direction. In the meantime, I had to work a ton of hours each week while I was putting it all together. Management gets paid for every hour they worked but we didn't get overtime wages after 40 hours. I didn't mind any of it, I was just interested in seeing If I could pull this off.

The inner-city kids were tough. Most came from single-parent, impoverished homes. All of them either knew or were related to someone in the area who was killed by gun violence. Most were involved in street gangs. Their neighborhoods were overrun with drugs, dealers, gangs, and graffiti. It's impossible to drive through some of these neighborhoods without noticing the poverty or the many houses that were abandoned and falling apart. These kids were smoking weed to cope with their situations. They were involved with gangs for protection. Some of them sold drugs for the neighborhood dealers because they didn't see any other way out of the impoverished neighborhoods and some of the money they made went to helping support their families. These kids were hardened by the way they lived and what they've seen throughout their lives. None of them feared jail. Some of them would look me in the eye and say "I ain't telling you shit, I'm gonna come here and do nothing for the hour and go home." I would usually just tell them "Well, if you ain't saying shit, neither am I." The silence usually lasted about ten minutes. I would never tell them they needed to stop smoking weed. Instead, I would ask them if the benefits of weed were worth the consequences. I would also ask "What is it that you're trying so hard 'not to feel?'"

Juvenile probation would refer or mandate these kids to treatment often with the expectation that we would miraculously cure them of their problems and send them back rehabilitated and abstinent from using any substances. I would meet these kids to assess their level of care needs and almost every one of them was so guarded and closed off to the idea of treatment. They didn't see a problem with smoking weed especially since it was legalized for medical use. They would ask why something that is considered to be medicine is not available for them. Most of them suffered from PTSD, anxiety, and depression and adults with those diagnoses were prescribed medical marijuana, why weren't they?

Some would say outright they weren't going to stop smoking weed even when faced with the consequence of extending probation or adjudicated to placement or residential treatment. I'm not an advocate for adolescents using marijuana, not in any way, but I also know without a doubt that providing these kids with treatment with the expectation of them arresting their use is in my eyes almost useless.

The kids from the suburbs couldn't be more different. Almost all had two-parent families, only a few were involved in the juvenile justice system and those that were, were scared to death to get in any more trouble. They lived only a few miles from the city but were in a completely different world. Their parents came to the assessment and usually asked a bunch of questions about substance use disorders. Some of them would call to check on their kids' progress, sometimes asking questions I wasn't allowed to answer because their kids were protected by federal and state confidentiality laws. It was easier to provide these kids with treatment, they were more receptive to it and most would eventually start turning in urines that were negative for any illicit substances.

It was hard getting the inner-city kids to participate in sessions, they were guarded and didn't trust me or any other adults. I was able to get through to a few once they felt a little more trusting. Getting these kids in a group setting was the hardest obstacle. The group sessions became show-off sessions where each kid would try and outdo the others. I sought advice from my supervisor and she was about as helpful as a rock. The kids at ARC were motivated to get privileges like weekend passes to go home to their families. The only thing I could use to try and get these kids in line was to speak with their probation officers but doing that would erase any possibility of gaining their trust.

I came to find the best way I could help these kids was to just hear them. I don't believe anyone other than their friends ever heard what they had to say. Whenever I spoke to their parents I heard the same thing over and over, "he never listens" or, "I can't control him." I remember the looks on the faces of the parents after I asked them if they ever really sat with the kids and let them speak and if they ever really heard them with understanding and compassion. These kids were from a completely different world than where I came from but all I heard when I listened to them was different parts of my own story of adolescence.

I could have been just another adult who told them how to live. I could've been just another person of authority who never heard them and watched as they went from juvenile justice and escalated to adult criminal justice. What I tried to do instead was show them all adults weren't trying to control them. I would be a voice of reason and try to help them realize some answers for themselves.

I still loved the job despite all the challenges. My biggest struggles were with my supervisor and her boss, the director of outpatient services. When I started they seemed to be about helping these kids. What it turned out was to get as many billable treatment hours from each client as possible. Some kids really didn't have a problem. They smoked weed once or twice a week, their grades were fine and they weren't involved with juvenile justice. I would keep these kids in treatment until they provided three consecutive urine drug screens. They would usually complete treatment and achieve their treatment plan goals between five and seven weeks.

My bosses, however, wanted me to place them in the group sessions with the inner-city kids. I knew that doing that would most likely going to cause them more problems rather than help them. The boss's reasons for getting the kids involved in groups was to be able to bill their insurance for more hours. I am not in this for the money. There isn't any money in it for counselors anyway, we are all paid way less than our worth. I was and always will be against providing unnecessary treatment for financial gain. They were relentless in their efforts but I never caved. If a kid would benefit from a higher level of care or more intense treatment, I would always make sure they would receive the level of treatment that will best suit them. I saw that my immediate supervisor and her boss were getting frustrated with me but I didn't care about them; I cared about the kids.

Chapter 92. Here comes the sun= *The Beatles*

In June, for Father's Day, Lindsey, Brandon, and Lauren took me to dinner. When we were done and I was getting ready to go home, Lindsey handed me an envelope with a card. When I opened it I nearly lost my shit. On the card was a picture from a sonogram with a baby in her womb. I felt that funny feeling in my throat before I started crying and BOOM, there I was crying like a baby after learning I was going to be a grandfather. I have to say, I told both kids repeatedly that if either of them was to make me a grandfather before I was sixty I was going to kill everyone, especially the person that got either of them pregnant. For whatever reason though, I was okay with this even though I was just fifty-six. I was incredibly happy for Lindsey and Brandon. We had an awesome family hug; it was the best feeling to be a part of my kids' lives and to be the patriarch of our growing little family.

I completed my last class and final internship in August and finally, after 6 years, I completed my MSW program at Temple University. What was supposed to take three years eventually took six. It felt like a lifetime but when all is said and done, I don't care how long it took. I have a freaking master's degree. Some things have happened as a result of being in recovery and also as a result of losing my business that are far beyond my wildest dreams. If the business never crashed, I'd have never sought higher education. If I ever even THINK about a Ph.D., someone please smack some sense into me.

I exhausted all available funding from student loans so I had to pay for the last three classes out of pocket. I had no way of coming up with the almost nine thousand dollars to pay for that. A friend suggested seeking donations from friends through a service called "Go fund me" which is an online service that people can use to fundraise for almost any cause. I had no other options so I tried it. I was overwhelmed by how much money I raised from it. My friends and family donated close to $3000! Temple helped too; they provided me with $2500 in scholarship funds. I was still responsible for around $3500 after all scholarships and donations from friends and I set up a payment plan to pay it off monthly.

I received a letter from the State with an opportunity to interview for the same position I had at SCI Coal Township at a state prison that was about three miles from my house. It was a pretty easy decision so I scheduled the interview. When I went for the interview, the manager of the drug and alcohol treatment division remembered me and went as far as telling me that my old boss Jen from Coal Township had wonderful things to say about me! I received a letter from the prison within two weeks offering me a position. I couldn't have been happier! After so much struggling for so long, things were falling perfectly into place.

BJ completed treatment and was working on a program of recovery. Finally. After writing her that letter I found myself wanting her to succeed. Of course, I had lots of resentments that had built up over time but I was tired of them. Having resentment is like drinking poison and hoping the person you have the resentment against dies from it. As BJ progressed in her recovery process I noticed my daughters both feeling better about her and wanting her to be involved in their lives. I invited her to come to my house on a few holidays so she could be with the kids and we could all eat together.

I stopped feeling the anxiety from the resentments I held on to for years and it was nice to have her there with us celebrating. The truth of our tale is neither of us was prepared to be involved in a relationship when we met. We both survived lifestyles that would have killed most and we both needed to recover from that and not jeopardize it by getting together when we did. Healing from our relationship and the divorce is our responsibility to ourselves. I feel that I should say that I've told the story about us from my viewpoint, I am sure she will disagree with quite a bit of it. She has her version as seen through her eyes. I've experienced a lot throughout my life. There were things I have had the pleasure of letting go of and there are some I am still in the process of letting go of.

I am happy that BJ has finally found her way back to recovery. I can't say that I am completely over the resentments but I can honestly say they no longer have control over my emotions and my feelings. If any of that shit comes up, I work through them and not around them. I never stuff them like I used to. I can now call BJ a friend, I have love for her and always wish her the best. I am happy to see her being a mother to our kids again. As of this writing, I am so proud of her, she recently celebrated 2 years of continued abstinence and recovery.

I took a break and started counting blue cars. It was a moment to appreciate how far I'd come since closing my business. At almost 57 years old, I felt grateful to be alive and to have a good relationship with both of my daughters. It wasn't long ago when I considered giving in to their requests just to be friends with them, but I held my ground and held them accountable when needed. Both my therapist and Bob advised me to stand firm, and though I argued with them, I now realize they were right.

I currently work as a drug and alcohol counselor in a state prison, doing assessments for a variety of inmates. Some have committed terrible crimes, while others are there for simple drug possession. Although it's not my dream job, I still love what I do and use my own experience to help those who need it most. I remind them that this could be either the beginning or the end of the line for them, and that treatment can work if they let it. I tell them that I once slept on the subway but now wake up in a bed, and that I am "always wonderful." Most importantly, I let them know that life is worth living and that recovery is possible.

Chapter 93. I've lived, a life that's full,
I traveled each and every highway,
And more, much more than this
I did it my way= *Francis Albert Sinatra*

Never in history has there been a song line that describes who I am better than this one. I have never lived by any specific rule or law, nor have I allowed any obstacles to stand in my way. I have never accepted anything as the way it has to be, nor have I accepted anyone's definition of me. While living my life my way wasn't always in my best interest, it was still better than living someone else's way.

I will never criticize anyone who chooses to follow the mainstream route to achieve their goals. Some people prefer this approach as it provides them with a sense of security. What I mean by this is that some individuals prefer to take the safest path and attain all that life has to offer them. There is nothing wrong with desiring stability. For instance, my brother opted for this approach, and as a result, he never had to sleep on a subway or face legal charges. He never experienced eviction or job loss or went through withdrawal. He has been happily married to his wife for 36 years, and his daughter is a successful, married woman with a master's degree and a thriving career.

It was never in me to take that path. It was there in front of me, but there was something in me that couldn't do it. I needed to explore the unknown. I needed to experience everything, good or bad, safe or dangerous. It didn't matter. I never had a plan or a destination. I lived in every moment as it happened and I have no regrets.

Nothing came easy. I fought for everything. Everything came with a price or a consequence. I remember almost everything that's happened to me throughout my life. The experience of writing this was amazing. I've relived moments in time that were long forgotten. As I remembered them I also felt everything that I felt as if I was back in the exact moment. I often wonder what life would have been like if I had taken the safer path. I wonder if I'd be the same person I am today. I don't believe I would.

If you were to ask anyone who knew me as a child growing up in Queens or as a musician in Los Angeles whether they would have ever imagined that I would be a person in long-term recovery from addiction, a parent, a grandparent, or a college graduate with both a bachelor's and a master's degree, I'm sure they would have laughed and thought you were crazy. Even now, there are days when I can hardly believe it myself. It's amazing to me that as I write these final words on August 10, 2023, I'm celebrating the anniversary of my twenty-fourth year of continuous abstinence from drugs and alcohol. I don't think I'll ever stop being amazed that I'm clean. Every year when my anniversary comes around, I feel a wave of gratitude for every experience I've ever had, both good and bad, because they all played a part in making me the man I am today - the man I can now say I'm proud of. I no longer feel the need to know why I was so insecure or why I never felt like I belonged. Today, I know that everything that happened to me played a part in creating the now peaceful soul that I am.

My daughter Lindsey has been married to her husband Brandon for almost four years. Lindsey is the most responsible of all of us. She gave birth to my grandson Jaxson on January 6, 2023. He's such a beautiful, perfect little guy. He's seven months old now and about ready to start crawling. He's been trying for a few days now. He smiles when he sees me. I make him laugh all the time. He loves hugs and kisses, he loves going outside, he loves his mom and dad, and his big brother Loki the Pitbull.

Lauren is now in her eighth month of pregnancy. She is living with me and getting on every little nerve I have but also makes me proud of her every single day. This young lady has survived through her private version of hell. She has grown into a beautiful, loving, understanding, strong young woman. I truly enjoy her company; I don't think there is anyone more like me in this world than her. She moved in along with her dog Gypsy and her two cats, Aurora and Pablo Escobar (Yes, my crazy kid named a cat after Pablo Escobar!). My wonderful, peaceful, quiet home is now a madhouse. The dogs completely lose it whenever someone walks past the house and I usually have to scream at the top of my lungs to get them to stop. Anytime anyone comes over, they jump all over them, and depending on who it is. Sometimes they get so excited they pee on my floor. The cats create chaos too. One of them will poop NEXT to the damn litter box if it's too full for him and the other one will jump on any furniture and she'll look me in the eye as she knocks shit over. Honestly though, I love it all. I make it seem like I'm grouchy all the time but I love all the animals and having Lauren here with me.

My life today is not perfect. I am still struggling financially and have aches and pains in parts of my body that I never knew existed. Although I'm not alone, I often feel lonely. I have many unresolved issues with my brother, and I wish we could sit down one day and just talk. Furthermore, I hope to develop a lasting and loving relationship with my niece, Victoria, since the fallout with my brother, our connection has been broken. I often let my emotions take me places where I have no business going. However, I long to find a way to love everyone, whether they were helpful or detrimental to my spiritual well-being. Despite all this, I still have the desire to achieve these things. I will never give up. I didn't give up when everything in the world was screaming at me to, so why would I do so now, especially when I have this peace in my heart and soul that makes my inner light shine ever so brightly?

I still haven't found my soulmate, whom I sometimes refer to as my "future ex-wife." She is out there somewhere. I am not currently in a romantic relationship, and people often ask me why. To be honest, I am not sure why I am not involved with someone. When I started classes at Albright College in 2012, I made a conscious decision not to pursue any romantic relationships while I was in school. I knew that getting involved would have distracted me from my studies. **I had no idea that I would be in school for almost eleven fucking years!** Nonetheless, being single for all these years has taught me a lot about myself. Some days I enjoy it, while other days I don't.

Over the years, I have learned to love and accept myself, warts and all. I have come to understand that I have a purpose for being here, and I have achieved a much better emotional and mental state than I have ever been in. If my "future ex-wife" ever does show up, I would be in a much better position to embrace her. Being single doesn't bother me, but I wouldn't mind finding someone and falling in love either. One of the greatest gifts I have received is the ability to sit alone at home, in silence, without any distractions. I no longer hear the negative voices in my head, and I don't worry about what others think of me.

I often hear people say "You can't love anyone until you love yourself" but I don't know about that. I have loved lots of people while I was suffering from severe low self-esteem and had an unadorned lack of love for myself. I've had mad love for so many friends like Dez, Tommy from Vertigo Children, Toby Julian from Hawaii, and Randy "Rockstar" Robertson. There are many women that I've had completely platonic relationships with for years as well. I love Linda, Angie, Anna, and Debbie with all my heart. Debbie passed away a few years back due to alcoholism and it was crushing. We all tried to help her but she didn't love herself enough. I loved Fran DiBella, we grew up together, and we came of age together in the New York City rock and roll club scene. It's been almost ten years since cancer took her away, but she forever lives in my heart.

There are so many stories that were not mentioned in this book, so many people and relationships that I left out, so I may have to at some point write another book. Until then, I will enjoy the peace within my heart. This once-tortured soul has found peace and comfort. The kid who needed to belong or fit in is now a man who is content with being the patriarch of my little and growing family and I know without a doubt that this is where I belong.

I need to say that I am not "one in a million." Rather, I am one of millions. What I mean is while my story is unique; I am just one of the many millions of people in the world who are in long-term recovery from the disease of addiction. However different our stories may be, we all share in common the strength to go through anything life throws at us and maintain abstinence while we go through it. There was a time when something as simple as tying my shoes in the morning was reason enough to get high and now, today, I can survive anything and maintain sobriety. This concept baffles so many people who don't understand the power of the disease of addiction. There still is a stigma that people should just be able to stop using at any time. I wish it were that easy but unfortunately, it is not. It took a village for me to find recovery. I would not be clean today without the support from the people I met in the rooms of Narcotics Anonymous. They were the village.

When I was in LA throughout the 80's and 90's I would often say it was my destiny to be drunk by noon and dead by thirty. People used to tell me to be careful what I wish for, I just might get it. Well, I call bullshit on that. I wanted to die for years until I realized I didn't *want* to die; I just didn't want to feel the pain anymore. For some reason, God saw fit to keep me around and experience all I've been through so I can help someone in need or someone who is feeling terrible about themselves and let them know that they're worthy and deserving of love despite anything they've done. Just like Bob, Kendra, and every sick and suffering addict I've ever worked with has done for me.

Chapter 94. And in the end, the love you take is equal to the love, you make- *The Beatles*

I don't believe there can be a more fitting song lyric for the final chapter of this book. To be honest, I thought I finished the book with the chapter before this but I woke up this morning and heard this song by the Beatles and just started writing. Throughout the many years of my addiction, I've taken more than I needed and, in my recovery, I've given more than I owe. I spent a lifetime in my addiction not understanding why I was here. I tried to believe that there was a God. I just couldn't understand why if he was what everyone said he was, then why he would keep me here when I never felt like I belonged. I continually asked why am I so different from everyone else. Why did Dez die? Will my brother ever see me as anything different than he does? Why am I so fucking evil? As I write this I think it sounds like such an undesirable existence and at times it was. I was never able to talk about any of this before I got clean and it took years after getting clean to truly address all my "issues". I know in my heart my parents loved me and I understand why it so often felt like they didn't. It took for me to be a parent to get that. I no longer question why I felt like I never fit in with the kids in my neighborhood when we were all so much alike in so many ways. When all is said and done, I know without a doubt that I had the disease of addiction before I ever picked up a drug. I am not a believer that either destiny or fate dictates our outcomes. There's a line in the bible, Ecclesiastes 9:11, that states "Time and unforeseen occurrence befall all" and I believe that to be my truth. I don't think I was destined to be the man I am today. This wasn't my fate. Dez wasn't "supposed" to die. There wasn't a reason for that to happen, it was just an unforeseen occurrence. How that affected the rest of my life and the things I've learned from it came over time and from experience. It wasn't "God's will" that I lost my business to gain humility. I'll never believe that a loving god will put anyone through the torture that I went through to learn that lesson.

If these things I am saying here are true, then that leaves a question. Why did all this happen? The only answer I can come up with is I don't know and nor do I need to. I am, however, grateful that it happened and for all I learned from it. To be honest, if the opposite was the truth and I come to find that God did make all this happen for me to become the man I am today, I'd be pissed. There were times in my life when I was so hurt that if I were to learn that anyone did that to me on purpose, for any reason, I don't believe I would be grateful for it. That's putting it lightly. I do believe, however, that God saw fit to keep me alive throughout it all. I hope I'm making sense here. I guess what I am trying to say is that God didn't make me live such a painful existence, but he allowed me to live *through* it and survive.

I am grateful I survived. I'm happy that I can finally share all this with anyone that chooses to read it. I'm writing this book not only to tell a story but also to share the knowledge that I've gained from the experience so that it may someday help someone. I've learned through the process of my recovery that there are a lot of people who grew up and lived feeling as I did. There's no way in hell that I can magically help them change any of that, I know this with certainty. There was never a time in my life either before or after I got clean that someone, could have told me that I deserved to forgive and love myself or that the things I believed about myself were wrong. If they did I'd never have believed them. What I needed to know was that I wasn't alone. I needed to know I was loved.

In closing this chapter, I'd like to share some of the knowledge I've gained from my experience through the time and unforeseen occurrences I've lived through. If you're a parent of a child, adolescent, or adult and they are suffering from addiction, please realize they're hurting. While consequences are necessary, and maybe as a consequence of their addiction they are not with you currently, you can still provide hope without enabling them. I wish that just once my parents told me they missed me when I was out there defiling myself. I wish they'd told me they're waiting for the real Michael to come home and when he's better he is welcome. I believe if the parents or other family of a sick and suffering addict said that to the person, it most likely wouldn't cause an immediate change, but it would provide some hope. When I was out there on my own I never felt hope because it was never provided. Hope was taken from me when I was told to leave and never come back. When I slept on subways, the lack of hope led me to self-medicate myself into oblivion because when I was sober the pain I felt was unbearable.

To the still sick and suffering addict, whether you're still using or in the process of recovery and still going through it, we get better. If not through the twelve steps or God, then through whatever it is that drives you to improve your life. Look deep into your soul because the good person you are lives there. Always has. There's a story about the beginning of civilization, the devil and his demons were thinking up ways to fuck up God's creation and they came up with the idea that taking our happiness from us was the answer. While discussing this they were debating on where to hide our happiness so we'd never find it. Finally, after a long debate, the smartest of all demons came up with the solution. He said they should hide happiness deep inside the human soul. They'll never think to look there. They'll instead seek to find it from outside themselves, from objects or other people, never knowing that they are carrying it within them all the time.

Our happiness is within us. Nothing we add to our lives will ever replace it. Not money, not objects like cars or houses, not others that we want to love us, nothing. It's in our spirit or soul, or whatever it is that you call it. It's there. We just have to find it. We have to choose to be happy. These wonderful words of wisdom were imparted to me from a person in long-term recovery and I have never had a story help me as much as this one. I heard this for the first time while at a meeting where I shared my twentieth year of complete abstinence from all mind- or mood-altering substances. We can learn at any time. Any old dog can learn new tricks.

I hope this story of my life reaches anyone who needs to hear the truth that anyone can find and enjoy recovery from addiction. We are all worthy of love and being saved. Anyone like me who has suffered from a tortured soul can enjoy life, happiness, peace, and recovery. It's all there, within our souls. If I were to be granted one wish, it would be that anytime someone asks how you're doing, you get a goofy smile on your face and tell them, *"I'm always wonderful."*

*In loving memory of: Dolores M Genna, James Michael Genna, Frances Genna, Ann, Ben and Carl LaGrassa, Lee and Ignazio Vinci, Robert McElroy, Domenic "Dez" DeRosa, Randy "Rockstar" Robertson, Francine DiBella, Debbie DiPietro, and Frank Mercurio.

Special thanks to Paul O'Conner, Joe & Dona Dmitrovic, Brian Bruce, Kendra Trufahnestock LCSW, James Hemperly Jr, Barbara Genna and Marty Mercurio. I would not be where I am today if not for you all.

To my sponsor, Robert McKendrick. I would not be the man I am today if you weren't in my life. Thank you for putting up with me all these years. Thank you for never giving up on me.

To my friend Ivan Neville. I'm forever grateful for the friendship we've shared since 1989. There isn't anyone alive who's lived through the lowest times with me except you. The fact that we're both still around to tell the story is nothing short of a miracle. I love you always.

Dedicated to Lindsey, Brandon and Jaxson Rodriguez, Lauren Kasey and Luka Michael Genna

Those that were loved and are no longer of this world: Joseph Drapala, Danny Palmer, Izzy Garcia, Thomas Fritz, Thomas Williams, Lynn Benalt, Michael Mogavero (Mikey Mugz), Michael Mostrocco, Jimmy Santoro, JoeyJean Sindoni, Nick (Big Nick) and Dale (Olive-oil) Oppedisano. I think of them often. All had a part in the theater that I call my soul. They've each in their own way had an impact on me.

Editing Consultant: Theodora Sakellarides

Cover Design: Molly Landon Robertson

2nd Cover Design: William Elex Poisel

Every Picture tells a story…

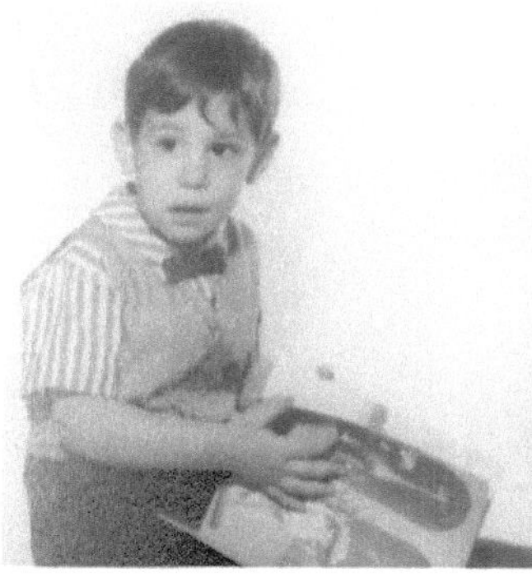 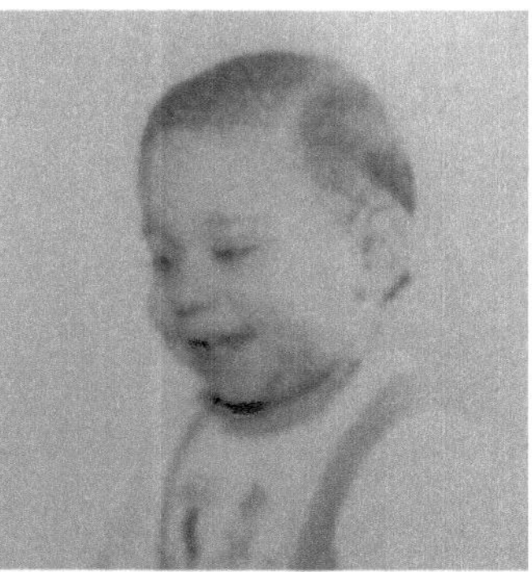

Look at those ears! I was definitely a cute baby, when I see these pictures I can't think of anything other than how much my daughter looks like me.

Left: Some of the 6th grade crew. Taken on the last day of school. Front middle, my neighbor Michael, to his left Joseph Drapala
Right: Between Michael and Joey is Nelson M and Scott W right to his left. Back row center is Danny Quinn and
to his right is Eric Olsen. The next picture is Eric and me. These were taken on the last day of 6th grade.
Can you believe this was the first day I smoked weed?

Mom and me on the last day of Jr. High School. She was so beautiful when she smiled.

This is the picture I showed my therapist. Sharing this picture with her literally changed my life.

This was just before joining the band Naztee Habitz. I was a beautiful kid, I wish I could see this back then.

Mikee Mascara 1987, 1988, 1991. I sure was WILD!

My only picture of Fran DiBella from back in the day. I remember the night we took these pictures, they were taken the 1st time I returned to NY from LA. I'm not sure if you can tell, I was drunk as fuck in this picture.

1986, the "Dez" days! I miss him all the time. Something in my heart tells me that me and him would've remained friends throughout the years, unlike most of the friendships I had during that time.

The Vertigo Children Days

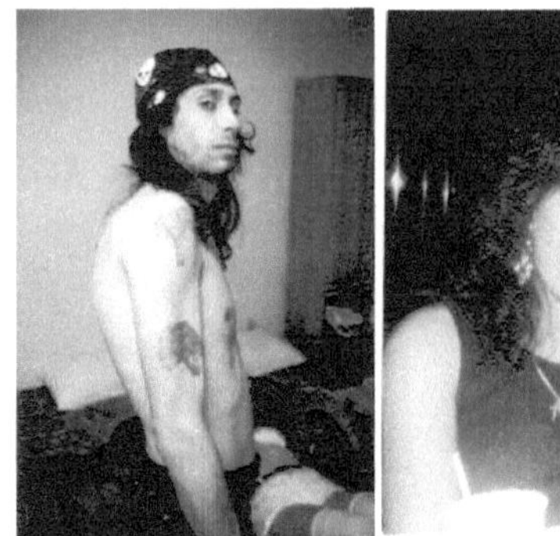

Oh mother, tell your children, not to do what I have done!! This picture describes how I looked in the midst of a binge (no clue who the passed-out woman is)! On the right is me and my friend Linda, (1986).

My last few times on stage in LA. First two pictures are from the world-famous Roxy Theater, and the one on the right is from some unknown club in the valley.

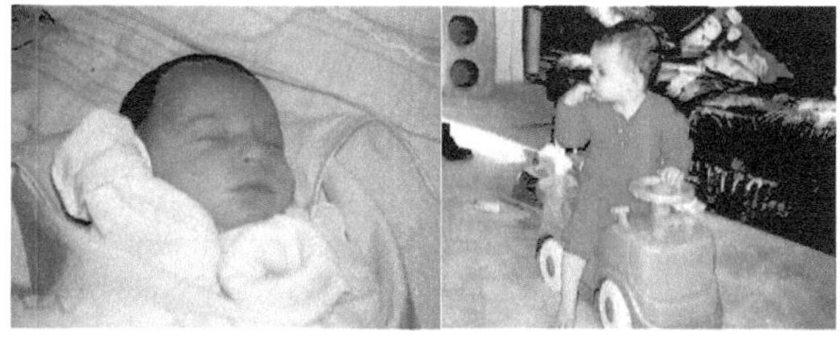

My beautiful first home. We lived here from 1999 through 2005. The middle pictures are of Lindsey at about 5 years old. The bottom row on the left is Lauren on the day she was born, the right is her at maybe 9 months.

This was the building we moved our offices to in 2003. I was on top of the world when we moved in and on the bottom when we moved out.

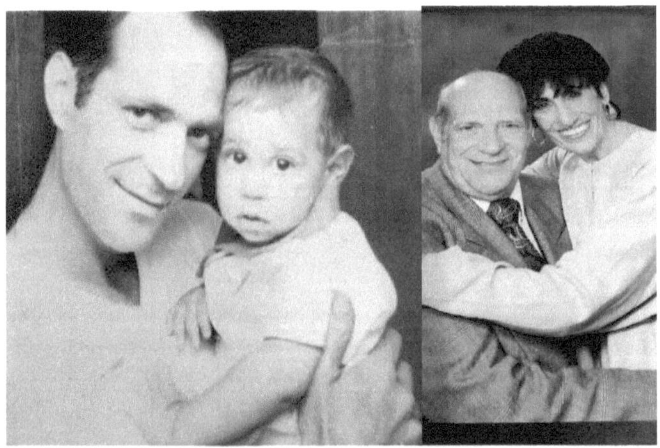

My favorite picture of my dad and me.   I love this picture of my mom and dad.

This was at the rehab where my pops spent his last days. I wish I could just have 5 more minutes with him. I'd get him in a headlock, squeeze his nose, and kiss his bald head! I miss my parents terribly.

The picture taken by the NYPD after my arrest for hopping the turnstile. The judge couldn't believe this was me when I appeared for the warrant for that charge in 2018!

Time goes by, way too fast. Left is from 2003 – right pic from 2021

They make life worth living.

On 5/22/2016, the "idiot with a GED" graduated college with a 3.8 GPA and a
Bachelors degree in Psychology.

All of us, The old head (Me), Lindsey, Lauren, BJ (2 years clean) and my beautiful grandson Jaxson Tyler Rodriguez. This was at Laurens baby shower, Luka Michael Genna is due in September 2023.

There's nothing more peaceful than a baby sleeping in my arms.

My Peaceful Soul